MOSTLY MURDER

The Portrait presented to the Author on his Retirement from Edinburgh University

Sir William Hutchison
President of the Royal Scottish Academy

MOSTLY MURDER

Sir Sydney Smith
C.B.E., LL.D., M.D.(Edin.), F.R.C.P.(Edin.)

With a Foreword by
Professor Keith Simpson, C.B.E.

DORSET PRESS
New York

TO KITTY

a good companion for half a century

Copyright © Sir Sydney Smith 1959
Foreword © Professor Keith Simpson 1973
All rights reserved.

This edition published by Dorset Press,
a division of Marboro Books Corporation,
by arrangement with Harrap Ltd.
1988 Dorset Press

ISBN 0-88029-306-3

Printed in the United States of America

M 9 8 7 6 5 4 3 2 1

Foreword to the Reissue

By PROFESSOR KEITH SIMPSON, C.B.E.

NO EXPERT IN THE ART OF MEDICAL DETECTION HAS EVER enjoyed the respect and affection of his fellow pathologists as Sydney Smith did, and few can have extracted so much fun from a macabre profession. His sparkle and enthusiasm turned the most drab situation into a tale, and his shrewd court tactics and alertness made him an expert witness few counsel would relish to tackle. His very remarkable experiences came to delightful fruition in 'Mostly Murder' and it is no surprise that there has been such an insistent demand for a reissue.

A New Zealander, he came to the famous Chair in Edinburgh, took 'time off' to organise a medico-legal system and Institute for Egypt, adding a colour to his life denied to most experts in his field, then returned to Edinburgh to add to his brilliance in the forensic field a natural flair for administration. He was undoubtedly the most popular Dean and lecturer in a medical subject this Scots School ever had—a reincarnation of Conan Doyle's Dr. Bell. Crimes of violence seemed to come his way as moths to a source of light, and he illuminated them in a way that gained a remarkable repute for him: his services were in demand to an extent that often bid fair to eclipse the Home Office performances of the great Spilsbury. Yet he retained a remarkable 'nose' for a good story, and no case every remained dull in his hands. Gifted with wit, he weaved stories from murders like those of the Sirdar of Egypt, the Merritt matricide, Sydney Fox, Anne Hearn in Dorset and the famous 'shark' case in Australia that any journalist would envy.

Here is the famous Ruxton case, a call to Ceylon, an affair with arsenic in Auckland, all told with an effervescence that compels reading. The book teems with criminal tales and asides that speak volubly for this great pathologist's zest and enthusiasm for the job he so excelled in. Pathologists like myself who knew him so well as an elder expert can see him vividly in these pages, recounting his tales with sparkle and his own unquenchable enthusiasm.

Preface

I SUPPOSE ONE SHOULD HAVE A REASON OR AT LEAST AN EXCUSE FOR adding another to the mass of new books which tend to submerge the reading public. My only excuse is that it amused me to recall a few of the more interesting cases with which I have been concerned during my professional life, and it seemed that other people might be interested to read my account of these varied investigations.

The book consists mainly of the story of these cases — a plain, unvarnished tale without embellishment or emotion. I trust that my readers will find something of interest in another man's work.

Many of the cases have appeared in the professional journals, such as the *British Medical Journal* and the *Police Journal*. These I have freely drawn from. I have to thank many police authorities for their help in letting me have material relating to cases dealt with by me.

In particular thanks are due to my old friend Gilbert Watson, who has helped me throughout in the preparation of the text and in the correction of the proofs.

SYDNEY SMITH

Contents

Illustrations

In Half-tone

In the Text

I

Three Small Bones

THE SEALED PARCEL CONTAINED THREE SMALL BONES, AND there was nothing strange about that. Similar parcels were continually delivered to the medico-legal section in Cairo. I dare say they still are. In that hot climate bodies are quickly reduced to bones, and in Egypt a lot of bodies fail to get a conventional burial. At least, they did thirty or forty years ago.

The police report that came with the parcel was no more remarkable than the contents. The bones had been found at the bottom of a well which had just been reopened after years of disuse. It was a chance discovery, the police had no reason to suspect anything sinister, and the bones were sent to my laboratory for a routine examination. They could have been the remains of some animal that had fallen into the well. The police asked me only to determine whether or not they were human.

After looking at the bones I was able to tell them more than that.

"They are the bones of a young woman," I reported. "She was short and slim. Aged between twenty-three and twenty-five when she died, which was at least three months ago. She had probably had at least one pregnancy, perhaps more. Her left leg was shorter than her right, and she walked with a pronounced limp. Probably she had polio when a child. She was killed by a shotgun loaded with home-made slugs, fired in an upward direction from a range of about three yards. The killer was standing, or sitting, in front of her, and slightly to her left. She was not killed outright, but died about seven to ten days later, probably from septic peritonitis due to the shooting."

That was the story of the three small bones, as I read it, and it gave the police something to work on. They made inquiries in the neighbourhood of the well about any missing young woman who limped. They soon heard of one, short and slim and about twenty-four, who had disappeared from a near-by village some months before. She had been married and divorced, had borne one child, and was living with her father until she disappeared. The police questioned him, and, as his answers were unsatisfactory, arrested him and charged him with the murder of his daughter. Then he broke down and confessed — but not to murder. He said he had killed her by accident.

"I was sitting on the ground in front of my hut, cleaning my gun," he said. "My daughter was standing in the doorway. I did not know the gun was loaded. Suddenly it went off — and she fell. I put her to bed and nursed her, but after a week she died."

"Why didn't you call a doctor?" the police asked him.

"Because I was frightened of getting into trouble for having the shotgun," he said. "I had no firearms permit. When she died I was even more terrified, so I hid the body in the well. It had not been used for a long time, and it did not seem likely that it would be used again. But after a few months I heard it was going to be put back into service, and I—I— "

Here he broke down, and that was understandable enough. Whatever the truth of his account of the shooting, there was no reason to doubt the rest of his story. In the dead of night he had gone down the well and removed his daughter's remains. The horror of this gruesome task is hardly imaginable. In that hot climate decomposition is so rapid that the corpse had almost completely disintegrated. Overcoming his nausea, he took away the remains and threw them into the Nile. He thought he had removed all traces, but he overlooked those three small bones. Unfortunately for him, they contained all the clues needed to bring his deed to light.

The solution to a mystery always looks easy — when it has been explained.

Two of those bones were hip-bones, the third a sacrum; when fitted together they formed a complete pelvis. No other part of the skeleton gives clearer evidence of sex, which in this case was obviously female. There was no more difficulty in determining her stature and build. The bones were small and light, so she was short and slight. They could almost have belonged to a child — but for the unmistakable evidence of her age. The crest of the hip-bone normally becomes united at about twenty-two to twenty-five; they had almost united here, but the union was still incomplete, so I could estimate her age with some precision.

Tiny fragments of soft tissue were clinging to the bones, and its condition told me that she had been dead at least three months. There were grooves in the bones, from which I could infer that she had had at least one pregnancy. Her limp was easily deduced. The right hip-bone was bigger and heavier than the left, and the cavity for the head of the femur was bigger on the right side. This meant that the right hip-bone had borne most of the weight of the body for a long time, which in turn implied that she had been lame in her left leg since early childhood or infancy. Polio was the most likely cause.

I knew the woman had been shot because there was a lead slug or pellet embedded in her right hip-bone. It was irregular in shape, so I guessed it was home-made. There was a grooved injury in another part of the same bone, and also a triangular fracture. Probably, then, these injuries had been made by similar slugs or pellets. If so, the weapon was presumably a shotgun. The spacing of the injuries indicated the dispersion of the shot, and from this I deduced that the range was about three yards. The grooved injury told me the direction and angle of the shot. It had been made by the passage of a slug from the front, backward and upward, and from left to right.

The grooved injury also contained the clue showing that she had not died immediately after she was shot. The margins of this injury showed a good deal of erosion of the bone, and that is a characteristic sign of suppuration. From the extent of this erosion I was able to deduce that the vital processes had been active for about seven to ten days after the shooting. Finally, the position of the injuries showed that at least one of the shots must have penetrated her abdomen. This and the definite evidence of infection made septic peritonitis the most likely cause of death.

My report was partly speculative, of course, but without speculation it would not have been much use. The police had nothing to go on except the bones, and it was up to me to try to give some direction to the investigation. That meant drawing inferences and making deductions as well as observing facts. In the event my report was confirmed in all particulars, except that the woman had been lame in both legs. The polio had evidently affected her right leg slightly as well as her left.

Forensic medicine is neutral. My report led to the arrest of the culprit, but it also bore out his plea of accidental shooting, and so cleared him of the murder charge.

I had never heard of forensic medicine when I decided to become a doctor. Nor for that matter was I drawn to the medical profession by a burning desire to relieve human suffering and pain. I merely picked on medicine as the most likely means of escape from a small New Zealand village into the wide world.

I was born on August 4, 1883, in Roxburgh, in the heart of the Otago gold-fields, where my parents had met. Like most other early emigrants, they had gone to New Zealand lured by the reports of the discovery of quantities of gold. Otago province was raw country, and those early colonists had to be tough.

My father was a cockney, born within the sound of Bow Bells; my mother a Yorkshirewoman, quite young when she emigrated with her parents but already a widow with six children when she married my father and started another family. I was the last of their children. Already in the eighties Roxburgh was a thriving village, a centre for gold-mining, sheep-farming, and fruit-growing, but still only a small place, with a population of a few hundred. It was not quite isolated, and stage-coaches carried passengers and mail, while heavy goods were drawn by horse-wagons and bullock-wagons. The roads were pretty bad — muddy in winter, dusty in summer. I remember when cycling to Alexandra, to visit my brother Horace, I had to start before sunrise, when the road was still hard with frost, because later in the day the wheels of my bike would have kept sticking in the mud. There was no railway. I did not see a train until I was nearly fourteen.

There were four churches in the village to undertake the spiritual needs of the people, four pubs for their temporal aid. One police constable enforced the law and carried out any other Government duty that might be required. As far as I know, there was no crime to engage his attention. One doctor looked after the health, not only of the villagers, but of every one living in the district within a radius of twenty or thirty miles.

Dr Mullen was a good all-rounder. He had to be, since he had nobody to consult in difficult cases. He seemed to be able to deal with all emergencies, but he did not like pulling out teeth. There was no dentist, of course, and conservative dentistry was unknown. Luckily for us, however, we had an efficient and indeed enthusiastic tooth-puller in the local blacksmith.

Tom Andrews was his name; he was a Scot, and a strong up-holder of the Church, who shod horses for a living and pulled out teeth for fun. He relieved me of more than one of mine, and I can still remember the smell of burning hoofs as he finished shoeing a horse before operating. I can also still smell the leather apron of his assistant, who held my head in lieu of an anæsthetic as I sat on the anvil. I can feel the searing pain of the application of the forceps, and can see the triumphant exhibition of the tooth, the whole tooth, and nothing but the tooth. I felt sure that a lump of my jaw must have been removed, and I was relieved to find no sign of it in the forceps. Tom Andrews always presented the tooth to his patient, who took it home and exhibited it as a souvenir. Like King James IV of Scotland, whose hobby it was to practise surgery, our blacksmith charged no fee for tooth-pulling, and frequently rewarded his patient for the privilege of operating on him.

So Roxburgh was small, rural, and isolated; but its population was highly cosmopolitan. The main reason for this paradox was that basically it was a mining community, and gold had attracted all sorts of people from all over the world. Many nationalities, professions, and trades, and most of the religions and philosophies, were represented. Mixing with them and listening to their con-versation about different parts of the world, hearing them relate their strange experiences and expound strange ideas, no doubt had a stimulating effect on a youngster living in the depths of the country.

Few of the gold-seekers reaped the reward they had antici-pated, and most settled down to some kind of steady if unexciting work. When I was born my father was a contractor to the munici-pality, engaged in making and repairing roads. Cheerful, tolerant, and kindly, he had a puckish sense of humour and was prone to practical jokes. His hobbies were amateur theatricals, the study of Shakespeare — whom he spouted on any occasion — and per-forming on the concertina. He was a good gardener, specializing in fruit and vegetables. He taught me chess, and we played together for several years.

My mother was a kindly disciplinarian and an active Christian. She cosseted and nursed her family and anybody else she thought in need of attention. Charity was part of her life, and she would have parted with her last penny to help a neighbour. She was a gardener of distinction, and I never think of home but in terms of flowers. In her later years, at an age when most women settle down to a sedentary life, she took up golf. Although a staunch teetotaller, she knew a good deal about wine-making, and we always had a good stock of home-made wines for special occasions. Very potent they were, too. I remember as quite a young child getting into the cellar and sampling them with a tin mug. I was found lying on the floor in a comatose state — I must have looked pretty bad, for instead of being punished I was put to bed, coddled, and made a fuss of.

My mother was also a bit of a quack. She had, however, a good knowledge of herbal remedies, and from her I acquired quite a lot of empirical medical knowledge long before my own studies began. She was a great believer in the application of hot fomentations for pain, the inhalation of various aromatic oils and balsams for chest complaints, the use of sulphur for inflammations about the throat, and so on. She knew all about vitamins long before the term was heard of, and often lectured me on the essential part played by fresh vegetables and fruit in keeping the blood healthy, as she described it. She had a brew for rheumatism made up of all sorts of ingredients, not unlike the witches' brew in *Macbeth*; but it seemed to have marked curative effects. Or perhaps her friends felt impelled in self-defence to get better, for it seemed a most noxious mixture.

Like all the other children in Roxburgh, I went to the village school. No secondary education was available, and it would have been an ordinary elementary school had it not had an exceptional headmaster — W. A. Reilly, B.A. (the magic letters ·doubtless increased his stature), to whom I always look back with considerable gratitude.

He was not only an unusually cultured man for a village schoolmaster, but an inspiring teacher. He taught most subjects, but was especially interested in history, particularly its more violent aspects; and he had the gift of infecting his pupils with his own enthusiasms. He was intensely patriotic, and left us in no doubt that God had been good to us in arranging that we should be British born. We put this characteristic of his to practical use on occasion. We found that a deft question could often deflect his attention from some difficult theme to the realism of high adventure, and this secured a respite until another day. I am sure he had "immortal longings" like Cleopatra, and, I suspect, an inner life like that of Walter Mitty. He gave lectures in the evenings to adults, and fought out the whole South African War, single-handed and step by step, on the blackboard in the village schoolroom.

A staunch imperialist and traditionalist, W. A. Reilly not only trained us to respect old customs but induced in us an ambition to see something of the world and get something out of life — to go out in search of adventure. More than anyone else, I think, he influenced me in the course of events that led to my making a career in medicine.

All my brothers had gone into various trades and businesses, and there was no family precedent for a professional career. The lack of educational facilities at Roxburgh made it an improbable choice. Our good dominie, busy with elementary classes, had no time to give the advanced instruction without which I could not hope to gain entrance to a university.

I thought of a medical career first as a means to an end. The end was to see the world, and if possible to get a place among the explorers and pioneers whom W. A. Reilly had inspired me to emulate. For this, I thought, one needed to become a specialist at something or other, and this led me to the idea of acquiring a university degree. I chose medicine because of its universality, because it seemed the master key that could open any door.

However, for a lad without any particular means, living in an out-of-the-way place like Roxburgh, the chances of qualifying seemed remote. I do not recollect having done much at school, except get into trouble, and when I left it was difficult to know what to turn to. As it happened, the local chemist at that time wanted an apprentice, and I thought that this was at least a chance to learn something that might be useful. In fact, I did not learn much. No tuition in science was available in Roxburgh, and I am afraid I got very little good from my time except to learn dispensing and certain other things that came in handy afterwards.

Fortunately, a gold-dredging boom broke out in the district, and as I had a capital of about a couple of pounds I took the opportunity to try my hand at high finance. I found it all very simple — much simpler, indeed, than it has been since. New shares were continually being issued, and could be bought by putting down a shilling per share on application and the same amount on allotment. In a boom everything goes up, and I was able to sell the shares at a premium subject to allotment. I was only seventeen at the time, and I managed to make what was quite a lot of money for a boy. My father was horrified, and kept warning me that if I went on I would burn my fingers. In the end I took notice of his words, and sold out and banked the money for the future. When my father saw how much I had made he was so impressed that he began speculating himself, taking up where I had left off. At that moment the boom came to an abrupt end, and it was my father's fingers that were nearly burned.

My apprenticeship to the local apothecary ended when the business was sold, but thanks to his successor I got a job as assistant to a chemist in Dunedin, the capital of Otago, at a salary of thirty shillings a week. In Dunedin I was able to get tuition, too, and I began to prepare for examinations. I became a qualified pharmacist at twenty-three. As the qualification entitled me to a reasonable salary, I was able to begin at once studying for the University of New Zealand entrance and medical preliminary examinations. After passing these I enrolled as part-time student in the Faculty of Science at Victoria College, Wellington, and took first-year chemistry and physics while holding the post of dispensing chemist in Wellington Hospital.

The passes that I obtained in chemistry and physics exempted me from taking these subjects in the medical first year, so I resolved to switch over to medicine. A fellow-student at Victoria College, named Tommy Horrax, had the same ambition, and, like many others all over the world, we decided that the best place to study for the profession was Edinburgh. If I was setting my sights high, I also knew of the existence of many excellent scholarships in that renowned school; and if I failed to win any of them I always had my qualification in pharmacy, which I could use for summer vacation work if necessary. Meanwhile I had enough capital to keep me going if I was careful. When I set off with Tommy early in 1908, at the age of twenty-five, I did not feel at all worried about finance. My thoughts were all of seeing the world, of life and adventure.

Edinburgh was all that we had expected — cold, foggy, wonderful. We admired the ancient 'castle' on Calton Hill — actually it was the old Calton Gaol — and the magnificent buildings, that we thought were different parts of the University (in reality George Heriot's School and Fettes College). But we were soon steeped in ancient history in exploring the real Castle, the High Street, Holyrood Palace, and so on. Tommy Horrax and I took digs together, and I can still hear in my imagination the mournful voices crying through the fog, "Co-o-o-al, tenpence a bag," and many of the other old street cries now heard no more.

I had to sit my chemistry and physics examinations and as I had studied these subjects to a fairly high standard I had hopes that I might not only pass but also win a Vans Dunlop scholarship. Then, to my dismay, I learnt that I was disqualified from entering for the scholarship because I had taken the qualifying courses outside the University. I felt that I had been robbed. However, there was another Vans Dunlop going in the same summer, in botany and zoology, for which I was eligible and, together with another man, G. A. C. Douglas, I won this scholarship, which was worth one hundred pounds a year for three years.

The Rectorial Election came on in the autumn, and in those days this event was fought on political lines. The Conservative Party nominated the Right Hon. George Wyndham, while the Liberals put up the Right Hon. Winston Churchill. We medical students thought it would be well to break away from tradition, and put up an independent candidate — Professor (later Sir) William Osler, an outstanding figure in the medical world.

The election was contested without inhibitions and with no holds barred. Our group was at a disadvantage in having no party funds to support our campaign, but we managed to secure supplies of the necessary fluid refreshment by well-timed raids on the headquarters of the other two parties, who suffered from embarrassment of riches. Many and gay were the fights we had, including the complete wrecking of the Conservative headquarters. Wyndham was elected, but we put up a very good fight — I think we polled more votes than the Liberals. We never interfered with the public in our scraps, and we found the police to be very good friends as long as we did not create too much dislocation of traffic or other public nuisances. Twenty years afterwards, when, as Dean of the Faculty of Medicine, I had to deal with cases of discipline, I found that my own experiences in these matters caused me to look with a tolerant eye on students' pranks and foibles. A little nonsense now and then is a very useful means of blowing off steam, and I trust that students will never become a docile body who have forgotten what Sir Walter Scott called the ancient pastime of high jinks. It is only fair to add that there is no sign of any such weakness at present.

Many of our teachers were world famous, and nearly all were memorable in some sort of way. Sir Halliday Croom was one of our more picturesque professors. He always appeared for lectures in full evening dress, white tie, and tails, with narrow trousers encasing what we described as his Chippendale legs. His subject was midwifery, and he had a fund of stories which enlivened his lectures. Since he told the same stories each year, his students were always prepared for them, and usually reminded him if he missed one. One of the best stories told of him concerned a lady who had been referred to him by a colleague.

"Did he examine you?" Sir Halliday asked.

"Yes, sir; he made a digitalis examination."

"Ah," said Sir Halliday, "then I trust he wore foxgloves." (Foxglove is the common name for the digitalis plant.)

The Department of Midwifery has always been a source of anecdotes; most of these cannot be told, but the Simpson story must be. "Granny" Simpson, as he was called — a nephew of the famous Sir James Young Simpson — held the Chair before Sir Halliday Croom. He was a practising Christian, and frequently handed out religious tracts before he gave his lecture. One morning the tracts were distributed as usual, and when he mounted the platform he received a terrific welcome — handclapping and stamping of feet and cries of "Congratulations!" This he attributed to the excellence of his pamphlet, forgetting that in *The Scotsman* that morning had appeared the information that Mrs Simpson had presented him with a son. The cheering abated, and Granny acknowledged the welcome thus:

"Thank you, gentlemen. Thank you for your evident appreciation of my little effort. I can assure you, however, that I had very little to do with it. It was almost entirely the work of Mrs Simpson — aided a little, just at the beginning, by the Reverend Dr Whyte of Free St George's "

Alexis Thomson, the Professor of Surgery, was another of our characters, greatly cherished by his students. Six feet of bluff good nature, Alexis could hold the attention of the class and inspire loyalty and enthusiasm in all of us. He was imperturbable. It is alleged that on one occasion, when he was operating, he stopped and said to the anæsthetist, "I don't know how the patient is doing at your end, Mr Jones, but he appears to be dead at mine."

In physiology we were fortunate in having Sir Edward Sharpey-Schafer, who had an international reputation in his subject generally, and particularly in connexion with hormones. He was also blessed with a salty wit. On one occasion when, at five minutes to the hour, we reminded him of the passage of time by the traditional method of shuffling our feet in unison he paused and said, "One moment more, gentlemen, if you please. I have a few more pearls to throw."

I could recount tales of most of our professors, for in those days professors seemed to be "characters," each with some distinctive attribute which was a source of interest and often of pride to his students. Nowadays professors seem to have lost those individual whims and eccentricities, and perhaps lost also some of the warm affection of their students. This may be a result of the increased strain which the large size of classes now puts upon professors — also, perhaps, of the decline of hero-worship among the young.

Perhaps the least impressive but certainly one of the best loved of our professors was Daniel Cunningham, who held the Chair of Anatomy. He was very learned, very kindly, but almost inaudible. He would wax eloquent on a description of the most minute anatomical objects, which he held up for inspection in an almost religious way, but I am afraid we caught very little of his divine fire. A more colourful character was one of his assistants who saw to it that we worked — Dr Jamieson, known affectionately to generations of students as "Jimmy." He always wore a black skull-cap and a sealskin waistcoat made from seals shot by himself at his Shetland home. He knew every student, and his life-history, and graduates returning to the University after many years would go up to the department to pay him their respects. He always knew them, remembered each one's Christian name, and often his father's name as well. I secured his friendship by winning the medal in Senior Anatomy, in which he was the arch-inquisitor. After I became Dean of the Faculty I made full use of Jimmy's extensive inside knowledge of students, and frequently consulted him when I was worried about a student's progress. He remained with us until well over the normal retiring age, and died only a few years ago. He had a sardonic wit, and was the subject of many tales. It is alleged that on his death-bed a well-intentioned visitor asked him if he had made his peace with God. "No," said Jimmy. "As far as I know, I had no quarrel with Him." With Jimmy passed away one of the last traditional figures in the school.

Jimmy's brother held the Chair of Anatomy in Leeds for many years, but at the age of seventy odd he was offered and accepted a similar Chair in Trinity College, Dublin. His old mother in the Shetlands was asked what she thought of the new honour to her son. "Oh, aye," she said. "It's well enough, but I wish that boy would settle down to a permanent job."

I enjoyed the whole course, securing a sufficient number of medals and prizes to prove my respectability and certain scholarships which, with coaching, kept me going comfortably enough. I graduated M.B., Ch.B. in 1912, with first-class honours and a research scholarship, and got married a week later. After our honeymoon I took a post for a month as locum tenens to a doctor in Fife.

It was a scattered mining and agricultural practice, and I found great pleasure in putting my training to practical use. One of my first cases established my reputation. I was called out to see a young man, the only son of a doting mother who said he was in a very dangerous state of health. "Come quickly, doctor, please." I went quickly, and examined the lad most thoroughly in a conscientious attempt to find out what was wrong with him. Finally forced to admit failure — to myself, anyway — I put him to bed and gave him something to keep him quiet. The mother was touchingly grateful. She said that never before had a doctor given her son such a thorough examination. She sang my praises far and wide — all due to the fact that I had not the foggiest idea what was wrong with the boy.

Another of my early patients, an enormous coal-miner, worried me for a different reason. There was no problem about diagnosis with him.

"Do ye pu' teeth, doctor?" he asked.

"Of course," I answered, looking more confident than I felt. The man I was standing in for had quite a local reputation as a puller of teeth.

"Well," said the miner, "get this yin oot for me."

I looked at the tooth — a second molar on the upper jaw. It seemed huge. I suggested diffidently that it was too good a tooth to lose, and that he should wait for a day or two until the dentist visited the town. Oh, no, not for him — he must have it out at once. A local anæsthetic? Not on your life. I got out the forceps, which are fortunately inscribed for the specific purpose for which they are designed — "Right Upper Molar", etc. — so at least I was able to choose the appropriate instrument. The rest was up to me.

I remembered the advice of my tutor in these matters. "For a tooth in the upper jaw try to push the forceps through the top of the head — for a tooth in the lower jaw try to push it right through the jaw." Having sterilized the forceps, I firmly encircled the tooth and pushed hard. Nothing happened. Again — with like result. Nothing, it seemed, would loosen that craggy projection. I then gave the forceps a rock-and-roll movement, and out came the massive ivory all in good order with roots complete. This I flourished before the patient, but his only remark was, "Ay, that's it, but it's the warst tooth I've ever had oot." I felt inclined to tell him that more probably I was the 'warst' dentist he had ever met.

It was in this post in Fife that I learned first what it was like to lose a patient. A young girl, beautiful and sweet-natured, was pregnant and suffering from continuous convulsions. I tried all the regular forms of treatment, emptied the uterus, and used every drug I knew to stop the fits. Finally I had to put her under chloroform. It was all to no purpose. She died holding my hand and thanking me for all I had done for her. For what, I thought — and I spent a miserable night thinking of the futility of medicine in certain circumstances. I am afraid that I worried too much about patients, and felt aggrieved when they did not respond to treatment. By the end of my month as a locum I was pretty sure I was not cut out for general practice.

Meanwhile, I had my research scholarship. My first choice of subject was ophthalmology, in which I had won a class medal, and I took a post as Junior House Surgeon (unpaid) in the Eye Department of the Royal Infirmary. In order to be sure that this appointment had the approval of the Faculty, I sought an interview with the Dean. At that time this happened to be Professor Harvey Littlejohn, who held the Chair of Forensic Medicine. He suggested that I should become an assistant in his department, where I could get ample material for an M.D. thesis. This post carried the munificent salary of fifty pounds per annum, and as it could be held conjointly with my scholarship I decided to accept.

And so it was, almost accidentally, that forensic medicine became my career.

2

Dr Bell and Sherlock Holmes

IN AN EARLY STORY SHERLOCK HOLMES TOLD DR WATSON THAT A
detective needed three things for success: the power of observation, the power of deduction, and a wide range of exact
knowledge. Precisely the same things are needed for successful
medical diagnosis, and it is not an accident that the original of
Sherlock Holmes was a doctor.

When I was a medical student one of our lecturers in surgery,
George Chiene, encouraged us to look for more than the conventional signs and symptoms before making a diagnosis. One day he
was discussing the subject of extroversion of the bladder — a
condition in which the abdominal wall has not closed properly,
and the bladder has not been properly formed. As a consequence
fluid from the kidneys is discharged on the abdominal wall. Eventually an operation is performed to reconstruct the parts, but until
then some form of absorbent diaper has to be used. Describing
such a case, Mr Chiene mentioned that the kilt was a most convenient dress for a boy so disabled, owing to the greater ease in
dressing him. Suddenly he looked up and saw that my friend
Tommy Horrax — who had taken his usual seat in the back of the
theatre, out of range of questions — was not paying attention.
The lecturer thought he would catch Tommy out.

"Now, Mr Horrax," he said, "if a woman came into your
consulting room, leading a boy of about ten who was wearing a
kilt and smelling of urine, what would you diagnose?"

Without a moment's delay my friend replied, "A Scotsman" —
which no doubt spoilt Mr Chiene's day. It certainly broke up the
class.

George Chiene did not invent this medical detective game. He
was simply following in the footsteps of an earlier lecturer to

medical students in Edinburgh, a very distinguished surgeon on the staff of the Royal Infirmary. This was Dr Joseph Bell, who had an almost uncanny gift of diagnosing not only disease but occupation and even character from a patient's appearance.

"This man," Bell told his students once, after only a glance at the patient, "is a left-handed cobbler." The patient gasped in surprise, the students stared wonderingly. "The worn places on his trousers," Bell explained, "could only have been made by resting a lapstone between his knees. The right side is more worn than the left because he hammers the leather with his left hand." Like a conjuring trick, it always seemed miraculous until it was explained, and then it was almost absurdly simple.

"Did you enjoy your walk over the golf-links to-day, as you came in from the south side of the town?" Bell asked another patient, a complete stranger who had never been to him before. Bell's out-patient clerk, although used to this deductive brilliance, was completely baffled until the surgeon explained. "On a showery day such as this the reddish clay at bare parts of the golf-course adheres to the boot, and a tiny part is bound to remain. There is no such clay anywhere else."

It was really quite elementary, as Bell himself used to tell friends and social acquaintances after startling them with a demonstration of his remarkable gift. Elementary, my dear Watson....

"Why," said a fellow-guest at a dinner party, "Dr Bell might almost be Sherlock Holmes."

"Madam," Dr Bell replied, "I am Sherlock Holmes."

So he was. That out-patient clerk whom he loved to puzzle, and who later qualified as a doctor himself, was Arthur Conan Doyle.

Something of what Conan Doyle learnt from Bell can be seen in a story like "The Five Orange Pips," in which Sherlock Holmes greets a visitor with the remark, "You have come up from the south-west, I see" — followed by the explanation: "That clay and chalk mixture which I see upon your toe-caps is quite distinctive." In another story, "The Adventure of the Norwood Builder," a young man bursts into the Baker Street consulting-room and introduces himself as John McFarlane. "You mention your name as if I should recognize it," the great detective chides him, "but I assure you that beyond the obvious facts that you are a bachelor, a solicitor, a Freemason, and an asthmatic, I know nothing whatever about you."

All this is pure Bell, and Conan Doyle gratefully admitted his debt. He did not succeed in establishing much of a practice in medicine, and took up writing in sheer desperation. Influenced by Gaboriau and Poe, he decided to try to create a new kind of fictitious detective. "I thought of my old teacher Joe Bell, of his eagle face, of his curious ways, of his eerie trick of spotting details," Doyle wrote in his autobiography. "If he were a detective he would surely reduce this fascinating but unorganized business to something nearer to an exact science. I would try if I could get this effect. It was surely possible in real life, so why should I not make it plausible in fiction?"

Therein lies the value of the Sherlock Holmes stories apart from their excellent entertainment. To-day criminal investigation is a science, and the plodding policeman gaping admiringly at the gifted amateur is an anachronism. This was not always so and the change owes much to the influence of Sherlock Holmes. An author may feel satisfaction when his fiction is accepted as true to life: Conan Doyle had the rare, perhaps unique, distinction of seeing life become true to his fiction.

To Holmes's three qualities necessary for a successful detective he might have added a fourth — the power of constructive imagination, always strictly controlled by the intellect, an essential quality when there are no more facts to be observed and no further inferences to be drawn. Holmes himself used this power successfully in "The Sign of Four" when he was baffled in his search for the missing launch. "I then put myself in the place of Small [the criminal] and looked at it as a man of his capacity would.... I wondered what I should do myself if I were in his shoes."

Doyle made it clear that there was nothing supernatural or even intuitive about the methods used by Sherlock Holmes; nor, by any means, were all his powers innate. His confidence in rejecting apparently probable inferences, and in drawing inferences that were apparently improbable or impossible, was due to his cult of prolonged observation and close examination of apparently trifling matters. By what his creator called "intense study and rigorous training" the master detective had perfected his ability to spot minute characteristics and instantly realize their significance until it was almost second nature.

The official police usually viewed Holmes's methods with thinly veiled suspicion, and indeed Conan Doyle sometimes pushed matters too far. Holmes's ability to distinguish a hundred and forty different kinds of tobacco ash — a subject on which he wrote, as we are told, one of his monographs — his assertions that "nothing has more individuality than a [tobacco] pipe save perhaps watches and bootlaces," that the true decade of a man's age can in normal cases be inferred from his handwriting, and that the handwriting of blood-relatives has similar characteristics — each of these imposes a strain on our credulity, and adds nothing to our regard for Holmes and his creator.

Full of significance and interest, however — especially to anyone concerned professionally with the detection of crime and criminals — is the anticipation of modern scientific methods of investigation. For instance, the use of the hand lens and the microscope; the measuring tape; the plaster casts of footprints; the extraction and examination of dust and the like from clothing; and the discrimination between bloodstains and other stains — in 1887 Holmes claimed to have discovered an infallible chemical test for bloodstains. "Why, man," he told Watson, "it is the most practical medico-legal discovery for years." Here we find the principle of using the chemical laboratory in criminal investigation.

But there is a puzzle for the attentive reader. Holmes first appears working in a chemical laboratory at a hospital. His knowledge of chemistry Watson reckoned as "profound." In his lodgings he had a private laboratory, and was fond of performing experiments there, often to Watson's great discomfort. His addiction to chemical science is, then, emphasized. Yet in not one of the detailed stories does he use his laboratory skill; in not one of these cases does he make a chemical test. His infallible test of bloodstains — discovered at the beginning of his career — was never called into action. All his cases were solved by quite other methods. Conan Doyle seems, indeed, curiously casual about scientific tests. In "Silver Blaze" we read that analysis of the stable-boy's supper disclosed the presence in it of powdered opium. The analysis was apparently conducted by the police (certainly not by Holmes), but we are not told how or where it was conducted. A still more strange example occurs in "The Naval Treaty." At the beginning Watson finds Holmes in his lodgings busy with a retort and a Bunsen burner, dipping into this bottle and that, and finally holding out a test-tube containing some fluid. "You come at a crisis, Watson. If this paper remains red, all is well. If it turns blue, it means a man's life." But that is all, a dozen lines or so; Conan Doyle passes on at once to the story of the vanished treaty, in the solution of which chemical analysis has no place whatsoever. We have here a hint of Holmes's use of chemistry in a criminal case, the last act in its solution, but not a word as to what the case was, nor as to what led up to that last act. So far as I know, this is the only hint of any such use by Holmes. It is difficult to imagine any case in which a man's life would rest upon the question of whether a fluid was acid or alkaline.

It may be, however, that Doyle was simply too anxious not to write above his readers' heads. When Dr Bell once suggested that Holmes should be matched against a germ murderer, and hinted that he knew of a case of this sort, Doyle replied that he feared that bacteriological murder might be too complex for the average reader to understand. For this reason, no doubt, most writers of detective stories at that time avoided scientific technicalities, and Doyle apparently took the same line. Nowadays the case is different; scientific trimmings are popular in detective stories, and lay authors sometimes risk using imperfect knowledge in an attempt to give the public what it wants.

Though he made scanty use of Holmes's or his own chemical knowledge, Conan Doyle's presentation of Holmes and his methods — his observation, his attention to details, however small, his cold, unemotional attitude, his power of diagnosing and grasping essential facts, his powers of logical deduction, his wide and exact knowledge, and the rest — served a serious purpose in turning the attention of the police and others towards the value of these methods, and of laboratory tests in criminal investigation. This may well have been his deliberate intention. In the latest story of all, "Shoscombe Old Place" (1927), Holmes tells Watson, "Since I ran down that coiner by the zinc and copper filings in the seam of his cuff, they [Scotland Yard] have begun to realize the importance of the microscope."

As a man Sherlock Holmes was hardly a lovable character, and in this respect he does not seem to have resembled his original at all. Joe Bell had a kind heart and a keen sense of humour.

"You must observe everything, gentlemen," he used to tell his students. "Use your eyes; use your fingers; use all your faculties before coming to a decision about anything." Once, while talking in this vein, he held up a tube containing fluid of a nauseous

The Author on Graduation (1912)

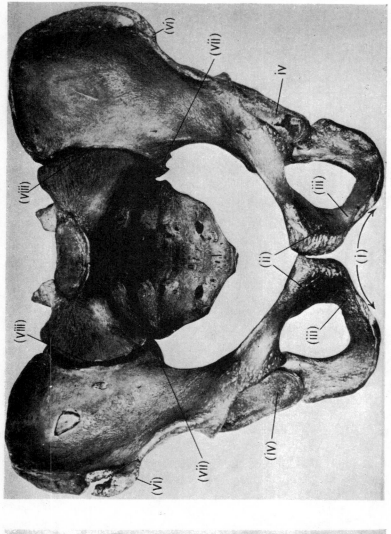

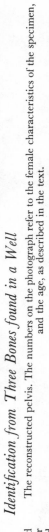

Identification from Three Bones found in a Well

The reconstructed pelvis. The numbers on the photograph refer to the female characteristics of the specimen, and the age, as described in the text.

The right hip-bone. (a) irregularly shaped lead slug embedded in the bone; (b) triangular piece of bone, displaced by a slug; (c) grooved fracture, showing erosion of bone due to septic infection after the passage of a slug.

nature. "Now, gentlemen, apply your powers of observation to this sample. Before attempting to carry out any chemical procedures, do as I do. Look at it — observe its colour, see whether it is opalescent or clear. Smell it: has it any particular odour that you can recognize? Taste it." Whereupon he put his finger into the glass and raised his hand to his mouth, making a grimace as he did so.

The sample was then handed round the class, and each student in turn looked at it, smelt it, put his finger in it, tasted it, and grimaced. When they had all finished Bell addressed them again:

"That, gentlemen, indicates the complete lack of observation in the members of this class. Not one of you observed that whereas I placed my forefinger in the glass, it was my middle finger that I put in my mouth."

There is another Joe Bell story, of which there are various versions, that he liked to tell against himself. According to one account, a patient walked into the out-patient theatre and Bell, after looking him over carefully, turned to his students and said:

"Now, here is an interesting case for us. This man, I should say, is a recently discharged soldier who was probably in the Royal Scots and had a good deal of service in the East. In the Army he was probably in the band, and, I have no doubt, played a brass wind instrument."

The students looked suitably astonished at these powers of deduction.

"Now," Bell continued, according to his habit, "how did I deduce this information about the patient? Did you notice that when he came in he stood rigidly to attention? No civilian ever does that, and a soldier, after he has been discharged for a time, also neglects to do so — hence I deduced that he had probably not been long discharged from the Army. You noticed, I hope, the deep tanning of his face and neck, and the tattoo mark on his arm. These things suggest that he saw a good deal of service in a hot clime, probably in the East, and it was there also that the tattoo mark was pricked on his arm, since it is not of a design which is likely to have been tattooed here. He is wearing a belt fastened by a buckle of the Royal Scots regiment. Of course, he may have acquired the belt by some out-of-the-way means, but the suggestion is that he may have been in that regiment. From his stature he would appear rather small for the regular infantry, and it was on that account that I suggested that he might have been in the band. Now, if you look at his chest and observe the way he breathes you will note that he shows all the signs of emphysema [dilation of the air-vessels in the lungs] — which may well be due to playing a large wind instrument: hence my suggestion that he had been a player of such an instrument for many years."

Bell then turned to the patient.

"Now, my man, have you been a soldier?" he asked confidently.

"Yes, sir."

"In the Royal Scots?"

"Yes, sir."

"For a long period?"

"Twenty years, sir."

"You have seen service in India?"

"Yes, sir."

"You played in the band?"

"Yes, sir."

"And can we take it that you played the euphonium or a similar instrument?"

"No, sir, the big drum."

A good enough story, which, whether true or not, indicates that the validity of the deduction drawn varies in accordance with the extent to which it excludes all other possibilities.

Observation and deduction alone are not enough, but must be supported by a wide range of exact knowledge. I blundered badly once through unpardonable ignorance. I was examining the clothing of a young woman who had made an allegation of a criminal assault, and there was a question whether certain articles of clothing had been taken off or torn off. I was examining the exhibits with a young advocate and, lifting a corset belt, I fastened it round my waist to observe the position of certain tears and stains. "Excuse me, sir," said the young lawyer, "but you are fastening it on the wrong side." I commended his powers of observation, which did him all the more credit as he was unmarried.

The necessity of taking nothing for granted was impressed on me as a student by Sir Norman Walker, the eminent specialist in skin diseases. In referring to the later manifestation of a disease that was relatively common at that time but is now, fortunately, less often seen, Sir Norman said:

"Gentlemen, in considering the origin of these conditions you must not be unduly impressed by the apparent respectability of your patient. Remember that every bishop was once a divinity student, and every admiral a midshipman."

There is nothing new in all this. Almost 2500 years ago Hippocrates stressed the importance of close observation of all details, and advised careful study of the whole patient and his environment before making a diagnosis. This advice is as valuable as ever in the general field of medicine. In the special field of forensic medicine it has exceptional significance.

The medico-legal expert, or specialist in forensic medicine, is not a detective. He may — and this is not his only function — use his knowledge and intelligence to help the police to solve a crime. In thus placing his expert knowledge at their disposal he does not usurp the duties of the police officers who are handling the case. They are responsible for the investigation, and it seldom happens that a crime is solved by a doctor or other scientist working in his laboratory alone. Basically his rôle is simply to furnish the police with specific information on matters of which he has specialized knowledge.

At the same time the part played by the medico-legal expert is not so circumscribed as that, for example, of an analytical chemist helping the police. He sees the case as a whole, not exclusively in its medical aspects. He observes, infers, and even speculates. To him, because of his special knowledge, a non-medical clue may have a significance that even an astute police-officer has not grasped. His peculiar experience and talents may enable him alone to deduce the correct interpretation of the facts.

The success or failure of an investigation depends often on the initial observations and actions of the police-officers who first appear on the scene of a crime. They are responsible also for protecting from damage everything that might be of useful interest to the medico-legal expert. For him a case often begins with a request to look at a dead body. The police may not know who the dead person is, and then they will want to be told of any detail that may help identification. They will want to know the cause and manner of death — whether it was due to natural causes or to violence; and if the latter, whether it is a case of accident, suicide, or murder. How did the person die? When did death take place? This may be very important if it is murder, and a suspected person claims an alibi. Where did death take place? The body may have been moved afterwards. Why did it happen? Usually only this last question, the motive, lies outside the professional scope of the medico-legal expert — but in certain cases, such as murder after sexual assault, he may be able to explain this too.

To find the answers to all these questions various facts have to be discovered and put together: the rate of cooling of the body, the onset and progress of stiffness (rigor mortis), post-mortem discoloration (hypostasis), the condition of food in the stomach and bowel, the state and composition of the blood, and many other matters of this kind. Hypostasis alone, although less written about than rigor mortis, can provide a variety of interesting information.

This post-mortem discoloration, or lividity, is caused by the sinking of the blood, under the effect of gravity, to the lowest vessels in the body. The gravitation begins as soon as the heart ceases to beat. The minute capillaries become distended with blood, and livid patches appear on the surface of the body. The discoloration starts soon after death, at first in small patches, which gradually fuse together into large areas. It is very distinct after twelve hours.

Normally the colour is at first bluish-pink, afterwards purplish; but in poisoning by carbon monoxide it is pink, by prussic acid light red, by certain other poisons chocolate-coloured, and in death from burning or cold it may be distinctly red. It is well marked in asphyxia, but less so in death from bleeding. If the body is moved before the blood coagulates the stains may change their position, but when coagulation in the capillaries takes place the stains are permanently fixed. This usually occurs in about six hours; but in death from choking or strangulation it may be delayed many hours longer.

The distribution of the stains depends on the position of the body. If it is lying on its back the whole back will be discoloured except the parts directly pressed on — for any pressure, however slight, prevents the capillaries from filling, and such areas are not discoloured. The position of any tight band, such as a collar band or a garter, or of wrinkles in a shirt, will be marked by the absence of discoloration. Such pale areas are sometimes confused with marks due to beating or strangling. Post-mortem stains must not be confused with bruises, which they often resemble, and in doubtful cases sections have to be taken for examination under the microscope.

Discoloration is only one of the important post-mortem signs from which vital information about the death may be discovered. Sometimes such medical data will simply confirm other facts and deductions already made by the police. On the other hand, it may be that when the medico-legal expert is called in there is no circumstantial evidence at all. I had a typical case in Egypt in the nineteen-twenties, when the body of a British official was found on the banks of the Nile, shot in the head. He was young, single, and healthy; with no known enemies, and free from any entanglements with the other sex; free from financial embarrassment and occupying a good position under the Egyptian Government. Apparently he had left his house after dinner, cycled out of town for about a mile, walked to the bank of the Nile, sat down, and either blown his brains out or had them blown out by someone else. There was no suicide letter, and no discernible motive for murder, but political murder was rife in Egypt at the time, and more than one British subject had been found dead in unusual circumstances. This case aroused a considerable stir in Government circles, and if it was murder the repercussions were likely to be serious. In the absence of any other evidence everything depended on the medical examination.

The bullet had entered on the right side of the forehead and emerged from the left side of the back of the head. Blackening and burning from powder round the wound showed that it had been fired from close quarters. There was no sign of any struggle on the man's body or at the place where he had been found. All this pointed strongly to suicide, but the lack of other evidence made corroboration desirable. After a careful examination of his whole body two details came to light: there was a small nick in one of the fingers of his right hand, and his waistcoat and shirt were unbuttoned. I deduced that the nick had been made when he caught the skin of his finger in pulling back the bolt of his pistol, and it seemed reasonable to infer that he had unfastened his waistcoat and shirt with the first intention of shooting himself in the heart. They were small points in themselves, but important as corroboratory evidence. The verdict was suicide.

The medico-legal expert may be called to give evidence either for the prosecution or for the defence. If his services are not co-opted by the police he may make them available to assist a person charged with the crime. And even when he is helping the police he should never be influenced by any police theory. His findings may very well destroy what had appeared a strong case against a particular person. They may also direct the attention of the police to a new line of investigation.

The scope of forensic medicine has not remained constant. At one time it included public health, but that has long since become a separate specialty. Similarly, psychiatry has absorbed much of the work that used to come within the scope of the medical jurist. Then even within his own field there has been a great deal of specialization. The forensic pathologist, the forensic serologist, and the forensic toxicologist are each well-nigh specialists in their own right, and ideally a combination of these should work together as a team.

By no means all forensic science is medical, and co-operation is often needed from the botanist, the zoologist, the entomologist, the geologist, and other specialists. The frontiers between various scientific disciplines are not always clearly marked, and through circumstances some anomalies have arisen. There is nothing medical about the identification of firearms from an examination of bullets and cartridge-cases; but there is no separate specialty of forensic ballistics, and this work has in my time fallen into the province of the medico-legal expert, because he was accustomed to dealing with bullets in relation to wounds, and because there was no one else to undertake it.

Forensic medicine — or medical jurisprudence, as it used to be called — is of great antiquity, being the offspring of two of the three oldest professions in the world. The Egyptian Imhotep (*c.* 3000 B.C.) was both Chief Justice and Court Physician, and may be regarded as the first known medico-legal expert. In early Greek and Roman times such medical and other sciences as existed were used in the administration of the law, and one of the earliest good books on the subject was published in medieval Italy.

Modern forensic medicine, however, grew up first in Germany and France. Britain was late in the field, and the first Chair — at Edinburgh University — was not created until 1807. This step was criticized in the House of Commons, one Member opposing it on the grounds that he could not understand what medical jurisprudence meant. In 1834 Alfred Swaine Taylor was appointed to a similar Chair at Guy's Hospital Medical School, and two years later he published the first of his great works on the subject, a book which I have had the honour of editing.

In Edinburgh it was usual for the Professor of Medical Jurisprudence to be also Chief Surgeon to the City Police. Sir Henry Littlejohn, Harvey's father, held both appointments when

Conan Doyle was learning the habits of observation from Joe Bell. Bell dabbled in criminal investigation, and worked with Sir Henry on a number of cases. Although a purely amateur detective without any official status, the original of Sherlock Holmes sometimes put the seal on his efforts by giving evidence for the Crown.

Sir Henry Littlejohn was another of Edinburgh University's 'characters.' A cynic with little faith in natural virtue, he once remarked tartly that he would wager he could push a wheelbarrow containing all the adult virgins in Edinburgh up the slopes of Arthur's Seat!

In 1906 Harvey Littlejohn succeeded his father in the Chair. He had previously given lectures to external students, and he made a great impression with his first lecture after his elevation. He was discussing a recent case of infanticide.

"Here you have, gentlemen," he declaimed, "an unfortunate child murdered by its unfortunate mother — only a girl herself, led astray by an unprincipled scoundrel and left to bear the fruits alone. As for that foul blackguard, the father——" Here Harvey launched into a torrent of invective that went on for quite a time. Then he stopped, and confided, "I have never let myself go like that before, because when I taught in the extra-mural school there was always the possibility that the father was in my audience."

He had a dramatic style of lecturing, and used to carry out reconstructions of his cases before us students. He succeeded his father as Chief Police Surgeon as well as Professor, and was an excellent witness for the Crown. Witty and caustic, with a tongue like a needle, he was a good mixer, very cocky and self-assured, and had an erroneous belief that he was a good bridge-player. At the University Club, I am told, the other members competed for the privilege of not having him as a partner. He had a fine stock of wines which he could not drink himself because of some stomach trouble, and as his assistant I was able to prevent some of these from going to waste. He was a leader in the field of forensic medicine, and a very good friend to me. In my work with him I saw a wide range of cases, and he encouraged me to examine all his material myself and to take an active, practical interest in the pathology of injury and all related subjects. Eventually he entrusted me with investigations, and in 1913 I had my first big case. I think it is worth retelling as an example of the work we were doing in Edinburgh in those early days.

3

The Hopetoun Quarry Murder

I N MY OPINION," SAID THE LOCAL DOCTOR, "AN AUTOPSY WOULD be a waste of time. Decomposition is too advanced."

The Procurator-Fiscal for West Lothian rejected the doctor's opinion, and the bodies were put in the mortuary at Linlithgow to await our arrival.

They had been found in a water-filled quarry near Winchburgh, on a Sunday afternoon in June 1913, by two ploughmen out for a stroll.

When they first saw the dark object floating on the water they thought some practical joker had thrown in a scarecrow from a neighbouring field. When they realized it was more sinister than that they took a long branch of a tree and pulled the dark object to the bank. They saw then that it consisted of two bodies tied together with window-cord. When they tried to lift the bodies out of the water the cord broke. The ploughmen then fetched the police.

The bodies were small, fully dressed, and unmistakably human. The fact that they were tied together strongly suggested foul play.

"We have no reports of any children missing from the neighbourhood," the police told us when we arrived. "As you will see, the features are unrecognizable."

We saw that all right, and presumably it was the reason for the local doctor's opinion that an autopsy would be valueless. In point of fact it made it more than ever necessary. These were unidentified bodies that had been dead for quite some time, and the police could not do much in investigation until they knew who they were.

We began with the clothing. This is the normal starting-point with an unknown body, and it usually produces clues. The character, cut, and style of the clothing, whether it is worn or torn and whether it has been mended — dust and debris in the pockets, the tag of the tailor or seller, name-tags, laundry and cleaners' marks — these and other details provide much information about the personality, social status, occupation, habits, and movements of the deceased. Often they lead to precise identification.

We did not expect so much in this case, because the garments were practically rotten from long immersion. However, as we took them off the bodies we saw that both the victims had been dressed alike — in shirts, stockings with garters under the knees, and boots. We saw also that the clothes were of cheap quality, suggesting that the victims were poor.

"That doesn't get us very far," said Littlejohn.

"No," I agreed, as I examined one of the shirts. "But look at this!"

There was a stamp imprinted on the shirt, very faded and hard to decipher, but I could just make out what it said.

It was the stamp of a poorhouse at Dysart, in Fife.

This single but quite dramatic clue was all we could learn from the clothing. At first sight the bodies themselves did not look as if they would have much to add. They had been almost wholly transformed into what is called adipocere.

When a body is left for a long period in water, or buried in damp ground, it undergoes a distinctive change. Human fat, which is normally semi-fluid, is gradually converted to a fat that is quite firm, like mutton suet. This is adipocere. The conversion is a slow process, but permanent when complete.

We were interested from a purely medical point of view, because extensive transformations are rarely come across, and these specimens were quite exceptional. In each body the formation was complete apart from the feet, which had been covered by the boots, and in which the adipocerous condition was therefore not so far advanced.

"How long do you think they were in the water?" Littlejohn asked me.

"Not more than two years," I suggested. "Perhaps only eighteen months, but hardly less."

He nodded agreement.

"Like to carry on by yourself?" he asked.

I said I would, and he let me do the autopsies on my own.

There is a regular drill for autopsies on unidentified bodies. The first thing is to determine whether or not they are human, and after that the sex and age. In this case the adipocere had preserved the shapes of the bodies unusually well, but their external appearance gave little or no indication of sex. One of them looked rather as if it was of a girl, but when I explored internally there was no sign of any female organs. I cut the groin, and found glandular structures sufficiently well preserved to be recognized as male. The other body, with less difficulty, proved to be of the same sex. This was, of course, what I had expected from the clothing.

It was a simple matter to discover their stature accurately by direct measurement. One was three feet seven and a half inches tall, the other three feet two; respectively the average heights of a boy of about six to seven and a boy of four. I looked at their teeth. The bigger boy had cut his first permanent molars, which usually erupt at the age of six. His central incisors were also fully cut, and as a rule these erupt a year later. The lateral incisors usually erupt at about eight, and in his case these were in process of cutting. All the others were milk teeth. I examined the growing ends of his long bones, and the state of these confirmed that he had been six or seven when he died. The smaller boy had all his milk teeth but none of his permanent teeth, which put his age between two and six. This margin was reduced by the fact that his first permanent molars were approaching the surface prior to cutting, so that he was well over two. The condition of his bones suggested an age between three and four.

Both boys' scalps were nearly bare, but in each case there were tufts of brown hair on the back which had been cut shortly before death. The elder boy had a small injury in the scalp, but no evidence of fracture; I could not say whether it had been inflicted before or after death.

In each case the internal organs were remarkably well preserved. Their stomachs were intact, and the contents — which I examined in our laboratory in Edinburgh — of great interest. In each stomach there were several ounces of thick material, including undigested and easily recognizable vegetable matter — whole green peas, barley, potatoes, turnips, and leeks; in fact, the traditional ingredients of Scotch broth. The extensive adipocere formation was responsible for preserving this valuable evidence over such a phenomenally long period. Its importance, of course, was that it helped to fix the time of death. The adipocere itself suggested this was eighteen months to two years ago. Assuming that the vegetables were fresh, the boys' last meal would have been eaten in the late summer or autumn of 1911.

I estimated that the meal had been eaten about one hour before death. This suggested that the boys lived locally, or at least that they had not been brought from a great distance to be disposed of. The force of this came home to me when we visited the quarry where the bodies were found.

It was extremely secluded. About a mile east of Winchburgh and a quarter of a mile north of the main Edinburgh road, it was hidden on the east and west sides by clumps of trees and bushes. About a hundred yards long and forty yards wide, it was filled with water to a considerable depth. It had been in disuse for several years, and was seldom visited by anyone; even in summer it was a dismal spot. The two ploughmen had gone there because one was a newcomer to the district and the other was showing him round.

We had to follow a long, winding cart-track to reach the quarry. It was the only way to it.

"How do you think the bodies were brought here?" Littlejohn asked.

He knew the answer as well as I did. The chances were that the boys had walked there, not suspecting that they would never walk back.

They had walked there with their killer.

Then surely they must have known him well. Probably he was a relative. Perhaps even a parent?

So we could give the police something to go on. We could tell them the victims' sex, ages, and heights; the colour of their hair, and the fact that they had it cut shortly before death; the contents of their last meal, and roughly when it had been eaten; that they were poor, and had been in a certain poorhouse not long before death; roughly when they had died; and, finally, how they had probably been brought to the quarry, and the sort of person who had taken them.

Almost at once the police discovered that two boys had disappeared from the neighbourhood in November 1911. One was nearly seven and the other four; both were of average height and build and had brown hair. Their father, a widower, had been in prison for failing to maintain them.

His name was Patrick Higgins. He had been a soldier once, and served for six or seven years with the Scottish Rifles in India.

When he returned home he took a job at the Winchburgh brick-works, and married a girl who also worked there. Their first son, William, was born in December 1904, and the second, John, in August 1907. Higgins drank heavily and neglected his family. His wife died in 1910, and soon afterwards the boys were getting relief from the Inspector of Poor at Wemyss, Fife. In January 1911 they were taken into the poorhouse at Dysart.

The parish applied to Higgins for payment, and when he refused he was gaoled for two months. He came out on August 24, and two days later he collected the boys from the Dysart Poorhouse and brought them back to the Winchburgh district. For the time being he boarded them in near-by Broxburn with a widow named Elizabeth Hynes, whom he had known since he was a boy. He himself slept sometimes in a lodging-house in the same town, some-times at the brickworks, where he cooked his meals in a rather barbarous fashion, using his spade as a frying-pan and making soup in the pail he used at his work. He earned twenty-four shillings a week, and apparently spent most of the money on drink. He promised to pay Mrs Hynes for the maintenance of his children, but did not give her a penny. She told the local Inspector of Poor, who went to the brickworks and warned Higgins that if he did not maintain his children he would be prosecuted again. At last, after they had been with Mrs Hynes for about a month, Higgins took them away, avoiding the widow by meeting them outside the house. He took the boys to the brickworks, tried to get them into a home, but refused to pay the required eight or nine shillings a week. Then, one wet and stormy night at the beginning of November, the boys disappeared.

It was early evening, said Hugh Shields, a miner, when he saw Higgins and the boys walk away to the east. Later Higgins re-turned alone. He and Shields went to a public-house together, and Higgins said, "The kids are all right now." When Shields asked where they were he said they were on their way to Canada.

Another miner, James Daly, who had known Higgins since he was a boy, confirmed the first part of Shields's story. It was on a Monday or Tuesday, he said, between 7 and 8 p.m., when he saw Higgins walk towards Winchburgh with his boys, holding the younger one by the hand. About three hours later Daly saw Higgins in a public-house.

"Did I not see you with your two boys to-night, Paddy?" he asked.

"Yes."

"Where are they now? Are they outside?"

"No," said Higgins. "I have got a good home for them now." He went on to tell Daly that he had caught the 8.30 train to Edinburgh, and in the compartment were two ladies, one of whom took a fancy to one of the boys and offered to take him. Higgins said he told her that where one went the other would have to go. Then, according to his story, the other lady, hearing the boys' mother was dead, agreed to take the other boy. Higgins said he had left the train at Ratho, and run back to Winchburgh to be in time for a drink. He told Daly he had not got the ladies' address, but they had his.

"You have no address," said Daly.

"Yes; Patrick Higgins, Winchburgh Brickworks."

The police found yet another miner, Llewelyn Richards, to whom Higgins had told the same story while in the public-house. Both Daly and Richards said Higgins was quite calm and rational and not at all peculiar or excited. Later that evening he returned to the brickworks to sleep, and told Alexander Fairnie, a brick-turner, the story of the ladies in the train. But some time afterwards, when Fairnie asked if he had had word of the children, Higgins replied that they had "gone to glory." Several months later he called on Mrs Hynes and told her they were both drowned.

Swiftly and surely the police collected the evidence against Higgins. More persons recalled being told the story of the ladies in the train, while others said Higgins had told them the boys were in a home or a school. The wardress of Dysart Poorhouse, who confirmed the boys' residence, identified the shirts. The police even succeeded in finding a woman who remembered having given the boys a meal of Scotch broth one wet and stormy evening in early November 1911.

Higgins was arrested within a few days of the bodies being found. He was taken completely by surprise — at his old lodging-house in Broxburn, at two o'clock in the morning. Four police-officers knocked up the keeper, who happened to be a new man and was not sure which of the lodgers Higgins was. He said one of the others, who had been there a long time, was bound to be able to tell him, and he went upstairs to ask him. This man was in a cubicle containing two beds. When the keeper said the man the police wanted had previously been in trouble for neglecting his children the man lying on the other bed sat up and said, "That's me they want, I believe." Then he rose, dressed, and went quietly off in the custody of the police, without showing the slightest anxiety or concern. When asked about his boys he said he did not know where they were. When cautioned he had nothing to say.

The trial was held in the High Court of Justiciary at Edinburgh three months later. It caused a great stir, for there had been nothing like it since Oscar Slater stood in the same dock four years before. The person in court who seemed least affected was Higgins himself. He simply sat there, expressionless, staring straight in front. The only time he showed any animation was when he entered or left the dock, and winked and nodded at acquaintances who were in court. For a man on trial for his life he looked extraordinarily unconcerned.

The defence did not question the identity of the two bodies or the contention that the boys had been murdered, but strove to discredit the evidence that Higgins had done the deed. In his closing speech his counsel argued that the case for the Crown rested only on suspicion, and that anyone else could have committed the crime. In addition to the plea of not guilty, however, the accused put forward a special defence that at the time he was alleged to have committed the crime he was insane and not responsible for his actions. He had a history of epilepsy, and all the evidence called by the defence was in support of the contention that he was of unsound mind when he killed the boys.

This was anticipated by the Crown, and when Harvey Littlejohn gave evidence he was questioned about the mental state of the accused. As Chief Surgeon to the Police, he had examined Higgins in prison, and he said he had found no traces of epilepsy, and thought Higgins a perfectly sane man.

"Would you call yourself a mental expert?" asked the counsel for the defence.

"Well," said Littlejohn, "perhaps *I* might not do so." He emphasized the personal pronoun in his usual cocky way, to the amusement of the court.

Two other doctors who had examined Higgins said they found no evidence of epileptic fits and thought him fully responsible for his actions. But several witnesses for the defence testified they had seen him having fits, and epilepsy was proved to have been the reason for his discharge from the Army. The last witness for the defence was Dr G. M. Robertson, lecturer on mental diseases in Edinburgh University and physician superintendent at the Royal Edinburgh Asylum. He said he thought Higgins's degradation might have been due to epilepsy, and that there existed in him a certain degree of mental weakness.

Lord Johnston, the judge, after a careful review of the evidence submitted, told the jury that their verdict should depend on whether they thought that Higgins was sane, and that he had been sane at the time the crime was committed. The jury retired for an hour and a half, and then returned for further direction in response to a series of questions they put to the judge. After another three-quarters of an hour they returned with a unanimous verdict of guilty, with a recommendation to mercy owing to the length of time that had elapsed between the murder and the trial, and to the want of expert evidence about the murderer's mental condition at the time of the crime.

There was a deep silence in court when the foreman announced the verdict. Higgins heard it without betraying the slightest tremor. When the judge called him by name he sprang to his feet, and he stood at attention in soldierly fashion while sentence of death was pronounced. He showed no sign of emotion until he was led down to the cells, when he looked back at his relatives and friends in court and gave them a smile and a wink.

Higgins was not reprieved, and on Wednesday, October 1, 1913, I went to see him hanged, as arranged by Harvey Littlejohn in his capacity of Chief Surgeon to the Police.

The city architect had erected the scaffold in the well of a staircase adjacent to the condemned cell. Higgins, a Roman Catholic, received Holy Communion in the early morning, and Mass was said in his cell, only a few yards from the scaffold, at seven o'clock. Canon Stuart, of St Mary's Cathedral, then said prayers continually till the end. The city magistrates, who were responsible for carrying out the sentence, arrived at the prison at about half-past seven. Their clerk exhibited the warrant for execution, and when Higgins had been identified as the proper party the Governor surrendered him to the magistrates and was given a formal receipt.

As at the climax to the trial, Higgins himself seemed less concerned than anyone else present. He stood up briskly for the preliminary pinioning operations, which began as the prison clock boomed out the hour of eight. The sound had hardly died away when the procession to the scaffold began.

It was a short walk — a few paces from one room to another — and Higgins was perfectly steady on his feet. After that it was a matter of seconds. Higgins's legs were pinioned, the white cap was placed over his head, the rope adjusted round his neck. All the time Canon Stuart continued to recite prayers. At the scaffold he repeated the words of the psalm "Into Thy hands I commend my spirit." Higgins began the response, "The Lord Jesus receive"—— but that was as far as he got, for then the bolt was drawn and the drop came.

I went down with the prison surgeon and examined the body. After it had been left hanging for the statutory period of one hour it was cut down, put in a plain black coffin, and buried in the prison grounds.

The sun was still shining when we went out of the prison and back into the world, where jolly crowds were setting off for the Musselburgh Races. Many of them had already watched what they could of the scene from the top of Calton Hill. Scotland had never been a great country for hanging, and an execution was always an exceptional event: this was Edinburgh's first of the century. Inevitably it was something of a Roman holiday. There was the usual macabre humour, and then a great hush as the clock struck the hour. All eyes were on the two towers, each with a flagstaff, at either end of the range of prison buildings. The black flag would be flown on one of them, no one knew which. The suspense lasted till three minutes past the hour, when the dark symbol fluttered out on the eastern turret. There was a general rush from those who had been watching the tower on the west. Then the crowds dispersed, and by the time we came out there were only stragglers left. Shortly before half-past eight these were dispersed by the police.

In the gatehouse of the prison the magistrates' clerk told representatives of the Press that death was instantaneous, that Higgins had been calm and composed to the last, and that he wanted it to be known that his sentence was just, and that drink had been the cause of his downfall and ruin. Canon Stuart also said Higgins was very anxious to let it be known that he admitted the justice of his sentence and had no desire to escape the consequences of his crime. "Drink and, through drink, neglect of religion have brought me down," Higgins had told Canon Stuart, who said that beneath his callous nature there was something good in the man, and that his apparent indifference had been assumed to cheer up his friends.

Finally the Governor published a letter he had received the day before the execution:

> I wish from my heart that you will accept this note from me, thanking you for your great kindness to me during my incarceration in the prison. Hoping you will excuse my blunt way of putting it, but, believe me, it is from my heart I say it. I also wish to thank Mr Ross [the chief warder] for his kindness. Hoping you will acquaint him with this note. I would also like you to tell him to thank all the officers that I have been under for their kindness and civility.
>
> Yours respectfully,
PATRICK HIGGINS

It was the first time I had seen a man hanged, and I found it rather an unpleasant experience; especially as I had been partly instrumental in bringing him to the gallows. Since then I have been present at other executions, but I have never lost the feeling of awe at seeing a man in full health walk into the room and knowing that in a matter of seconds he would be dead.

Death, said the prison doctor, was instantaneous, but when I felt the pulse of the executed man, still feebly beating, I wondered at the calm certainty with which my medical colleague pronounced his verdict. No doubt with the neck broken, and the spinal cord severed, death is as nearly instantaneous as may be; but the moment when a person dies every cell in the body is alive, and it is post-mortem persistence of life in the tissues that enables us to form an opinion about the length of time that a body has been what we call dead. I wonder just when life as a whole ceases. When a person is hanged the heart, as in the case of Higgins, usually continues beating for a longer or shorter time after death; and it has often been debated among biologists whether, with the blood still circulating, momentary consciousness might be present after the neck is broken.

In decapitation also it is a question whether the head as it falls into the basket still retains enough consciousness to wonder what is happening to it. In France there has been great controversy about momentary persistence of life after beheading. After the execution of Charlotte Corday, on July 17, 1793, it was said that

> one of the executioners held up her head by her beautiful hair and slapped the face in front of the crowd. The face, which was pale, had no sooner received the slap than both cheeks visibly reddened, and her countenance expressed the most unequivocal marks of indignation. Every spectator was struck by the change of colour, and with loud murmurs cried out for vengeance on this cowardly and atrocious barbarity.

That is the description given by Dr Sue, a prominent medical authority in Paris at the time. Dr Sue and many other physicians and surgeons after him, both in France and in Germany, held that there does remain in the brain of a decapitated head some degree of thought, and in the nerves some degree of sensibility, and they quoted the case of Charlotte Corday as proof of that doctrine. But we shall never know what a head really feels when it leaves the body — or rather, if any of us finds out it will be too late by then to pass the knowledge on.

There is a story, possibly apocryphal, that when Sir Everard Digby was executed for complicity in the Gunpowder Plot the executioners took out his heart and exhibited it to the people, exclaiming, "This is the heart of a traitor" — whereat the head was heard to articulate quite distinctly, "Thou liest."

One result of the Higgins case was recorded in doggerel in a university magazine at the time:

> Two bodies found in a lonely mere,
> Converted into adipocere.
> Harvey, when called in to see 'em,
> Said, "Just what I need for my museum."

As a matter of fact the responsibility for the body-snatching was mine. When I was doing the autopsies at Linlithgow I thought we ought to keep a specimen of such perfect adipocere formation for teaching purposes. I suggested it to Littlejohn in a low voice, for there were two police-officers in the mortuary with us.

"Good idea," he murmured. "I'll clear the decks, and then you go ahead."

He went over to the police-officers, who were standing by the door, and asked them to go outside with him so that they could confer on the case. The officers did not need to be asked twice, for the proceedings on my bench were hardly congenial.

As soon as they were outside I helped myself to some choice specimens and parcelled them up. They had still not come back when I finished my work, so I put the remains in the coffin provided, and screwed down the lid.

"I've packed up the stomachs to take back to Edinburgh," I told Littlejohn when he and the police-officers came in again.

"Good," he said, looking at all my packages with some surprise. "What else have you got?" he whispered on the way out.

"The two heads, a leg and an arm from each, and all the internal organs," I answered with a little pride.

"Good God!" Littlejohn exclaimed, and nearly tripped himself up.

There was not much motor transport in those days, and we went back to Edinburgh by train with my parcels on the luggage-rack. The train was crowded, and it was a hot day. We had the window open, but pretty soon the other passengers began to wrinkle their noses, sniff, and look at one another's boots. No wonder, for the smell was mephitic. The atmosphere grew thicker, and I could see that Littlejohn was getting uneasy. The true source of the stench was bound to be discovered in time. But the train reached Edinburgh before then, and we got safely home.

We put the purloined specimens in the Forensic Medicine Museum at the University, and you can see them there to this day. They are still used to illustrate adipocere formation to students. So complete is their state of preservation that most of the details — including the small injury to William Higgins's scalp — can still clearly be discerned.

4

Adventures in Egypt

FORENSIC MEDICINE FASCINATED ME FROM THE START. AS A career it had nothing like the openings of ophthalmology, but when I had to choose between the two I never had a doubt. I had been doing both when I entered Harvey Littlejohn's department — ophthalmology at the Royal Infirmary in the mornings, forensic medicine at the University in the afternoons. When I found I could not do justice to both I dropped ophthalmology — and, because forensic medicine is such a narrow specialty, took up public health as a second string.

I got my M.D. with honours in 1914, with a gold medal and the Alison Prize. Meanwhile I had taken my Diploma of Public Health, so I was sufficiently well qualified to be in a position to take a decent job. Just then the Egyptian Government decided to give its Principal Medico-Legal Expert, Dr Hamilton, an assistant. I applied and was accepted, and then had to wait for the appointment to be ratified. As usual in Cairo, there was a long delay. I was growing tired of waiting when I received a cable from my old friend Tommy Horrax, who had gone back to New Zealand, telling me of a vacancy in the Government Health Department there. "Shall I apply on your behalf?" he finished a rather long cable. I sent back one word: "Yes." A few days later I went to London for an interview with the High Commissioner for New Zealand, and some weeks later we sailed.

It was July 1914, and I had no idea the world was on the verge of war. We were already in the Red Sea when it began. When we reached New Zealand I was posted to Dunedin as Medical Officer of Health for Otago. I volunteered for military service at once, but the Health Department would not release me. However, I was transferred to Wellington and given the rank of captain, then major, in the New Zealand Army Corps, with military duties at various camps in addition to the ordinary civil health work.

The principal camp was at Trentham, and I was told it was in the grip of a serious epidemic of typhus. I found the camp grossly overcrowded and devoid of the ordinary amenities. Men were falling out by the dozen, and the adjoining racecourse buildings had been turned into a temporary hospital. Typhus thrives in overcrowded and insanitary conditions, but after I had examined the camp and the sick men I came to the conclusion that the cause was not typhus at all. This opinion of a new and inexperienced medical officer was not received by my senior officers with much warmth, and I was asked what I knew about typhus. I probably knew as much or as little as the rest, but that was not the point. I said, "There is not a louse in the camp." Typhus cannot spread without lice.

I tentatively diagnosed the disease as cerebro-spinal meningitis, and this was subsequently confirmed bacteriologically. I then had the job, together with the engineers, of getting the camp converted into a permanent camp with water-supply, drainage, laundry, baths, drying-rooms, and so on. There were no further cases of meningitis.

After a time I had the idea of setting up a mobile laboratory and team for use in Gallipoli. I proposed to have a well-equipped laboratory on a motor-truck with a couple of experienced sanitary engineers, a chemist, a bacteriologist, and ancillary staff. I modestly suggested that I should be C.O. of the unit. I had the plans all complete when we heard from the War Office that such a unit would not be acceptable, but that they would welcome one medical officer as a reinforcement to their existing units. Our tuberculosis officer went.

I continued my work in New Zealand until 1917, when Dr Hamilton died suddenly in Cairo, and the Egyptian Government cabled offering me his post. This carried with it a lectureship in forensic medicine in the School of Medicine in Kasr el Aine. The New Zealand Government agreed to release me, and I sailed on a troopship in medical charge of New Zealand reinforcements for the Middle East.

The medico-legal section in Cairo, of which I took over control, was attached to a department of the Ministry of Justice called the Parquet, whose head was the Procurator-General. There is no similar body in England, but in some respects it is not unlike the office of the Procurator-Fiscal and his associates in Scotland.

The Parquet was responsible for the investigation of crime, and for that purpose it controlled the police. Its officers, who had the status of magistrates, examined witnesses under oath, and ordered arrests. The chief of the Parquet or his substitute decided whether to send a case to the courts for trial, and when he did the Parquet official acted as prosecutor. All this followed the French system rather than the British, and in fact the criminal law of Egypt was based on the Code Napoléon.

The medico-legal section was an essential part of the organization, and we were full-time Government officials. When I took charge the staff consisted of two Egyptian doctors and a number of clerks and attendants. Both doctors were well-trained, reliable men, who had been in the section for some years. They presented a nice contrast of types. Ahmed Amer was a countryman, of the landowning class, with family estates: he knew the *fellaheen* well. Mahmoud Maher was a townsman, much more sophisticated and polished, and a member of a famous political family: one of his brothers, Ahmed Maher, was assassinated while Prime Minister in 1945. Both these men were tremendously helpful to me, especially in initiating me into the customs of Egypt, which often bore closely on our work.

The scope and amount of this work was considerable. We had to review practically all important crimes throughout the country; and at that time there were about a thousand cases of murder and as many attempted murders every year. When I arrived the section was greatly hampered by not having a laboratory of its own. All analyses and other scientific activities were carried out either in the Government analytical laboratories or in the School of Medicine. Luckily both Arthur Lucas at the Government laboratories and W. Morris Colles at the School were interested in the application of science to medico-legal problems, and were very valuable collaborators. Nevertheless, I thought better work would result from a closer union between the medical and other scientific departments, and quite soon I not only managed to secure laboratories attached exclusively to my section, but was lucky enough to get Colles transferred from the School of Medicine to take charge of them. These laboratories grew rapidly. Photographic and X-ray installations were added, and I had some of our clerical staff trained as technicians. Within a few years we had probably the finest medico-legal installation in the world. I should think it was certainly the busiest.

I have a dermatographic skin.

Strike me on the arm, for example, and in a few minutes the skin will accurately reproduce the form of whatever weapon you used.

This peculiarity is neither harmful nor useful — in the ordinary run of things. But it was worth more than a parlour-trick to me almost immediately after I took over my post.

The case was not of great importance in itself, but it had a high significance to me. The commandant of one of the principal prisons in Egypt was charged with ill-treating a prisoner by beating him with a whip. Dr Amer examined the prisoner, and reported that there were marks on the body that in his opinion had been caused by a whip. The defending counsel said this report was ridiculous, and procured reports to the contrary from no fewer than six senior medical men. Two of them were British practitioners of consultant rank.

The case was referred to me. I examined the prisoner, and agreed with Dr Amer.

At the trial I suggested that there should be a conference between the medical witnesses on both sides before I gave my evidence. This was agreed to, and we had the prisoner brought before us for a joint examination.

"Now look at these scars," I said. "These tram-lines are typical whip-marks. And look at the way they curve round the limbs — only a whip could make marks like that." I pointed to the ends of the scars. "See how each scar terminates in a fine line," I said. "And look at the marks of the knots on the lash at the end of the whip."

The six doctors appearing for the defence were not convinced.

"Well," I said, "there is one way to prove it." And I picked up the whip.

They looked a bit startled, as if wondering whom I proposed to use as a guinea-pig. Their eyes opened wider when I brought the whip down on my own arm.

"I have a dermatographic skin," I explained. A few minutes later my arm showed it — and proved my point. The marks on my arm were exactly similar to the scars on the prisoner's body.

The two British doctors agreed that this was good enough, and immediately withdrew from the case. A Syrian doctor followed. The remaining three — two Egyptians and a Greek — refused to be convinced. The trial went on, and I was called to give my evidence.

I took the whip with me to the witness-box, and repeated my demonstration in open court. The prison commandant was found guilty of the charge.

It was a simple enough case, but it was a remarkable help to me in playing myself in. Although I did not know it then, it created much interest among the younger lawyers in Cairo. When I visited Beirut over thirty years later one of them who was also on a visit there reminded me of the case and told me about its effect on them — not because of my spectacular demonstration with the whip, but because I, a whole-time Government official, gave evidence in favour of a prisoner against a senior Government official.

The function of the law, however, is to establish truth. Any expert witness, whether called by the defence or by the prosecution, is acting as an agent of the law. The Crown has many advantages over the accused, including virtually unlimited financial resources; and when there is a conflict between experts the court is probably more likely to believe the witness for the prosecution. All the more reason for him to be strictly impartial. He should not think of a conviction as a victory, of an acquittal as a defeat. He should state the facts — and his interpretation of the facts — fully and frankly, without considering whether they strengthen, weaken, or even destroy the Crown's case. His evidence may be crucial: on it may depend the liberty or even the life of a fellow human being. His responsibility is indeed great.

It was exceptionally great in Egypt, because of the general lack of reliance placed on the evidence of witnesses to fact. Truthfulness was considered something of an idiosyncrasy, and evidence on oath a marketable commodity; so the evidence of an alleged eye-witness was received with much less confidence than it is in Britain. Therefore laboratory evidence assumed an importance of the first magnitude, on the understanding that, while men may lie, inanimate things cannot.

This was brought home to me forcibly in a case of murder in Cairo in which it was all-important to fix the time of death.

The victim was a Frenchman, and therefore the Procurator-General asked me to examine the body personally at the scene of the crime; for in any case in which a foreigner was murdered by an Egyptian there was always the possibility of political repercussions.

In Egypt at that time, under the capitulations, foreigners enjoyed certain rights in connexion with criminal and civil proceedings. If a matter affected foreigners alone it was dealt with by their consular courts, while if both a foreigner and an Egyptian were involved the proceedings took place in the mixed courts. In this case a doctor appointed by the French Consul was assigned to act with me in the post-mortem examination. I, of course, was acting for the Egyptian Government.

The man had been murdered in his own house, which was rather oddly constructed. It consisted of a line of four self-contained rooms, each opening separately from a veranda. The victim was found in the end room, on his own bed, with severe injuries of the head. The mosquito-net was down, and was considerably torn in the area where the head had been. He had evidently been attacked while asleep.

It was known that he was a bad character, and in the habit of letting rooms for immoral purposes. The room next door to his, if not replete with all the accessories of high-class profligacy, as Kai Lung puts it, was at least furnished with most of them, including a large ottoman couch covered with gay Eastern trappings. On the table were the remains of what had obviously been an excellent meal for two, consisting of several courses elegantly served. Two empty champagne glasses and two glasses that had contained liqueur brandy, a cigar-stump, and three cigarette-ends smeared with lipstick completed the picture. A man and a woman had dined and apparently spent the evening in the room. The meal had been supplied from Shepheard's Hotel, and on inquiry there it was learnt that it had been served to the couple in their room at nine o'clock the previous night. Their names were easily ascertained. Both were married, but not to each other, and occupied good positions in Cairo society. If the crime had been committed while they were in the house they would necessarily have to give evidence, and this would undoubtedly lead to a scandal and the breaking up of at least two families. Unless it was demanded by the requirements of justice, there was no object in making public their presence there that night. Quite apart from the general investigation, the time at which the crime occurred was a matter of great importance to them.

The body had been found about midday, and we examined it in the early afternoon. There were seven separate bruises on the right side of the head, and as they were roughly parallel it seemed fairly clear that they had not been struck in the dark. Probably the first blow had stunned him, and the others were given to make certain of his death. There were no signs of a struggle. The electric light was not on. The body was clothed in a shirt such as is worn in the daytime, and on the feet were socks held up by suspenders; there were unused pyjamas in the room. From the post-mortem discoloration and other marks on the body it was evident that it had not been moved after the infliction of the fatal injuries.

On a table in the room were the remains of a light meal. The dishes were still unwashed. We found that the stomach contained food of the same nature as that in the room; it showed practically no signs of digestion, and appeared to have been taken about an hour before his death. The body was completely stiff, but the stiffness was just beginning to pass off. It was May, and at that time in Cairo rigor mortis begins to pass in about twenty-four hours. The initial softening therefore suggested that death had taken place about twenty-four hours before. A slight stain over the region of the appendix, due to commencing putrefaction, supported this suggestion. I concluded that the man had been attacked during his after-lunch siesta, and that death had taken place between one and two o'clock in the afternoon. Further, it seemed probable that the assailant was familiar with the run of the house and might have known his victim.

My French colleague agreed with me in all matters concerning the mode of death, but disagreed absolutely about the time. "*A midi? Jamais de la vie!*" he said vigorously. He contended that death had taken place late the night before.

I had had considerable experience in fixing the time of death in Egypt, and I felt quite sure I was right. I went over in detail the circumstances that had led me to my conclusion. I reminded him of the position of the body and the way it was dressed; the position of the injuries and the way they were inflicted; the nature and state of the food in the stomach; and, above all, the state of rigor mortis and the commencing putrefaction.

He did not dispute any of these points. "Then why," I asked, "are you so sure that he did not die yesterday afternoon?"

"Because," he said simply and devastatingly, "I know a man who saw him alive last night."

This was something of a facer. However, I had learnt in Egypt that when the evidence derived from the scientific consideration of material things all pointed to one conclusion, and this was opposed by the evidence of an eye-witness, then the eye-witness was either mistaken in his belief or deliberately lying. I said so. But my colleague refused to budge. The eye-witness was a personal friend, he said, who certainly would not have invented it and was far too reliable to have made a mistake. We therefore sent in two separate reports, agreeing in everything except the time of death.

No one's life depended on the point as yet, but our difference of opinion was of some social importance to the loving couple in the adjoining room. Happily, they and their respective families were spared exposure by the prompt arrest and confession of the dead man's servant, who had disappeared after the crime. He told the police that his master was a sexual pervert, and had been using him for immoral purposes: not that he minded this, but he was highly incensed about what he considered his master's attempt to do him out of the proper remuneration for his services. He had become so angry that at last he had waited until his master had retired for his after-lunch siesta and had then attacked and killed him with a poker while he was lying on his bed.

This confession corroborated my estimate of the time of death, and the evidence of the eye-witness could be ignored. The innocence of the lovers was established completely, and they were not called upon to give evidence, but, I trust, continued to command the confidence of their respective spouses. I expect, however, that the discovery that there had been a bloody corpse next door to them, while they in silken dalliance lay, did nothing to add to their peace of mind.

A much more striking example of the importance of laboratory evidence in cases where there were eye-witnesses occurred when a man was shot dead in Alexandria. This time a man's life was at stake.

The first I knew of it was when I received a bundle of bloodstained clothing. According to the Parquet's report that came with it, the case was virtually complete, and I had only to supply confirmation to make the murderer's conviction certain.

Two men had seen him do it. They had seen him and his victim standing face to face when he fired a revolver or pistol, and the victim clutched his left leg, turned, and fled. They had seen the accused give chase, and fire again, this time from behind. At that, they said, the victim grasped his right leg, staggered on for about a hundred yards, and then fell to the ground. He was nearly dead when he was picked up, and he died on the way to hospital.

The story of the two eye-witnesses was circumstantial enough, but the police were not so easily satisfied. An autopsy was performed, to see how this story stood against the medical evidence. It came off very well. Two bullet-wounds were found, one in each leg. On the left leg the wound was said to have been inflicted from the front, on the right leg from behind. One bullet had perforated a main artery of the thigh, and the victim had died from hæmorrhage. With this excellent corroboration from the autopsy, the remains were buried and preparations for the trial were made. The clothing was sent to me to complete the prosecution's case.

But I could see at a glance that something was wrong. The bullet-holes were there all right, and the bloodstaining was copious. The clothing all round the bullet-holes had been soaked. But that was what was wrong. The bloodstaining was confined to the parts of clothing that would have been in contact with the wounds. The rest of it was not stained at all.

This could mean only one thing. If the victim had been upright when he was shot he had fallen immediately and not run away. If he had stayed on his feet the blood would certainly have run down his legs. The alleged eye-witness story of the hundred yards' run between wounds was plainly false.

Something else was wrong, although I could not be quite sure about this yet. The bullet-holes did not look as if the shots had been fired either from the front or from behind. They seemed to show that they came from the victim's left side.

I asked for an exhumation.

"I think you'll find he was only shot once," I said.

So it proved. The man had been struck by a single bullet, fired from his left side. It had passed almost horizontally through both legs. It had not come from a revolver or pistol at all, but was probably a high-velocity rifle-bullet. It had fractured both thigh-bones in its passage. This meant that the victim must have fallen at once — he could not have staggered a yard.

It was clear from these deductions that the evidence of the men claiming to be eye-witnesses was false.

I was called by the Crown at the trial, and related what I had found and what I thought it meant. To my surprise the counsel for the defence elected to cross-examine me at great length about firearm wounds and ballistics generally. At last he was interrupted by the judge. "Has it not yet dawned on you, Abdul Bey," he said, "that the principal witness for the Crown has completely demolished the case for the Crown?"

This case, which was typical of many in which I had to bring out evidence in favour of the accused although I was a prosecution witness, improved my reputation for impartiality. Thus I succeeded in winning the confidence of the legal profession and the public, and before long consultants ceased to be called in as expert witnesses for the defence. Eventually our reports came to be accepted without reserve by both prosecution and defence, so that it was only in highly important cases that I had to appear in court personally. This may have made life a little easier, but it also increased my responsibility. When our findings were accepted without question, it was not enough to be scrupulously accurate in our presentation of the case; we had, in our deductions from the observed facts, to draw attention to any point which could in any way be helpful in the defence of the accused.

Often I was able to scotch a case before it came to trial. One that I remember very well was somewhat similar to the shooting at Alexandria that I have just described. The main difference was that this time the accused was a policeman, and he did not deny firing at or even killing the deceased. He only maintained that he was innocent of the charge of murder.

Again the case began for me with a bundle of dead man's clothes. Again I was only expected to confirm what had already been discovered and deduced.

Most of the facts were agreed by every one. There had been a robbery, and the culprit was seen running away. The policeman called to him to halt, but the man ran on. The policeman fired, but could not see the result of his shot. The fugitive apparently got away. However, his dead body was found later in a plantation some distance from where the shooting had taken place.

So far so good. The dead man could have struggled on after being wounded, and died in the plantation of the wound inflicted by the policeman's shot. But the local doctor, who made a postmortem, said there had been two shots. He found two bullet-wounds.

One was in the left thigh. The shot had evidently been fired from the front, and the doctor found the bullet embedded in the muscles at the back of the thigh.

The other bullet had struck the victim in the back. It had passed through the body in a roughly horizontal direction, and made its exit at the lower part of the abdomen.

"He was shot twice," said the local doctor. "First from the front at rather long range, secondly in the back — probably after he had fallen on his face." If the policeman did that it was tantamount to murder.

The policeman swore he had only fired once. That was, he said, when the fugitive was running crouched down along a wall. After that he lost sight of him.

The policeman was well thought of by his senior officers, who found it hard to believe he could have murdered the man. But there were the wounds, one in the front and the other in the back, and the medical evidence was so strong that the policeman was arrested and charged with murder.

That was the position when they sent me the clothing, which consisted of a shirt and an outer garment called a *galabieh*. All the police reports came too. I looked for three bullet-holes in the *galabieh*.

I found one.

It was the entrance-hole of the bullet in the back.

I should have found the exit-hole of this bullet in the front of the *galabieh*. No trace. I should also have found an entrance-hole in the front of the *galabieh*, made by the bullet that had lodged in the man's left thigh. But — no trace.

I looked at the shirt, and found plenty of holes.

First there was the entrance-hole of the bullet in the back, corresponding with the only hole in the *galabieh*. Then there was the exit-hole of this bullet, in the front of the shirt. Then there were a number of in-and-out holes, connecting this exit-hole with the last of the holes in the shirt — the entrance-hole of the bullet that had entered the front of the man's left thigh.

It was clear to me now.

The local doctor had reasoned that if he found two wounds inflicted from different directions — one from the front, the other from the back — two shots had been fired. In fact, there had been only one shot.

I reconstructed the shooting in my laboratory. I put the dead man's clothes on the lay figure, and adjusted its position so that it could have been, as the policeman said, running crouched against a wall; in other words, running while bent double. In that position each time the runner raises a leg the thigh comes almost in contact with the abdomen. When the lay figure's left leg was raised the problem was solved.

The policeman had, as he said, fired only one shot. It had hit the fugitive in the back. It had passed through the pelvis and made its exit from the front of the abdomen just when the victim's left leg was raised. After passing through a few folds of shirt the bullet had re-entered the body at the front of the left thigh, and passed backward into the muscles.

I had the body exhumed, examined the wounds, and found that the injuries could all have been inflicted in this way. When I made my report the case was dropped and the policeman returned to duty.

After I had been in Cairo for some years I received a visit from Professor Harvey Littlejohn, who was so interested in my laboratory that he did not have time to see the Pyramids. When I showed him round first he looked with some puzzlement at about a dozen sets of identical apparatus ranged along a bench.

"What are all those there for?" he asked.

"For Marsh tests," I said.

"I can see they're for the Marsh test," said Littlejohn brusquely. "But why have you put up so many?"

"They're all cases of murder," I explained.

Littlejohn was speechless. He could hardly believe that any laboratory would have so many cases requiring Marsh tests running at the same time.

For the Marsh test is the standard test for arsenic.

What Littlejohn saw was not exceptional. I do not think there was a day during my eleven years in Cairo in which no case of arsenic poisoning was under examination in my laboratories.

Murder by poisoning was very common in Egypt, but there was none of that picturesque subtlety about it that novelists and historians have taught to us to associate with the East. Most cases, indeed, were extremely crude. As in all other countries, the most popular poison was arsenic, the easiest both to administer and to detect.

I gave evidence for the Crown in many hundreds of cases of arsenic poisoning, none of which was sufficiently interesting to deserve recollection here. Reports from my department were accepted by both parties, and there was never any difficulty in proving the guilt of the accused; and things that happen every day become commonplace.

There is always an exception, and one case of arsenic poisoning was memorable in a peculiar way. A middle-aged man came to Cairo from his home in the country, very ill, and died soon after he arrived. He had all the signs and symptoms of acute arsenic poisoning, including vomiting and diarrhœa. I performed the post-mortem examination myself, concluded that it was another arsenic case, and proved it by chemical tests on the contents of the stomach. I sent my analytical findings to the Parquet in the normal way. I did not know at the time that the Health Department had decided that it was a case of cholera, and had issued orders that the body was not to be touched.

Cholera is a disease highly dreaded in the East, and the most stringent precautions are taken to reduce the danger of infection. No post-mortem examination of a victim of the disease is permitted. The Department of Health was therefore very upset when it learned that a post-mortem had been performed, and that I had certified that death was due, not to cholera, but to arsenic poisoning.

Having declared it to be cholera, the Department refused to consider the possibility of error. I was confronted by an irate official, who threatened me with dire consequences — "for," he said, "not only did this man die from cholera, but several members of his family did also." He went on to say that the Department had already isolated their house and the village where they lived, and had taken all the other precautions that were required whenever a case of cholera occurred.

I was sure about the cause of death, and the fact that other members of the family had died with the same symptoms as my man did nothing to make me think the Department of Health might be right. On the contrary, having found arsenic in the body that I had examined, I felt fairly certain that his wife, daughter, and elder son had died from the same cause, and that we were dealing with wholesale murder.

I eventually obtained authority to exhume all the bodies, and found, as I had expected, that arsenic was the cause of death in all of them. The murderer proved to be the younger son, who had been disappointed by his father's refusal to sanction his marriage and made a clean sweep of the whole family.

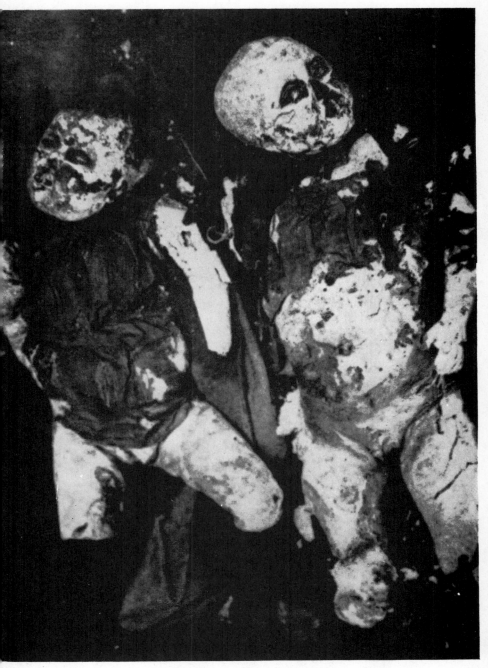

The Hopetoun Quarry Murder

The bodies of the two children found in a disused quarry. They
are completely transformed into adipocere.

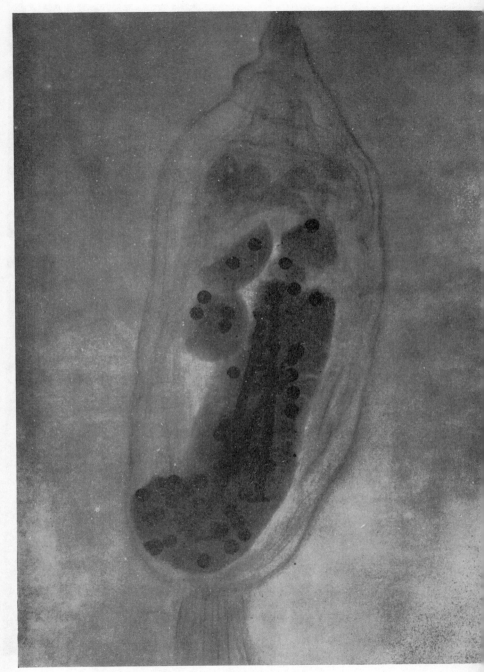

A Cob of Maize filled with Nails and Arsenic and used for poisoning Buffaloes

Rayah and Sekina: Multiple Murder for Gain

The photograph shows the mummified corpses of four of the victims.

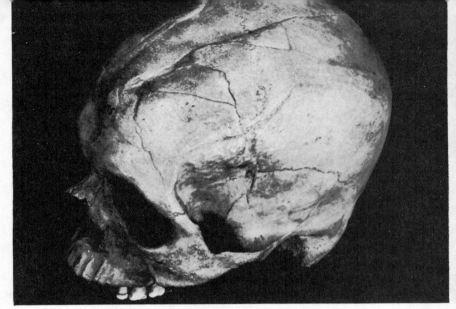

Multiple Injuries to the Head accompanied by a Complete Recovery
[*p.* 268]

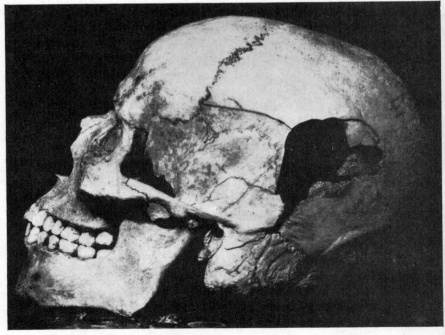

The Skull in the Mokattam Hills—The Identification of Abd el Wahib
[*p.* 94]

The Murder of the Sirdar

A reconstruction of the crime by the Egyptian police.

The Murder of the Sirdar: Vice seized on the Premises of One of the Accused

A cartridge is placed in position. It was from this vice that particles of lead, zinc, copper, and nickel were obtained.

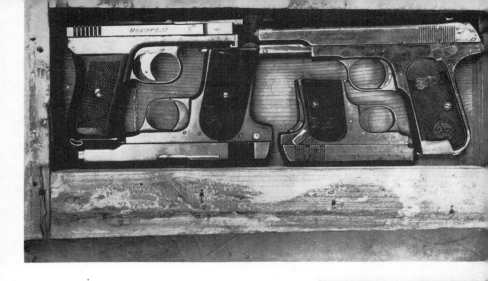

The Sirdar Case

(*above*) The lower part of the door in the house of Mahmoud Rachid, showing the lower panel removed, and the four seized pistols fitted into the secret cavity.

(*right*) A bullet extracted from the body of the Sirdar and one found in the magazine of the seized automatic.

(*below*) The panel removed to show the marks caused by the sights of the pistols.

Identification of a Rifle-cartridge found in the Desert

A and C. From a rifle seized in connexion with the case.
B. From the scene of the crime.
The arrows show the identical nature of the markings.

[p. 117]

Bullet turned inside out on striking an Iron Plate

[p. 272]

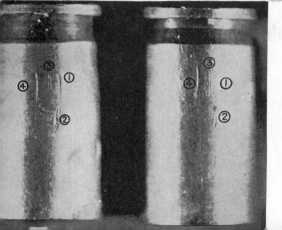

The Sirdar Case

A. Cartridge-case found at the scene of the crime.
B. Cartridge-case fired from one of the weapons found with the accused.

It is, perhaps, a mark of civilization and progress that in more advanced communities crimes of revenge tend to be greatly outnumbered by crimes committed for gain. Revenge was a more common motive in Egypt than in Europe, and arsenic was used not only to poison an enemy but also to poison his cattle. To livestock the poison was usually administered in powdered form in the hollowed-out core of a cob of maize. A more gruesome method of animal destruction was baking a cake of maize with the incorporation of needles or nails. The sharp points caused laceration of the animal's gut and death from peritonitis within a few days.

Other popular poisons besides arsenic included the seeds of thorn-apple and henbane. These were usually mixed with crushed dates or figs or given in coffee. They were rarely used with murderous intent, but usually just to make robbery easier. One traveller would meet another on some desert track, and be offered a handful of mashed dates in which a quantity of henbane seeds was incorporated. They would talk together for a while, and then the victim would feel drowsy and fall asleep. While he was unconscious he would be robbed of all his belongings. He would wake up, if he was lucky, to find all his clothes and belongings gone. I have had as many as a dozen such cases in hospital at the same time.

Exhumations also were frequent enough to become commonplace. In a hot climate bodies have to be disposed of within twenty-four hours of death, and consequently suspicion often reached the authorities only after the burial.

Outside Cairo an exhumation was carried out with a certain ceremony. I always travelled with my retinue of attendant, clerk, and guard, and as the *Tabeeb el Shareh* (legal doctor) I had the privilege of having the train stopped anywhere I liked. At the appropriate place I was met by the local mayor and other officials, and we all trooped off to the grave. When it was opened the body, or what was left of it, was examined in the open air. Interested villagers were kept at a respectful distance by the police. When I had finished my work I was usually entertained to lunch.

This was a meal of great magnificence. Often there were ten or more courses, including perhaps a whole roast lamb. As principal guest I needed to be in good gastric training, for if I declined a dish the whole course was sent away untasted by anyone. The meal was usually devoured hard by the scene of the autopsy, and often before the remains had been reinterred. Their gruesome proximity never seemed to affect the conviviality of the occasion.

Most burials were made on the surface, a small cairn being built over the body, which was not enclosed in a coffin. Decomposition took place very quickly, and generally after a month or so nothing was left but the bones. The rapidity of putrefaction, along with Egyptian murderers' general fondness for disposing secretly of the bodies of their victims, caused difficult problems of identification. Often we had to try to discover personal identities from mere fragments of tissues and collections of bones.

A typical example was the case of an elderly landowner who disappeared when apparently in good health. His son and heir — known to be a bad character — was suspected of having murdered him. But there was no body, and therefore no case. The police went on probing, and after several months someone informed. He said the landowner had been murdered by his son, and the body dismembered and buried in a field beside a canal bank. He told the police where to dig.

They went and dug, and unearthed a skull, some fragments of bones, and a mass of decomposed tissue. There were also a few bits of clothing, which were found to be portions of a fancy waistcoat in common use by Egyptians of a somewhat better class than the *fellaheen*. That was all the police could tell me when they sent in the remains.

I began with the skull, which was obviously human and complete with lower jaw. Following my usual routine, I looked first of all for the dead man's race. I measured the length, breadth, and height of the skull, and examined the lower jaw plate and nasal bones. I found that it was neither European nor Negro, but almost certainly Egyptian, which in certain measurements lies between. That did not help much. Then I looked for the sex, and could be fairly sure it was male. I was able also to make more than an informed guess at the dead man's age. All the sutures were closed, and that alone put him at over sixty. He had no teeth in his upper jaw, and there was evidence of extractions a great many years before his death. In the lower jaw, too, all the teeth on the right side had been lost for a number of years, although on the left side three molars had survived. I examined their upper surfaces, and found clear evidence that they had been grinding against upper molars. This meant that the dead man had worn an upper denture.

I went all over the skull for any trace of the scalp, and on the right side I found a very small portion which had been converted into adipocere. Embedded in this were many hairs. They looked black, which seemed unlikely for a man of this age; so it was, for they were grey at the base of the shafts, showing that he had been in the habit of dyeing his hair. I tried to determine the precise nature of the dye, but could find only that it was not mineral but was probably one of the aniline compounds.

So much for the skull. Next I sorted out the bones. There were six portions of long bones, all human and apparently belonging to the same body. They had male characteristics, and were fully ossified; more evidence that the dead man was elderly. I reconstructed the long bones as well as I could, and from them the skeleton. This gave me an estimated body length of five feet nine inches.

There were two other points of interest about the bones. The first was that there were marks of pressure on the lower end of each shin-bone. This meant that he had been in the habit of squatting, the native Egyptian's usual method of resting. The other point was that the bones were marked with transverse cuts and nicks. This was highly significant, for it was the first sign of possible foul play. The cuts had apparently been made by a fairly sharp knife, and the nicks could have been from an instrument like a moderately sharp adze. The usual way of dismembering a body is with a sharp knife for the soft parts and an adze for the bones.

Rummaging through the mass of decomposed tissue, I found two more pieces of bone, and these told me how the man had died. They belonged to the hyoid, the small bone at the base of the tongue. It had been fractured in two places — one at the top of the left horn, the other where the right horn joined the body. The fractures alone meant nothing, for they could very easily have occurred when the body was broken up. But when I examined them more closely I found tiny amounts of adipocere in the fractured ends. This meant, beyond all doubt, that the fracture had occurred before the body was buried. It is difficult to fracture the hyoid in any manner except one, and that is by grasping the neck. The obvious assumption was that the man had been strangled to death. This was borne out by some fragments of ossified thyroid cartilage that I found as well, and which looked as if they had been damaged by pressure on the neck.

Adding it all up, I reported that the remains were probably of an elderly Egyptian male, about five feet nine inches tall, who had had all his teeth except the left lower molars extracted many years before death; who wore a denture in the upper jaw, and was in the habit of dyeing his grey hair black with one of the aniline dyes; and who had probably been killed by manual strangulation. His body, I added, had been dismembered with a strong, sharp knife and a fairly sharp adze. The remains had been buried in a damp place at least six months before they were dug up.

My description tallied exactly with that of the missing landowner. Not only that, but the police searched his house again and found hair-dye, with pot and brushes, and an upper dental plate. They sent the dentures to me, and I placed them in the upper jaw. It was a perfect fit. More, the molars on the left of this denture were worn, while those on the right were not; and the worn edges fitted exactly into the surfaces of the surviving molars in the lower jaw. I thought this made the identification conclusive. The court thought so too, when the landowner's son was charged with murder.

In that case, of course, my job was to confirm rather than discover the identity of the remains. My description of the man could definitely be confirmed or refuted by witnesses who had known him when he was alive. In many cases, however, the police had no clue at all to the origin of the remains. Identification then was more difficult. That it was not impossible I have shown in the case of the three small bones found in a well related at the beginning of this book. In such cases the most valuable clues were often individual peculiarities, such as congenital deformities or defects due to injury or disease. Two further cases may illustrate the point.

In the first I received only a skull, which had been found partially buried in the bank of a canal. It had no scalp or hair, no tissues of the face, and no lower jaw. Some adipocere adhering to the base indicated that death had occurred at least six months before. Embedded in this adipocere were some small fragments of bone, which proved to be the body and horns of the hyoid. The right horn was fractured, and adipocere had been deposited in the fractured ends: therefore the fracture was present before burial; from which it was safe to assume that the victim had been strangled.

But who was the victim? There was no history of anybody missing, no hint as to who the person could be. Moreover, when I carried out the usual examination, it proved to be more difficult than usual to establish the primary facts of sex and race. But the cause of this difficulty proved the best clue.

The right side of the face was bigger than the left. The right forehead was fuller than the left, which was slightly flattened; the eye-sockets were unequal; the upper jaw was larger on the right side. These and other differences gave the face a distinctly squint-like appearance.

The lack of symmetry was even more pronounced at the base of the skull. When I examined this two things struck me at once: the difference in size of the occipital condyles — the surfaces that form the joint between the neck and the skull, and rest on the spinal column — and the difference between the mastoid processes, to which the main rotating muscles of the neck are attached. The right occipital condyle was much larger than the left. The left mastoid process was much larger than the right.

These abnormalities could only have been caused by one thing. Some time in infancy, probably at or about the time of birth, the principal rotating muscle on the left side of the neck had contracted, causing the head to be tilted towards the left shoulder and the chin turned to the right. In other words, I was able to report that the owner of the skull had suffered from birth from the condition known as wry-neck.

I was able also to deduce that the person was an Egyptian woman in her early twenties, but it was the neck deformity that solved the case. The police inquired until they heard of a woman with wry-neck who had disappeared from a village near by, and about whose disappearance the husband had made many false statements: he was arrested, charged with murder, and convicted.

In another case of this kind I received from the police a number of bones, including both the skull and pelvis, which they had found. They were from an unknown person, and the authorities wished to get some hint of their identity. It was not difficult to deduce that they were the remains of an Egyptian woman of about middle age and about five feet four inches tall. This information had a certain value, but was not likely to help the police much. There were, however, several details of a personal nature which were more helpful. For example, her teeth were covered on the right side, both top and bottom, with a thick layer of deposited salts. This indicated that the right side had not been used for chewing for a considerable time, no doubt on account of a gum-boil or other inflammatory condition of the gum or jaw. On the same side she had a decayed second molar that must have caused great pain for a considerable period. Such dental information could be expected to be of some value in identification, but it was as nothing compared with the evidence of her eyes — or rather her eye-sockets, for, of course, only the sockets remained.

When I examined them I saw that the left socket was smaller than the right in both diameters, and the floor seemed to bulge more inward, giving a less roomy cavity. The opening for the optic nerve in the left side was extremely small — in the right it was of normal size. The inference was that she had had only one eye. She had been blind in her left eye, which had atrophied or been removed in early childhood. The cause of death could not be decided.

The laboratory findings led to a complete change of direction in the investigations of the police, and before long they discovered that a one-eyed woman had disappeared from a neighbouring village about a year before. Her eye had been removed in early childhood, and, strangely enough, the doctor who had removed it was still practising, and able to give evidence about the deceased. She had suffered severely from a painful condition of the jaw, which had prevented her from sleeping. When she disappeared it was thought she had committed suicide, but her body had never been discovered.

5

Murder as a Business

THE BONE WAS HUMAN ALL RIGHT. I THOUGHT IT WAS PART OF a leg. I could not tell the body's age or sex. It had probably been buried a year or so before.

That was all I could say about the single bone that was sent to my laboratory from Alexandria in the summer of 1920. I had no idea that this was the beginning of one of the most fantastic cases of my career.

The bone had been discovered by chance. A gang of workmen were digging a trench in a side-street, and one side of the trench collapsed. Among the debris one of the workmen saw the bone. He fished it out and gave it to the police.

When I said it was human the police took charge of the excavations. Other parts of a human body were unearthed, and they seemed to come from under the house beside which the trench was being dug. I was asked to go to Alexandria, and under my direction an examination of the inside of the house was made.

It was a poorly constructed building with an earthen floor. This was dug up under my supervision, and I began to realize something of the worries of an archæologist when disinterring choice relics of the past. The difference was that our relics were anything but choice, although some of them might have been once.

The first body we found was quite near the surface. It was female, quite young, and in a fairly good state of preservation; evidently it had not been buried very long. The cause of death was strangulation.

The next body, which lay close beside the first, was similar to it. So was the next — and the next. We were digging up a mass grave.

There were seven bodies in a row, and when we had cleared

that we found another layer underneath. Fourteen bodies, packed like sardines, under the floor of one room.

They were in various stages of putrefaction, but the longest any of them had been there was under two years. They had all been strangled, and some of them still wore the cords, like neckties, that had been used to choke out their lives.

Fourteen adults had been murdered and buried under this house within a space of two years. The police had no inkling of the crimes until the road-trench caved in and the workman found that single bone. How could so many persons have gone to the house and disappeared for ever without anyone's suspicions being aroused?

I examined the bodies as they were dug up, to try to find an answer to this question. It soon emerged.

They were all women, all Egyptians, and their ages ranged from eighteen to beyond middle age. They had been circumcised, so they were of the Moslem religion. Most significant of all, although some had apparently borne children, they had all retained their pubic hair. This was normally removed by married women as a measure of hygiene. It was kept by only one class of women, I believe for aphrodisiac reasons, and that was prostitutes. This fact had often helped towards the identification of bodies by establishing a woman's status or profession.

No one could disappear so easily as a prostitute. No one was easier to murder.

But prostitutes are usually known to the police, and we could identify most of them. Meanwhile the owners of the house, two women named Rayah and Sekena and their husbands, were arrested. Not until their trial did the whole story come out.

It was customary for women, and especially women of this class, to put most of their money into gold and other ornaments which they carried on their persons. They regarded this as safer than putting their savings into a bank or investing them. The practice was certainly more decorative. Unfortunately, it made their financial status obvious, and this exposed them to danger.

Rayah and Sekena had picked their victims carefully. They had all done well in their profession, and wore indisputable evidence of their success. Nor did they need to be told to put on their finery when they were invited to go to the house to meet a very rich landowner. They had nowhere safe to leave their gold and jewellery, anyway, so of course they wore it all.

Once in the house it was easy. The woman was given coffee or other refreshment while waiting for her prospective client to arrive, and the husband of Rayah or Sekena slipped a noose over her head from behind. Practice makes perfect, and there was no noise or fuss after the first few times. The murdered woman was stripped of her clothes and jewels, and her body joined the others under the floor. Until there were fourteen.

The two women and their husbands were convicted and sentenced to death.

The extraordinary amount of crime in Egypt, especially crimes of violence, gives a rather distorted idea of the Egyptians. So far from being cruel or brutal, they are mostly a good-natured people.

My work took me to all parts of the country, and I came into contact with all classes. I found the country folk — the *fellaheen* — simple, hard-working, humorous, and rather pleasant. Their main relaxation consisted in having a cup of coffee, accompanied by much argument, in the café, and in the propagation of large families. They were, however, fanatical when roused, and were comparatively easily excited into mob hysteria.

Their living conditions were, by our standards, appalling. Each village consisted of a collection of mud huts massed together. In each hut the man, his wife or wives, children, and domestic animals lived a simple communal life. The huts had little light and no ventilation, mud floors and no furniture: generally the family sat on the floor, slept on the floor, and ate on the floor. None of the roads was properly made. In the ordinary dry weather every movement on them raised huge clouds of dust, and when it rained they were seas of mud. Piped water supplies were practically unknown, and all water had to be brought from the village well or from a canal in large jars balanced on the women's heads. Sanitary arrangements were as a rule entirely wanting, the latrine attached to the mosque being the only convenience in the village. There were a few better houses with two storeys occupied by the more prosperous villagers and officials.

Once I had to inspect a house in Upper Egypt in which a *fellah* had been killed. It was in the hot weather, and the house had been closed for several days. As I entered the floor seemed to me to be swaying, and I thought I must be in for an attack of giddiness. I closed my eyes tightly; when I opened them again the floor still seemed to be heaving. I then noticed that my white drill trousers were almost black half-way up to the knees with masses of fleas. The apparent floor movement was due to the jumping of millions of these insects.

I rapidly removed myself to the house of the Parquet agent — who was in the fortunate position of having a bathroom — got into the water, and shook my clothes over it. I drowned thousands of fleas, dusted myself with Keating's Powder, and did my job in comfort. In those days, before the advent of D.D.T., I never travelled without first dusting out my socks and the inside of my pants with Keating's. This kept me fairly clear for the day.

Among the contributory causes of crime in Egypt were included plurality of wives and ease of divorce.

Although the right to marry four wives is sanctioned by Islamic law, the Prophet did not introduce polygamy. He merely recognized a prevailing custom, and at the same time limited its scope. Polygamy was originally world-wide, and is still practised in many Eastern countries other than the Moslem states.

Originally it was the privilege of the aristocracy, and it had a certain prestige or snob value: a man's social standing was to some extent gauged by the number of his wives. From the upper classes the custom gradually descended the social scale to the workers and peasants. In Egypt when I was there it was to a great extent confined to the *fellaheen*. To them polygamy had an economic value, since an extra wife meant an extra pair of hands. In the upper classes it meant merely additional expense, and most Moslems, like most Christians, have found it difficult enough to control one wife, let alone four.

In addition to the unsatisfactory situation of women arising from polygamy, there is the further social insecurity inherent in the ease of divorce. Under Moslem law a wife may be divorced by the husband without legal formalities, so that it was possible for a man to have an endless chain of wives, divorcing the eldest and recruiting a young substitute whenever the fancy took him. But there was a snare for the man in this ease of divorce. Often he would send a wife packing in a fit of anger, and then want her back when he had cooled down. Under Islamic law, however, if the divorce was a so-called 'triple divorce' he could not remarry her until she had been married by another man and again divorced. This requirement led to the development of a new profession. Men would undertake to marry and divorce a woman

simply to enable her to remarry her former husband. For this
service they received a fee, but demanded nothing more so far as
one knew.

Sometimes, of course, there was a misfire. In one case I knew
of, a man divorced a beautiful young wife in a fit of pique, and at
once took the necessary steps to legalize her return to him. The
husband of convenience obliged to the extent of marrying the
woman, but then told his employer that on second thoughts he
preferred to keep her himself. The former husband could do
nothing about it except to secure the divorce by means of a heavy
bribe. I do not know what happened to the double-crossing
second spouse, but his trickery doubtless reduced his expectation
of life.

When a wife was divorced she retained the custody of any
children of the marriage until they were seven if boys or nine if
girls, and during this time the father had to pay for their maintenance. Often a father poisoned or otherwise destroyed such
children in order to get rid of this financial burden — a barbarous
practice indeed, but not confined to the East, as the case of
Patrick Higgins will have shown.

Child-murder was provoked also by the system of plurality of
wives. One wife often destroyed the offspring of another in order
that her own children might inherit. The Moslem law of inheritance is very rigid, and greatly restricts the power of the
individual to dispose of his property. The respective proportions
of the estate inherited by wives, sons, and daughters were laid
down by law, and murder within the family could increase the
share of the survivors. In one case, for example, a man's second
wife poisoned the two sons of a former wife and finally the husband,
in order that her own child should inherit.

Inheritance apart, polygamy was a potent cause of domestic
unhappiness and jealousy, and therefore of crime. Usually the
newest wife was the youngest and prettiest, and became the husband's favourite. But the senior spouse wielded more authority
— and was more able to cause mischief.

Zenab was a senior spouse, the elder of two. I do not know if
she was attractive, for when I met her first she was very, very dead.

She had been on bad terms with her husband for some time,
and after a serious quarrel she disappeared. Her relatives went
to the police and said her husband had murdered her.

There was no evidence except that she was missing, but that was sinister enough. In Egyptian villages wives did not just go away — there was nowhere for them to go. So when Zenab's husband said he did not know where his wife was the police arrested him and searched his house. They found nothing, but that was not surprising. In such cases the body was usually buried secretly or thrown into the Nile. There was a rumour that Zenab's body had been cut up and taken away in a sack, but no traces to support this could be found. At last the police gave up, and Zenab's husband was released.

Her relatives continued the search, and Sayeed, her brother, began a vigil by a disused well some distance from the village. He was seen there day after day, as if he was keeping an eye on it, although he was completely blind. Hence some reserve by the police when, after six weeks, he told them he thought his sister's body had been thrown down the well. But they had it drained, and, sure enough, parts of a human body were found in a sack weighted with stones.

The body was decomposed, and the features were unrecognizable, but the relatives swore it was Zenab. The husband swore it was not The police arrested him again and charged him with murder.

It was not quite cricket, but they put a stool-pigeon in his cell. He told his fellow-prisoner about the case, and said it was a put-up job. Sayeed and the others had probably stolen the body from a tomb and dumped it down the well to frame him.

"Are you sure it is not Zenab's body?" the stool-pigeon asked him.

"Sure? Of course I'm sure, because I know where her body is! It's in the cesspit of the village mosque."

"How did it get there?" the stool-pigeon asked.

"It was thrown there by the people who murdered her," he confided. "By the relatives of my second wife."

Of course, none of this would be admissible as evidence, but it was good information.

As usual, the cesspit leading from the mosque latrine was the only method of sewage disposal in the village. The police opened it three days after finding the body in the well, and again parts of a human body were discovered.

It was almost the same story over again. The body was decomposed, the features were unrecognizable. This time, however, the relatives of Zenab swore that it was not her. They could hardly have done anything else after being so emphatic that hers was the body in the well.

When he saw that the police were worried about the second body Sayeed came up with a theory that would make everything nice and tidy. He suggested that the second body had been taken from a tomb by the husband's relatives and thrown into the cesspit to support his version of the affair.

But which tomb, the police asked, had the body been stolen from?

"From the tomb of my daughter, Fatma," said a man named Foda, coming forward just at this point. "She was buried about the time Zenab disappeared. Now her body has been stolen."

Zenab's husband was not at all put out by this.

"Then Fatma's is the body found in the well," he said. "Zenab's relatives stole it from the tomb, and threw it down the well to frame me."

"Impossible," said Foda. "My daughter's body was not stolen from the tomb until after the body in the well was found."

The case seemed to be getting rather complicated, and at this stage I was called in. My brief was to try to identify the two bodies, and in particular to find out which, if either, was Zenab, and which, if either, was Fatma.

I have mentioned that in Egypt bodies were not usually buried, but were placed without coffins in tombs on the surface of the ground. These little tombs, built of mud brick, were a prominent feature of the landscape. Of course, putrefaction was extremely rapid, and if conditions were dry — and they were at this particular place — in six weeks a body might be expected to have lost its soft parts completely, and to show nothing but a skeleton. Certainly no adipocere could have been formed.

The first important thing I found when I examined these rather gruesome remains was that both bodies still contained soft tissues, and in both cases certain parts had been converted into adipocere.

So if either body was that of Fatma her father was lying. If it had not been removed until after the finding of the body in the well, as he said, there could not have been adipocere. If, on the other hand, it had been taken from the tomb within a day or two of burial and then thrown into either the well or the cesspit adipocere could have been formed to the extent found. I concluded that Foda was a liar, and that the body of his daughter had been removed soon after burial, probably with his paid connivance.

Was Fatma's the body found in the mosque cesspit?

I reckoned the age of the woman in the cesspit to be between thirty-five and forty; Fatma was under thirty. I calculated the height of the body to be not more than five feet; Fatma had a sister said to be about the same height as herself, and when we measured this girl we found she was five feet three inches. There were several decayed teeth in the body from the cesspit, and two or three had been lost by extraction; Fatma was said to have had a complete set. All pubic hair had been removed from the woman in the cesspit, so she had been married; Fatma had died a spinster. Finally, together with the remains in the cesspit were two plaits of hair, with ornaments attached, and some portions of clothing; in Egypt before a body was buried all hair ornaments were removed, the hair was unbraided, and ordinary clothes were taken off and burial clothes put on.

Undoubtedly the body in the cesspit was not Fatma's.

Could it be Zenab's?

Zenab also had had a sister, said to be of about her own height. We measured her, and found she was a little under five feet. Zenab had been about forty years old, and was known to have several decayed teeth and to have lost two or three by extraction. She was married. The plaits, hair ornaments, and clothing from the cesspit were identified as hers. One of the feet found among the remains corresponded with a shoe that had belonged to Zenab, and there was a sack that had belonged to her husband. So I concluded that Sayeed and her other relatives were lying, and her husband had told the truth. Up to a point, anyway. The body in the cesspit was Zenab's.

What about the body in the well?

Age, under thirty. Height, about five feet four. Teeth complete and free from decay. There were no fragments of clothing, so the body had probably been prepared for burial. The hair was long, unbraided, and devoid of ornaments.

All this fitted perfectly with what we knew of Fatma, and the complicated case began to unravel itself. Both bodies had been cut up before disposal. I could not say definitely how either had died, but in the body in the cesspit I found dislocation of both horns of the hyoid. It looked as if Zenab had been strangled.

Just when I thought my part of the investigation was finished, the police received fresh information about the two plaits of hair found in the cesspit. It was said that they did not belong to the body at all, but had been cut from the head of a girl in the village who suffered from a disease of the scalp.

If true this piece of evidence would go some way to undermining our identification of the cesspit body. The police investigated further, and the girl was produced. Sure enough, she had the scalp disease, and her hair had been cut off.

"Is there any way of finding out whether or not the plaits were cut off from her head?" I was asked.

"Nothing could be easier," I replied. "You cannot cut off hair without cutting off the roots." I examined the plaits again. All the roots were present. "This hair was not cut off," I said. "It came out by putrefaction."

So ended the last attempt at deception by Zenab's relatives. As the dead woman's husband had told the stool-pigeon in prison, they had tried to frame him with Fatma's body, which they had taken from its tomb soon after burial, no doubt bribing her father to let them. They had thrown it down the well, and left it there — guarded by the blind Sayeed — long enough to become unrecognizable. Having gone to these highly criminal lengths, they had to stick to their story and deny the identity of the body in the cesspit as Zenab's, and even invented false evidence to support their denial.

You might say they had got themselves into a mess by their vile conduct, but to seek a moral in the story would be unwise. If they had not tried to frame Zenab's husband he would never have disclosed where her body really was — the body would never have been found, the murderer never brought to justice.

For on just one point Zenab's husband had lied and her relatives told the truth. She had not been murdered by relatives of his second wife. He had killed her himself.

He was duly tried and convicted.

Another gruesome case began early one morning in May when an engineer working on the wharf at Alexandria fished a sack out of the sea. It contained the lower half of a human body, naked except for a pair of men's socks with suspenders attached, but indubitably female. Later the same morning another sack was washed up, containing the upper part of a woman's body, clad in a chemise and red dress, and this followed the first one to the mortuary. There the two halves were put together, and it was evident that they were portions of the same body. It had been divided by means of a saw through the middle of the abdomen. There were two severe wounds on the head, with fracture of the bones and damage to the brain. They looked like cuts from a moderately sharp axe, and it seemed to be definitely a case of murder and dismemberment.

She had been a good-looking European woman of about thirty years of age; blonde, of medium height, and well developed. She wore a wedding ring, but did not appear to have borne children.

The weather in Alexandria in May is quite hot, and rigor mortis would normally begin to disappear in about twenty-four hours. This body was still completely stiff, and its general condition suggested that it had been dead for about eighteen hours, and in the water for much of that time. Clotted blood in many of the vessels indicated that some hours had elapsed after death before the body had been cut up and thrown into the sea. Post-mortem discoloration showed that she had been lying on her back during these hours. The stomach contained a quantity of partially digested bread, oranges, meat, and rice, the condition of which suggested that she had been killed about an hour after she had eaten it. All this pointed to the probability that she had been killed the evening before, that her body had somewhat later been sawn into halves, placed in sacks, and thrown into the sea round about midnight.

The effects of the tide, currents, and wind were investigated and made it fairly certain that the body must have been thrown in from the shore or from a boat some miles along the Ramleh front. Watermen, when told the probable time, gave a fairly close approximation of the place where it might have been thrown in. The sacks were rice sacks printed "Base Supply, Basra," and had obviously belonged to the British Army.

As the dead woman's features were sufficiently recognizable for the purposes of identification, she was put on show with her face left bare for the public to see. After a few hours, since she was still unidentified, the police decided to take photographs. The official photographer was summoned — and recognized the woman himself! She had been a prostitute, and the photographer had been one of her clients. His identification was confirmed by a police-officer, who was apparently another of her clients. This led to some macabre ribaldry, and it was a current joke that he had made the identification from the first sack.

The woman was a Rumanian professionally known as "Emma."

Inquiries revealed that she had left her lodgings a month before to live with a Levantine named John Kay, who had a villa on the coast within the area suggested by the watermen. He was a contractor to the Army, and dealt in sacks disposed of by the Army authorities. When questioned he agreed that "Emma" had been living with him for about a month, but said she had left his house at 6 p.m. on the day before the sacks were washed up. He explained that she had taken all her belongings and did not return. He admitted that the socks on her feet were his, and said that she had been in the habit from time to time of wearing his socks in the house.

It seemed highly improbable that any young woman of this sort would have travelled to town wearing a man's socks and suspenders and there was enough suspicion apart from this for the police to make a thorough search of the house. It proved disappointing. Many sacks were found similar to those used to dispose of the body, but such sacks could have been on the premises of any sack merchant. There were no signs of a struggle, and no clothes or articles belonging to "Emma." No bloodstains were found, and a minute search failed to reveal either an axe or a saw or any similar instrument that might have been used either in the murder or in dismembering the body.

Apart from the sacks, however, there were a number of suspicious circumstances. The cook said that the woman had eaten a meal of meat, rice, bread, and oranges about five or six on the evening of her alleged departure. Dogs had been heard barking in the house about midnight. John Kay's wife, who had been in England for a considerable time, had recently cabled her husband that she was returning to Alexandria. A servant said Kay had borrowed a saw from him and not returned it, although Kay denied this. Kay was arrested, and I was asked to inspect the house to see if any possible clues had been overlooked by the police.

Eight days after the sacks were washed up I went to the house with the local Parquet officer and senior police-officer. I stopped them at the front door. A brown stain on one of the upper panels looked to me like blood.

"It's definitely blood," I said, after a rapid examination.

"Can you say if it's human?"

"I'll take a specimen and test it in the lab. But look here," I went on. "There's more blood on the jamb."

There was some splashing on each side of this stain, and below it a line of blood ran down the edge of the door. It looked as if some object saturated with blood had struck against the edge of the door when it was open.

I looked again at the panel, which was lightly streaked with two bloodstains, each about five inches long.

"They could have been caused by some bloody object brushing against the door from left to right," I said. That meant passing from the inside to the outside of the house. "Such as a sack carried over the left shoulder." I measured the distance from the stains to the ground, and found it was about forty inches. "By a man of average height," I added.

I took a few paces into the house, and then turned round.

"When the left foot goes forward," I said, suiting the action to the words, "the left shoulder moves to the left." I finished the step so that if I had been carrying a sack it would have brushed against the stains on the panel. "Right step forward, shoulder to the right." I went forward again. "Left step forward, shoulder to the left." This step took me past the door-jamb, with my imaginary sack now level with the stains there.

I cut the bloodstained areas out of the door, and, as always when collecting such specimens, put them in containers, labelled and sealed them — every official had his own personal seal — and gave them to the police to deliver to my laboratory in Cairo. Then we continued the examination of the house.

"These are the Army rice sacks from Basra," said the local Parquet as we went into the entrance hall. "There's nothing else here."

There was the tiled floor, which I examined closely. I found that some of the tiles were cleaner than others.

"It looks as if this part of the floor has been washed recently, but not the rest," I said.

"Nothing has been washed since we took over the house," said the senior police-officer.

I removed some of the cleaner tiles, tested the cement between them — and got a reaction for blood.

We went on and searched the rest of the house, but without finding any more bloodstains or signs of a struggle. We came back to the hall.

"I think she was killed and cut up here," I said.

"But the blood?" questioned the Parquet.

"It's a problem," I agreed. The amount I had found in the material between the tiles was small. It would have been a very messy operation, and there should have been a great deal of blood about. Why was there so little trace?

I examined the pile of sacks. There were many of them, and not a sign of blood on any. I went over them again, this time turning them inside out. Still nothing at first — and then I saw it. Near the bottom of the interior of one of the sacks was a heavy round bloodstain about seven inches across. There was a smaller but similar stain opposite, on the inner surface of the other side of the sack.

"Something was put in the sack for a short while and then taken out again," I said. "Some object heavily bloodstained on one side. Then the sack was laid flat so that the two sides came into contact, and the bloodstained area on one side soiled the other."

"Any idea what sort of object?"

"It could have been a human head," I said, "judging by the size of the stain." I showed them some hairs I had taken out. "It looks as if the whole body was placed in the sack, head downward, with a lump of sandstone, but shortly afterwards taken out again."

We intensified the search, and eventually found more traces of blood in the back premises of the house. I found one stain on a piece of timber, another on a garden roller, a third on some stones. The trail led to a disused covered well. We opened it up, and on the bottom we found fourteen sacks. They were the same kind as those in the house, and they gave a general reaction for blood. We found also some articles of clothing — a dress, underwear, shoes, stockings, a hat, and a handbag containing articles of value — all of which were identified as having belonged to "Emma." In addition, the well yielded up two Army puttees, attached to a bit of piping jutting out on its side. One of these was profusely stained with blood. From the way the stains were disposed it looked as if the puttee had been wrapped three times round an object that was bleeding on one side — an object of the size of a human head. All these bloodstains later proved to be of human origin.

I now had enough information to be able to put forward a tentative reconstruction of the crime.

When John Kay heard that his wife was coming back to Egypt he told "Emma" that she would have to go. A quarrel ensued, and it ended with the murder of the woman. This occurred about

6 p.m. — an hour after the evening meal. Kay killed her in the hall with a number of blows on the head with a hatchet. He covered the body with sacks, and left it until about midnight. Then he tried to push it into a sack, but it was too big; so he took it out again and sawed it in half. He probably did this in the hall, the bulk of the blood being retained by the sacks on which the body was lying; he had already bandaged the head with a puttee to prevent excessive effusion of blood. He placed the two halves of the body in separate sacks and carried them out through the front door to the sea, which was three or four hundred yards away, and threw them in. The set of the current and tide carried the sacks to the harbour, where they were discovered the next morning. Meanwhile Kay cleaned up the hall and washed part of the floor to remove traces of blood. He took out fourteen sacks, which had been soaked with blood, and threw them down the well. He overlooked the sack in which he had first put the body, because it was not obviously bloodstained on the outside. He used the well also to dispose of the bloodstained puttee and all the woman's clothing and personal effects.

No doubt because of the French legal influence, reconstructing a crime was a more common procedure in Egypt than it is in Britain. When I gave evidence at Kay's trial the full court — judge, counsel, witnesses, and accused — adjourned to the scene of the crime to see a practical demonstration. I did my reconstruction step by step, carrying a loaded sack on my shoulder to represent the body when I showed how I thought the bloodstains had been made on the front door.

John Kay watched it all with an expressionless face. What were his thoughts? It was an interesting speculation, for obviously he was the only person present who knew exactly what had taken place. After his conviction — he was sentenced to penal servitude for life — I was told that he had admitted that the reconstruction was remarkably accurate. But he never revealed what he had done with the hatchet and the saw.

6

Mobs and Riots

THERE HAD BEEN A FAIRLY STRONG NATIONALIST MOVEMENT in Egypt since 1905, but during the 1914-18 war this subsided to a great extent. Two days after the Armistice, however, the nationalist leader, Said Pasha Zagloul, asked permission to go to London to put Egypt's case for independence. His request was turned down by the Foreign Office. That was probably the British Government's first great error of judgment in its post-war dealings with Egypt, although by no means the last. As an immediate result Zagloul went into action.

Riots broke out first in Cairo and Alexandria, then in the provincial towns, and finally throughout the country. Zagloul and three of his lieutenants were deported to Malta, and the rioting became worse. Trams were overturned, street-lamps demolished, shops smashed and looted, and many Europeans stoned and assaulted. In rural areas trains were held up, railway-lines and rolling-stock destroyed, and telegraph-lines cut. Eight British officers and men who had been on leave at Luxor were taken off a train and butchered.

By this time the whole country was in the throes of mass hysteria. Houses were burnt down in the cities, barricades erected in the streets, and murder and violence stalked abroad. There were many dreadful occurrences, but these had better be left undescribed. The situation in Cairo was very grave, and numbers of Egyptians as well as of foreigners were killed. From our flat in Savoy Chambers we could hear, night after night, the sound of rifle-fire in the streets.

When the riots were at their worst my mortuary was in a dreadful mess. Dozens of bodies of persons killed by gunshot or otherwise lay piled on the floor, sometimes two or three deep. I had to examine large numbers of Egyptians who had been shot by the authorities, and also from time to time the body of some one of my friends who had been assassinated. As I did not want to strain the loyalty of my staff too far, I did most of the work myself. The autopsies were necessarily curtailed, and I contented myself with observing the main injuries and issuing death certificates.

Officials were all armed, and I found it very irksome to carry a heavy automatic pistol or revolver at the hip while wearing a suit of white cotton with the temperature approaching eighty to ninety degrees. I managed to get to my office regularly, although the route to it was through the Sharia Mohammed Ali, which was not a healthy spot. I walked as a rule with my well-tried and trusty bodyguard, Hamid Osman, following two or three paces behind. I met many a mob shouting, "Down with the British!" but was never actually molested. Like Agag, I walked delicately, of course, and saw to it that I gave no cause for interference.

There was only one other British official in the building where my office was located — George Hughes, the Chief Inspector of Parquets — and from day to day there were rumours of rioters preparing to invade the premises. There was only one staircase leading to my laboratories, and I kept about fifty large bottles of sulphuric acid in my office in case of emergency. I felt moderately sure that if an attack was made up that narrow stairway my sulphuric acid would hold it up until help arrived, but I was very glad I never had to take such a drastic measure.

On one occasion when the riots were in full swing my assistant and I were returning from Kasr el Aini hospital when we heard the roar of a mob of some thousands marching towards the Residency, shouting their usual mixture of English, French, and Arabic slogans: "*Ishtaklal el Tam* [complete independence]!" "*A bas l'anglais!*" "*Vive Zagloul Pasha!*" and, oddly enough, occasionally "Long live Cromer!" The driver of our carriage promptly turned his horses to avoid trouble. We managed to stop him, and got out before he drove furiously away.

We took refuge in the Government Laboratory in the Public Works garden, and from the roof had a splendid view of the surging mass of dancing, gesticulating rioters. The roar of an excited mob swelling into greater and greater volume as it approaches nearer and nearer has an extraordinarily exciting and frightening effect. This effect is enhanced by the knowledge that there is nothing that one can do about it. I had my automatic with me, looked at it, and put it back in my pocket. I thought what a futile little thing it was when dealing with a mob. I remembered the advice of an old-stager who said, "Never show a gun unless you are prepared to shoot, and to shoot to kill. Otherwise leave it out of sight, or it will only increase your danger."

The laboratory was not attacked, and the crowd dispersed sufficiently to let us get on our way again. Unfortunately, we ran into it again as we approached Abdin Palace, and I thought, as we became surrounded, that anything might happen. The situation was critical. At that moment two mounted troopers of the Australian force came into the square. Their rifles remained in their holsters, and they were armed apparently with nothing but long canes and their distinctive slouch hats. As they approached in a nonchalant way, skilfully using their canes with encouraging cries such as "*Imshi!*" the raging crowd of thousands wilted away like snow in sunshine. It was a marvellous example of practical psychology.

In general, and even when anti-British feeling was at its highest, I was on good terms with the Egyptians. I mixed freely with the young intelligentsia, and had several friends among them. They talked politics to me without restraint, perhaps because they had the idea that New Zealand was another country under the iron heel of England.

It was customary in those early days for the First Secretary of the Residency to ask the views of senior officials about the state of feeling in the country. When he discussed the political situation with me during the period of unrest I suggested that a straight-out offer of Dominion status, with an independent Government such as we had in New Zealand, would be seriously considered by the thinking classes and would stand a good chance of being accepted; but it would have to be an equal partnership, with a freely elected Parliament. The Secretary said, "Very interesting, but what about Zagloul?" I replied that it would make a very good impression if we allowed him to return in time for the elections, so that they could make him the first Prime Minister. He mentioned the name of another firebrand, also in exile, and I said I would like to see him as Egyptian Ambassador to the Court of St James's. "Do have a whisky and soda before you go," said the Secretary, which I did and went. But I am convinced that we and

Egypt could have been good friends to-day if we had invited her into the Commonwealth as an equal partner then.

Eventually the riots were suppressed, but they broke out again several times during the next five years. Students of law and of medicine were particularly troublesome, and frequently went on strike. I used to lecture to both, and once, when I was crossing the Kasr el Nil bridge on the way to the School of Law, I ran into some of my class carrying the usual banners and yelling the usual slogans like "Death to the British!" One of the mob saw me coming, and quickly detached himself and ran up. "Don't go to the School to-day, Professor," he said. "There is nobody there — we are having a revolution." After having stopped the revolution long enough to save me from a long and unfruitful walk he rejoined the mob, and continued to shout for death to the British. I thought it was very good of him, and rather characteristic in a way. All the same, Professor Robson, who also lectured at the Law School, was shot in the back and killed while he was walking home a few days afterwards, and I had the melancholy duty of examining his body.

During the main period of unrest between 1919 and 1922, there were some thirty murders or attempted murders of British officials or soldiers by means of firearms, and five more by means of home-made bombs. Though many of the outrages occurred in daylight in thickly populated areas, in not one case, so far as I remember, did a single eye-witness ever come forward to identify a suspect, nor did any member of the public try to help the police in any way. As no personal motive was involved — it did not matter to the political assassin who his victim was, so long as he was British — it was extraordinarily difficult to bring home the crimes to any individual. In none of these cases did the police obtain a single useful clue to the identity of the assassins. But in my laboratory I was slowly collecting information that I hoped might one day lead to the identification of the assassins through the weapons they used.

As it happened, our first gropings into what was then the infant science of forensic ballistics helped the authorities only in a negative way, saving them from making mistakes; and I did not get much thanks for that.

Zagloul Pasha was on a lecture tour of Upper Egypt, and in a riot some Egyptians were shot. The Parquet investigations led to the conclusion that all the victims had been shot by Zagloul's supporters. Dr Amer examined the bodies, and did not feel sure that this was correct. The clothing was sent to the laboratory for examination. The marks on it did not appear to have been made by revolver bullets or a charge of shot. They were more in keeping with the square-shaped slugs used by the Ghaffirs, an irregular force attached to the police. I was able to clinch the matter when I discovered an actual Ghaffir slug adhering by blood to the inside of one of the garments. I reported to the Parquet my opinion that the men had been shot by Government agents, and not by members of Zagloul's party. This report was obviously most inconvenient for the Government, since they were convinced, and had made public statements, that the Zagloulists had caused all the trouble. I was sent for by the Procurator-General.

"Why, doctor, do you suggest that the Government Ghaffirs are responsible for these deaths by shooting? I have conclusive evidence before me that the supporters of Zagloul Pasha are entirely and solely responsible. Every shot was fired by members of that party."

"That may be, Excellency," I said, "but if those people were shot by Zagloul's supporters, then they must have been furnished with Government arms and ammunition."

"I'm sorry," he said, "that you take that attitude, and I would like you, in view of the evidence I have put before you, to reconsider your report."

"Excellency," I said, "my report concerns what I actually found, and is not subject to revision. What you do with it is no concern of mine, but I cannot alter it."

That was that. The impending prosecutions were dropped, and I'm afraid my report was shelved, since I heard no more of it.

On another occasion during a riot near Alexandria a number of people were killed. The injuries were certified to be due to the discharge of small arms of low velocity such as revolvers, and were presumed to have been caused by members of the mob. The victims were buried. Later I was asked to exhume the bodies, about fifty in all, to see if any information could be obtained that might identify the weapons used.

The bodies were badly decomposed, and only fractured bones and fragments of missiles were available for identification purposes. My assistants and I examined all the remains as carefully as we could, though the bodies had to be run through like machines on a conveyor belt. I collected quite a number of bullets or parts of bullets, and when I cleaned these up I found that they were all derived from ·303 ammunition.

The cartridges used by the military authorities at that time were charged with cordite, as a propellant, and a compound bullet, as a projectile. The bullet was composed of a lead core with an aluminium tip, the whole enclosed in a strong cupro-nickel jacket. What ballistic reason there might be for the aluminium tip I do not know; but it was very useful to a medico-legal expert, since the bullet often broke at the junction of the lead and aluminium, leaving the tip in the body. No other military force used such bullets, and they were all made in British ordnance factories.

I found enough to prove that the ammunition used was British official ·303 cartridges, and that the bullets were fired from British Army rifles. In other words, the whole of the deaths were caused by British weapons — presumably in the hands of British troops, but that was no concern of mine.

This report finished the investigation, which up till then had been directed towards proving that the deaths were due to shooting by members of the mob. By this time, I am afraid, I was not looked upon with any favour by either the military or the civil authorities.

There was an amusing sequel. Among the projectiles which I found in the bodies there were a few bullet-tips composed not of aluminium but of paper pulp. I reported this fact to the War Office in London, suggesting firstly that some contractor was using paper pulp as a substitute for aluminium, and secondly that, since the paper-pulp tip seemed to serve the same function (if any) as the aluminium tip, it might pay them to discontinue the use of aluminium. I received a courteous reply thanking me for my suggestions. The paper pulp, the War Office said, was substituted for aluminium when the aluminium supply gave out early in the War. In answer to my suggestion that the use of aluminium might profitably be discontinued I was assured that the light metal tip conferred on the bullet certain ballistic pro-perties which were invaluable, but were not divulged to me. Nor, said the War Office, was I right in thinking that it would be cheaper to use paper than aluminium, for the pulp had to be put through several processes and thoroughly sterilized so that wound infection should not take place. This struck me as an exceedingly delicate thoughtfulness for the victims of the shooting, not unlike the perfection of the 'clean' atomic bomb at the present time.

In February 1922 the British Government formally ended the protectorate and declared Egypt an independent sovereign State. The Sultan assumed the title of King, a new Constitution was drawn up, and the country acquired every semblance of independence. British authority, however, was undiminished. The British High Commissioner advised the King. Each department of State had a British Adviser to the Minister. British judges sat in the courts together with Egyptian judges, and every senior official in the administration had a British colleague to advise him. There was no heavy-handed demonstration of British authority; but the authority was always there, and advice given had to be taken. It was supported by an army of occupation.

I found the senior British officials a splendid body of men, not particularly brainy but scrupulously honest and just. They all spoke and wrote Arabic, some of them with great fluency. They were required to pass a test in that language within a short period after their engagement. They were, of course, incorruptible, and their word was always kept. The people used to swear most impressively "on the word of an Englishman," and it was very interesting to see how quite ordinary young men from British schools and universities thus impressed their personality on the Egyptian people.

Joining the Government service as I did, as the head of a special section, I was not required to take any test of my knowledge of Arabic. This was just as well, for I am shockingly bad at languages. I managed to pick up enough for my ordinary requirements, but I never became really good. One of my Egyptian colleagues was kind enough to say once that my Arabic was fairly good in its way, but in common with most other "Englishmen" my verbs seemed to be restricted to the imperative mood.

The declaration of Egypt's independence did not end the political unrest, rioting, and murder. Martial law, which had been continuously in force since 1914, remained.

My wife and I had a holiday in Luxor, and we were there when Howard Carter was busily engaged in examining the tomb of Tutankhamen. The Winter Palace Hotel was practically besieged by representatives of the Press of the world, thirsting for any scrap of news. Lord Carnarvon had given *The Times* exclusive access to the news, and this led to a most embittered and undignified contest. Personally I have always found it wise to take the Press into one's confidence when engaged in work that requires careful handling — they can usually be relied on not to publish matters needing discretion if the reason is explained to them, but are liable to publish all kinds of rubbish if they are kept in the dark. In Luxor it was a perfect dog-fight. We were personal friends of Merton, the *Times* representative, and got a certain amount of inside information which, though it added greatly to our interest, exposed us to the frenzied zeal of journalists searching for the slightest peg on which to hang a story.

Two months after entering the antechamber, Carnarvon and Carter opened the sepulchral chamber. In it were four golden shrines, one inside the other, and within the fourth the sarcophagus. When the lid of this was raised the outer coffin of the Pharaoh was exposed. Inside it were two others, the innermost of pure gold weighing three hundred pounds. Thus was revealed the royal mummy, lying in state with a golden portrait mask, golden trappings and rings, bangles and pectorals of gold encrusted with jewels and ornamented with enamels. These followed the treasures from the antechamber to the national museum in Cairo, and if there were nothing else of interest in the country just to see them would make a visit to Egypt worth while.

Lord Carnarvon never saw them. He died in April 1923, several months before the coffin was opened; killed, it was currently reported in Cairo, by a curse on anyone who broke the seal. It was rumoured — quite falsely — that this curse was inscribed on the entrance to the tomb. There were other casualties besides Lord Carnarvon, including Howard Carter's pet canary, and these were widely regarded as proof of the efficacy of the curse.

Most Egyptians believed to some extent in magic. Once our cook refused point-blank to touch a pair of pigeons that a friend of ours had sent because, he said, "Mr Macpherson's cook has the evil eye, and the birds would make you ill."

Belief in both evil and good spirits, and in the necessity of guarding against the former and propitiating the latter, played an important part in all matters to do with health, marriage, childbirth, and everyday affairs. Many maladies and troubles were ascribed to possession by evil spirits, and amulets and charms to ward these off were used by nearly everybody. Tattooing and scarification were in common use for the same purpose, and even to-day many Egyptians bear scars on the outer sides of the eyes, the results of incisions made in babyhood as a protection against demons. Nor are these superstitions confined to ignorant peasants. You may still see a resplendent car belonging to some high official or businessman sporting a ring of blue beads on the radiator-cap to keep devils away.

Ordinarily the use of charms, amulets, incantations, and so on is quite harmless, and no doubt it has some psychological or suggestive value; but always there is a tendency for some form of black magic to arise, with its horrible rites and ceremonies, often involving human sacrifice. It is only when damage is caused that the law is invoked, but injury or death occurs too often to allow any dubiety to exist about the desirability of suppressing magical practice in any society where it survives or arises.

In one sad case that I remember in Egypt a young child was killed in the process of exorcism. The infant had a history of convulsions; and the mother, believing these to be caused by possession by an evil spirit, went not to the doctor but to a person more learned in these matters. He confirmed her diagnosis, and advised her to drive the 'afreet' out by sitting the child in a pan and lighting a fire under it. The child died of burns.

Imagine my surprise many years later, in Scotland, when I had to examine a child that had died in suspicious circumstances and found severe burns on the backside and heels exactly similar to those I had seen on the Egyptian child. When asked to explain the burns the foster-mother eventually admitted that she had sat the child on the stove and lit a fire under it in exactly the same way — not ostensibly to drive out an evil spirit, but to see if it would stop the child's persistent crying: but wherein lies the difference? Holding sick children over a smoky fire is practised in many countries, and I have been told that it is regarded as most efficient in driving out a persistent evil spirit.

The superstitions of Egypt were inevitable in a society where all children were brought up by mothers who were totally ignorant of life outside the nursery and the kitchen. A woman in Egypt in those days had no status in the world. Her education was neglected entirely, and she seemed to be taught nothing of the ordinary ways of life. She hardly ever appeared at any social function, and when she did she was always veiled. In the country districts the veil was a heavy black arrangement with a brass nosepiece that rendered the wearer sufficiently unattractive, as it was meant to do. The shame of being seen by a man when unveiled had to be avoided at all costs — as witness the peasant woman who was disturbed when bathing, wearing only a gown, and who instinctively raised the garment over her head to conceal her face from lewd masculine eyes. In the towns, among the better classes, the veil had become diaphanous, and this, of course, lent the wearer an added glamour. Now it has disappeared almost entirely, and with it has gone a great deal of the mystery of womanhood in the East.

In the summer of 1922 we went home on leave. During my absence some dry bones and fragments of clothing were found in a cave high up in the Mokattam Hills, just outside Cairo. They were not identified, and, though signs of injuries were seen in the skull, it was assumed that they might have been due to a fall. One of my assistants in the medico-legal section reported to this effect, and the Parquet ordered the remains to be buried and the clothing destroyed. But one of my staff, who knew my peculiar liking for examining fragments of material, which he no doubt considered a harmless idiosyncrasy, stored the remains to await my return from leave.

There they stayed until shortly before I came back, when the Parquet evinced intense interest in these remains. Instructions were given to have them exhumed, but nobody knew where they were buried. An inquiry was opened, and this led to the discovery that they never had been buried, but had been put in a sealed container under lock and key in my store and were there still.

The Director of Public Security took charge of them, and after they had been re-examined by several officials they were held over until my return. They were then returned to me to see whether it was possible to get any information about the identity of the deceased and the manner of his death. I was left completely in the dark about the reason for the renewed interest in the case.

The remains consisted of practically a complete skeleton and some articles of clothing, including a jacket, *galabieh*, sweater, vest, cotton drawers, and a pair of socks. After examining all this I reported that the skeleton was of an Egyptian with slight Negroid characteristics, male, about twenty-four years of age; that he was five feet five inches tall, strongly built, with dark, curly hair; and that he had a complete set of good teeth and also a peculiar extra incisor tooth on the right side of his lower jaw. I said I thought he had been struck twice over the head by a right-handed man, standing in front of him and to his left, with an iron bar or other heavy instrument about three-quarters of an inch broad. I thought the first blow caused him to fall, and the second was struck while he was lying on the ground. Then his throat had been cut. I estimated that the murder had taken place three or four months previously. I suggested that the victim had been a domestic servant to a European, and that probably his employer had been a British official named Gayer Anderson; or, if not, that he had some relationship with a servant in Gayer Anderson's employment.

This report hit the Department of Public Security like a bomb. I could not understand the reason for their excitement since they had told me nothing of the case, but later I learned that the identification was crucial in corroborating the testimony of an informer. This man had given them a great deal of information which, if confirmed, might be of considerable value in their investigation of certain political murders.

The informer had told them that a secret society to which he belonged had decided to murder Gayer Anderson, an official in the Ministry of the Interior, and had assigned a rôle in the crime to Gayer Anderson's servant. But some of the conspirators had begun to suspect that the servant was in touch with the police, and they decided to get rid of him before he could betray them. Then, said the informer, they lured him to the Mokattam Hills, interrogated him, and then killed him by beating him over the head with an iron bar, and hid the body in a near-by cave.

It was the mention of the locality that led the authorities to renew their interest in the remains, but this interest waned after the material had been examined by several officials without result. They were absolutely dumbfounded when, after examining the same remains, I not only confirmed in detail the informer's description of the man, and his occupation and how and when he was killed, but made the identification complete by actually naming his employer.

As a matter of fact, it was extraordinarily simple, and it shows how a reputation can be gained on very slight grounds. But I was not in a hurry to lose this reputation, and so, when a Security Department official asked me how on earth anybody could get such confirmation by looking at a mess of bones and clothes, I just said that we had our methods and left it at that. I kept them guessing until the murderers were brought to trial.

The prosecution had no difficulty in establishing the identity of the victim of the crime. The evidence of friends and relatives confirmed every detail of the physical conditions referred to in my report — his age, his stature, the colour of his hair, the abnormality in his teeth, and so on. The identity card of the missing servant was produced, and it gave his height as 163 centimetres (five feet five inches) and his age as twenty-four years.

There was nothing very remarkable about the way I had formed my theory of how the victim had been killed. The two injuries on his skull — a depressed fracture above the ear and another fracture in front — were typical of blows from a heavy instrument with a small striking area. No weapon had been found when I made my report, but afterwards, under the direction of the informer, a heavy file was dug up, and this was exhibited at the trial. Its diameter was about three-quarters of an inch. I had not seen it before; but I had taken the skull with me to court — a thing that, of course, would not be allowed in this country — and I asked permission to compare the file with the main injury to the skull. The court agreed, and when I put the end of the file in the depression in the skull it fitted as accurately as a key in its lock.

My suggestion that the victim's throat had been cut when he was lying on his back was based on the distribution of bloodstains on the clothes round his neck. It was his clothing, also, that indicated his status of domestic servant. The sweater, a garment used in the East almost exclusively by the British, pointed to the nationality of his employer.

But his employer's name — how on earth had I found that out?

From the man's socks. They were of rather fine cashmere, such as no servant would buy, and inside each was a small piece of tape bearing the name of Gayer Anderson.

Civil unrest died down in 1923, and in July martial law was at last brought to an end. Zagloul was allowed to return from exile in time for the new elections, and in January 1924 he became Prime Minister. In September he went to London for talks with the British Government. These soon broke down, and events moved swiftly towards a crisis.

When it came it could hardly have been more dramatic. On November 19, 1924, Sir Lee Stack Pasha, the Sirdar (Commander-in-Chief) of the Egyptian Army and Governor-General of the Sudan, was shot in broad daylight while driving through the streets of Cairo, and died the following day.

This was the culminating point in the series of political crimes that had begun with the attempted murder of Captain Combe in November 1919. It was also to lead to the climax of my five years' work on forensic ballistics.

7

The Murder of the Sirdar

IT IS WELL KNOWN THAT FINGERPRINTS IDENTIFICATION DEPENDS
on the fact that no two fingerprints are exactly alike. The
identification of inanimate objects depends upon a precisely
similar general rule. The differences may be slight, even microscopic; but they always exist. From irregularities in a piece of
typing it is possible to identify the particular typewriter that was
used. From the marks on a bullet or cartridge-case can be identified the particular weapon that fired the shot. That is the basis
of forensic ballistics.

The earliest instance I have seen of this science being used in
the investigation of crime is recorded in the autobiography of
Henry Goddard, a Bow Street Runner, who solved a case by
relating a pimple on a bullet to a tiny hole in the mould in which
it was cast. That was in 1835. Little further progress had been
made when I became interested in 1919, and so far as I was concerned it was still a virgin field. I learned later that Major Calvin
Goddard, of the Ordnance Reserve of the United States Army,
was interested in the same problem, and he published a most in-
formative article based on his own researches in the *Military Surgeon*
in February 1926. Lucas, at the Government Laboratory in Cairo,
shared my interest in the subject, and thought it should be a
branch of forensic chemistry; but since the identification of the
missile was closely associated with the examination of the body of
the person shot, I considered it essential to undertake the ballistic
investigations in our own laboratories. Bullets were our concern
once they entered the body and it seemed reasonable to try to find
out from them all we could. Our opportunities for research were
exceptional: the steady and copious supply of shooting enabled us to
test, correct, and increase our knowledge without intermission.

Every bullet tells a story. Modern firearms are designed to make the bullet come out spinning like a top, because it flies farther and straighter as a result of the spin. The spin is imparted in the barrel by what is called rifling, a series of spiral grooves sloping to the right or left. The elevated surfaces of the bore, projecting between the grooves and called 'lands,' cut into the surface of the bullet as it spins its way along the barrel. When it emerges, therefore, it is marked by grooves corresponding to the lands of the barrel, between which are elevations corresponding to the barrel's grooves.

The grooves in the barrel vary from one make and type of weapon to another, in number, direction, pitch, width, and depth. Thus the Webley Service revolver has seven grooves sloping to the right; the Colt, six sloping to the left; the Smith and Wesson, five sloping to the right; and so on. It follows that every used bullet bears marks that are characteristic of the make and type of firearm from which it was fired. But that is not all. When we studied used bullets under a microscope we found that in addition to the regular type-marks, there were individual differences in one or more of the lands and grooves and which were specific to a particular weapon. Also there were usually marks caused by slight faults or patches of rust in the barrel, or by metallic fouling.

To discover whether a spent bullet was fired from a suspected weapon we worked out a routine technique. First we used the weapon to fire a number of rounds of ammunition of the same make into a roll of cotton-wool or bag of rags. Next we examined each of the test bullets together with the crime bullet under a comparison microscope. When we began work we had no such instrument, but improvised one of our own. Later we took advantage of the design of Charles E. Waite, another American pioneer in forensic ballistics. With the comparison microscope we compared the bullets, groove by groove. We found not only general similarities but also evidence of tool-marks, scratches, slight erosions, and other almost imperceptible defects in the barrel. Of course, not all the marks on each bullet were reproduced on the others, because scratches caused by particles of metallic fouling alter from shot to shot. Only when several test bullets had shown the same mark did we consider it characteristic.

Comparison was more difficult when the crime bullet had been flattened or otherwise distorted by impact, but in general we

could decide whether a weapon submitted to us was or was not
the one from which a particular bullet had been fired.

Identification was much easier if we were supplied with the
cartridge-case as well. Again we made comparisons with test
cartridge-cases after firing a number of rounds into cotton-wool.
Every used cartridge-case bore marks made by the firing-pin on
the copper cap — marks which varied in position, form, and
depth — and by the breech-block, against which it was forced
backward when the bullet was driven out of the weapon. Any
file- or tool-marks on the breech-block were reproduced on the
base of the cartridge and cap. On the cylindrical surface of the
cartridge there might be marks caused by irregularities or tool-
marks in the breech or slide. When an automatic pistol was used
there were also marks made by the extractor hook and the ejector
on the rim of the cartridge-case.

The most important fact about automatic pistols, from our
point of view, was that the cartridge-case was automatically
ejected after a shot was fired, and therefore that it was usually
left on the ground at the scene of the crime.

It could prove as incriminating as if the murderer had left his
visiting-card.

In the early political murders the bullets extracted from the
bodies of the victims were mostly ·45-inch calibre with a heavy
cupro-nickel coating — a type of ammunition such as is used in
automatic pistols. However, in none of these murders were any
cartridge-cases discovered at the scene of the crime. I thought at
first that an automatic pistol might have been fired from a pocket
inside the assassin's gown or *galabieh*, so that the cartridge-case
would have been retained there when ejected instead of dropping
to the ground. But a number of these bullets bore marks showing
that they had been fired from a barrel with seven right-handed
grooves. This rifling is typical of the Webley ·45 revolver. I knew
that the weapon could not have been a Webley automatic, as this
has six grooves. So by a process of exclusion I deduced that
automatic ammunition had probably been fired from a revolver,
as it normally can be: revolver ammunition, on the other hand,
cannot be used with an automatic pistol unless the rim is filed
down.

Although we were handicapped by not having any of the
cartridge-cases, the examination of the bullets themselves under

the comparison microscope showed that many of them had been fired from a particular weapon. This weapon, which was first used in November 1919, ceased to be used after March 1922 — although it was to reappear later, as I shall relate. It was fairly safe to assume that the various murders had been committed by either a single individual or an organized gang. This theory was supported by the fact that the type of ammunition used could not be bought in Egypt at the time.

The next batch of assassinations was more satisfactory from my point of view, as cartridge-cases were always found at the scene of the crime. By examining these and the bullets I was able to deduce that different weapons were used from time to time, but one particular pistol, a ·32 automatic with markings suggestive of a Colt, was involved in them all. The presence of this weapon over and over again made it very likely that the murders were the work of an organized gang.

The ammunition used was apparently from a common stock, and scratches on the cartridge-cases suggested that the magazines of the pistols had been loaded and unloaded many times. It seemed reasonable to infer that the weapons and ammunition were kept in a central store, handed out to the assassins for a particular crime, and, on its completion, handed back again for storage.

I reported that I thought the murders were probably the work of one gang, that the weapons were stored in some central place, and that if these weapons could be seized I would be able to identify those that had been actually used in certain murders, of which I specified seven.

I felt quite sure I would be able to identify the ·32 Colt automatic. Not only did each of the six grooves in the barrel have its own distinctive features, but there was a highly individual fault in the muzzle end of the barrel that produced a characteristic scratched groove on every bullet that was fired from it. The imprint of this fault lay between two of the normal grooves on the bullet, and was broader than the marks of the barrel's lands and quite different from them.

The authorities were completely baffled, however, and none of these crimes had been solved when the Sirdar was murdered.

He was returning home in his car from the War Ministry, at about 1.30 p.m., accompanied by Captain Patrick Campbell, his aide-de-camp. Fred Marsh, the chauffeur, slowed down when about to pass a tram-line in the heart of the city, and the trap was sprung. Many shots were fired, and all three occupants of the car were hit. Marsh did not stop but accelerated, and the ambushers chased the car for fifty yards, firing as they ran. Then they shot their way through the crowd, wounding an Egyptian policeman. They had a taxi waiting, and before driving off they threw a bomb to prevent pursuit. It did not explode, but they got away.

On the following day the Sirdar died from shock and hæmorrhage.

I examined the car, reconstructed the crime, and considered the material evidence. This consisted of nine cartridge-cases, found at the scene of the crime, and six bullets that had been extracted from the bodies of the victims.

The cartridge-cases were all ·32 automatic pistol ammunition. The marks on them showed that three different types of automatic had been used, and three of the cases bore extractor and ejector marks characteristic of a Colt.

The bullets were all ·32 automatic pistol ammunition, with a heavy cupro-nickel jacket. In five of them — including the one that had killed the Sirdar — a cross-shaped cut had been made in the tip to convert them into expanding or 'dum-dum' bullets. These bullets had been fired from three different types of weapon — a pistol of the Mauser type, with four right-handed rifling grooves; a pistol of the Browning or Sûreté type, with six right-handed grooves; and a pistol of the Colt type, with six left-handed grooves.

The bullet that had killed the Sirdar bore the marks characteristic of a Colt. The pistol was evidently in a bad state, with the lands worn, for the normal rifling grooves could hardly be seen; but on the bullet there was a clearly marked scratched groove, lying between two normal grooves and broader than them, which betrayed a fault in the muzzle end of the barrel.

I had seen this scratched groove before. I had seen it many times — and when I compared the bullet microscopically with other crime bullets in my collection I was sure that the Colt ·32 that had killed the Sirdar was the same weapon that had been used repeatedly in previous political murders and attempted murders.

I reported to the Parquet accordingly, and said that if this weapon was seized I would be able to identify it.

Meanwhile the police were making great efforts to track down the assassins. Many arrests were made and houses searched without result. The escape taxi was found, however, and information was received that the crime had been planned and executed by a secret society led by a lawyer named Shafik Mansour. A notorious nationalist, he had been among the accused in the murder of a Prime Minister in 1910, and was arrested again after the attempted murder of another Prime Minister in 1914. In both cases he escaped conviction, but he was later deported to Malta and did not return to Egypt until the end of 1919. He was an important personage in nationalist circles, and had openly advocated assassination as a political weapon. He and his associates were very likely suspects, but no evidence was found against them, and the investigation came to a complete standstill. It was then decided to employ a spy to try to get some kind of lead.

The man engaged, Helbawi by name, had been one of those convicted for the attempt on the life of the Prime Minister in 1914, and he had been serving a sentence of penal servitude. With his record he had no difficulty in getting into touch with the gang responsible for the murder of the Sirdar. Two of the gang were young students, brothers named Enayat; and Helbawi thought they were most likely to confess and implicate the others if they knew they were likely to be convicted themselves.

It seemed to us that if these two could be forced into flight the chances were that they would take their weapons with them — and if we could get the weapons the rest would be easy. So Helbawi was instructed to tell the Enayats that the police were about to make an arrest, and to advise them to flee the country. He was to suggest that the safest way out was by taking the train to Tripoli. The Tripoli line was selected in order that the arrests could be made in the desert, where escape was impossible; besides, in territory controlled by the Frontier District Administration much less formality was needed in connexion with arrest and imprisonment.

Helbawi played his part perfectly, and on January 31, 1925, the Enayats boarded a train at Alexandria bound for the west. Later that day the train was stopped in the desert, the brothers were arrested, and their carriage was searched. But no weapon or ammunition could be found — until one of the police-officers accidentally kicked over a basket of fruit. Out fell four automatic pistols and a quantity of ammunition.

The weapons and ammunition were at once brought to my laboratory for examination. Two of the pistols — a Mauser and a Libia — were of ·25 calibre, and therefore of no interest so far as the murder of the Sirdar was concerned. The other two were both of ·32 calibre. One was a Sûreté, the other a Colt. Both contained bullets of which the tips had been cut to convert them into dum-dum. Both weapons were clean, well oiled, and well cared for, but there was a trace of rust at the muzzle of the Sûreté pistol that might be expected to obscure the identification marks on bullets fired through it.

It was a tense moment in the laboratory as I prepared to fire test bullets from the two pistols into cotton-wool. The Chief of Police, the Director of Public Security, and other officials were all there waiting for the result. There was still no real evidence against any of the gang, and if the test failed it was unlikely that they would ever be brought to justice. It was, moreover, an unusual feature of a murder investigation. Now it is a routine method in shooting cases; then, so far as I know, it was a novel type of investigation.

I fired the test shots, and then compared the bullets and cartridge-cases with those brought to me from the scene of the crime.

The evidence on the bullets fired from the Sûreté pistol was not quite conclusive. The grooves were identical in width and pitch, but there was more scratching between grooves on the test bullets, and no outstanding characteristic fault or detail. There were grounds for strong suspicion, but I could not give a definite opinion on a comparison of the bullets alone.

The comparison of the cartridge-cases told a different story. A series of scratches on the surface, a deep nick in the edge of the cap caused by the ejection bar, curved marks on the smooth surface of the cap caused by the breech-block — these and other markings were identical on test and crime cartridge-cases, and proved beyond all doubt that three of the crime bullets had been fired by the Sûreté pistol.

The evidence of the Colt cartridge-cases was also very strong. The extractor and ejector marks were characteristic of any Colt pistol, but there were also details of a purely individual nature. I used twenty-four other Colt pistols as controls, and in no other case was an exactly similar extractor mark produced.

The evidence of the Colt bullets clinched the matter. Like the crime bullets, the test bullets did not show clearly marked rifling grooves, owing to the bad state of the barrel and the worn lands; but there was no mistaking that broad scratched groove caused by a fault in the muzzle end of the barrel. Under the comparison microscope the details of the marking on the test and crime bullets proved identical. I was able to say with absolute certainty that this pistol, and no other, had fired the bullet that had killed the Sirdar.

Finally I examined the ammunition that had been seized from the Enayat brothers on the train. The cartridges were of three brands — the same brands as those of the cartridge-cases found at the scene of the crime. The tips of the bullets had been treated in exactly the same manner as the crime bullets. In each case the tip showed a saw cut which penetrated into the lead and a file cut which increased the width of the saw cut.

On the strength of my report the police decided not only that they had caught the right men but that they now had enough evidence to convict them. Faced with all this, the Enayat brothers came to the same conclusion, and confessed.

Both brothers had been among those arrested on suspicion immediately after the crime. Then they had denied everything, and had been released with the rest because there was no evidence against them. They repeated their denials after being arrested in the train. It was only when they were told of the identification of the murder weapons that they broke down and confessed.

The younger Enayat — he was only nineteen — confessed first, and, doubtless hoping to save his own life (although I was assured no such promise was made), implicated in his confession the other members of the gang. The older Enayat — he was twenty-two — at first denied everything, but when he discovered his brother had confessed he broke down and, bit by bit, reluctantly, told the whole story.

As a result of the Enayat brothers' disclosures the police arrested six other members of the gang — including the leader, Shafik Mansour.

The houses of these men were all searched, and in that of one — an engineer named Mahmoud Rachid — a box of tools was found. These included some saws, two vices, and fifty-three files, varying in fineness from rasps to key files, all of which were sent to me for examination.

One of the vices had pieces of zinc fitted to the jaws to prevent the teeth from marking an object held in them. In each piece of zinc there was a groove made by clamping some object of the size of a ·32 cartridge, and in each groove there were traces of brass. This was more or less suspicious, but no good as evidence by itself. I took the vice to pieces, and in the joint I found some dust containing bright metallic particles. On analysis the dust showed traces of lead, copper, zinc, and nickel, identical with filings from the seized bullets. This combination was extremely suspicious, although a working mechanic might conceivably have had traces of all these metals among his tools.

I found nothing on the saws, but there were traces of brass on several of the files. I was able to report that all the tools required for cutting the tips of the bullets were present in the box, and that they were of the same nature as those actually used; and that the dust contaminating the tools was the same as the dust that would be produced by cutting the bullets. There was, therefore, a strong presumption, but no conclusive proof, that these were the tools used.

Mahmoud Rachid strenuously denied all knowledge of the case. So did Shafik Mansour, whose main interest seemed to be in the forthcoming general election. He was a Member of Parliament, and hoped to be allowed to visit his constituency to defend his seat. But he became less concerned about his political career when he heard that the Enayat brothers had implicated him in their confessions. The conspirators had sworn a solemn oath not to betray one another, and he had been sure they would keep their word. But now he lost his nerve. Thinking the others were in the adjoining cells, he stood at the window of his own cell and shouted, "Deny, all of you, for your safety lies in your denial." Then, no doubt realizing the imprudence of shouting such compromising words, he began to act as if he were mad. He walked up and down his cell, delivered a speech, and tore his clothes. The prison authorities asked me to examine him.

The first time I saw him he was not excited, but seemed dull and listless. His answers were sensible and clear, although he complained that his memory was deficient. He had been sleeping badly, his blood-pressure was up, and his reflexes much diminished; otherwise he was quite normal. After leaving the cell I went back and watched him through the spy-hole: he was then wringing his hands and lamenting, and gave the picture of complete despair, but this seemed to me to be no sign of madness, as the poor devil had good reason to despair. I recommended that he should not be interrogated again for a while, and suggested that a special warder should be detailed to keep him under continuous observation. He was given a better diet and transferred to a more comfortable prison, where I saw him three days later.

He was still sleeping badly and did not eat much, and he complained of headaches and many other pains. He answered questions sensibly but was in a dull, apathetic state. His memory for recent events was extremely bad, and the whole of his mental faculties appeared dulled. He said he had overheard in the first prison that he was to be flogged, and he was afraid he would die if this happened. He had also heard there, he said, that the King had given orders that he was to be hanged, and this made him very agitated. I asked him if, as a lawyer, he believed such things could happen without a trial. He started crying — he always did when reminded of his status as a lawyer — and said he did not now believe what they had told him. Altogether he was extremely anxious and depressed, but the expectation that he would shortly be executed was not likely to have a soothing effect on him. Dr Johnson told Boswell, "Depend upon it, Sir, when a man knows he is to be hanged in a fortnight, it concentrates his mind wonderfully," but in Shafik's case the concentration was not obvious. I felt rather sorry for him, but sympathy was banished by the fact that he was responsible for the cold-blooded murder of several of my friends whose butchered bodies I had had to dissect.

I recommended that he should be kept quiet, without interrogation, and that he should be given exercise outside the prison. He was still under this treatment when, less than a week later, he suddenly decided to confess.

In any reputable country confessions are rightly the subject of suspicion, and are examined by the courts with rigorous care. Corroboration from other sources is considered desirable, and if there is any hint of compulsion or influence the confession will be refused admission as evidence. In Great Britain no statement by an accused person is admissible unless he was properly cautioned before making it, and no cross-examination of a person under arrest is allowed before he is placed on trial. In Egypt also the courts would accept a confession only if they were sure it was really voluntary.

In the Sirdar case the prosecution relied to a great extent on the confessions of the accused persons and information drawn from the laboratory. The confessions of at least four of the conspirators were used in evidence. I had intimate knowledge of only one of these — it was the most important — and I know that this one was entirely voluntary. I saw Shafik many times before and after he confessed, and had long conversations with him; and never once did he even hint at improper pressure. It is true that he regretted having confessed, and the next time I examined him he was in very poor shape. He told me he was fed up with the waiting, and wanted to be hanged at once to get it over. He said his brain was going. Eventually he calmed down, and I recommended that he should be taken for drives through Cairo and given certain meals outside gaol. Eventually I was able to report that he was fit to be put on trial. He admitted to me that he had been feigning madness, but dropped it because it was too difficult to keep it up.

I advised the prison authorities not to question Shafik, but when he was in a talking mood he let everything out. He admitted complicity in some of the previous political murders and attempted murders in which the same Colt ·32 had been used. He told also where the gang kept their arsenal. He said the firearms and ammunition were stored in a secret receptacle in a door in Mahmoud Rachid's house.

The police searched the house again, and found the door. The hiding-place was a cavity under the bottom panel, which could be unscrewed. The door was sent to me for examination.

The panel had originally been fixed in position with glue and with two nails on one side and four on the bottom. The bottom nails were still there, but the side nails had been removed and replaced by screws. The nail-holes in the bottom were ragged and irregular, and round them were many large and small punctures and scratches. I assumed they had been caused by attempts to replace the panel after removal. The nails at the bottom of the panel had to be forced into the holes, and as it was difficult to get them all in at the first attempt various scratches and punctures had been made. Many of these marks were distinctly old, showing that the hiding-place had been in use for some time. There were so many of them — thirty could be counted round one hole — that it was clear that the panel had been removed and replaced many times.

The cavity was empty, but there were some interesting dents in the wood inside. I tried replacing the murder weapon — and, sure enough, some of the dents corresponded exactly with the fore-sight and back-sight of the pistol. By trying it in different ways I found that there were twelve sets of these marks, the Colt having been placed in the receptacle in four different ways.

There were many other marks caused by hard substances being forced against the wood, and several corresponded with the sights of the Mauser found on the Enayat brothers. The cavity accommodated the four seized pistols comfortably.

After this find Mahmoud Rachid confessed, and, like Shafik, he admitted his complicity in previous crimes in which the same Colt ·32 had been used.

The trial was held at the end of May, six months after the Sirdar was killed. Eight were accused of murder, or incitement to murder, including both the Enayat brothers, Mahmoud Rachid, and, of course, Shafik Mansour. Mahmoud Rachid qualified his confessions, while Shafik Mansour denied his completely. He said that while in prison he had been possessed by a nervous excitement or trance, and nothing he said under this could be taken into account.

The case for the Crown depended upon the confessions of the accused, the evidence of the police-spy Helbawi, and the medico-legal reports. Only the last could be fully relied on, and they had me in the witness-box for a long period.

"Is it easy for anyone to convert an ordinary bullet into a dum-dum?" was one of the questions I was asked.

"Anyone can convert it if he has the necessary tools," I answered. Then I produced photographs of specimens, and volunteered to make a dum-dum before the court. The offer was taken up, and I was handed the files and vice found in the house of Mahmoud Rachid. I fixed the vice to the court desk, inserted a bullet, and with a file made it dum-dum in a few seconds.

Then they produced the door. It was placed on trestles in front of the judge's bench, and the lawyers gathered round as I showed how the pistols had been stored and how the dents on the inside corresponded exactly with the sights of the Colt. I was still holding this weapon when the Procurator-General asked his last question:

"Were any of these pistols used in this case?"

"The Colt has a fault in its barrel which makes a special groove on any bullet fired through it," I answered. "The bullets taken from the Sirdar's chest and from Captain Campbell's have this special groove." Quite instinctively I raised the murder pistol above my head as I added, "I declare definitely that they were both fired from this Colt."

I was the last witness for the prosecution, and my evidence was not challenged by the defence.

The closing speeches were made on June 1, and the court announced that it would deliver judgment the next day at noon. As a matter of fact, it did nothing of the kind. Under Egyptian law if any of a group of several accused was sentenced to death the dossiers of all were submitted to the Mufti.

"The dossiers have been transmitted to the Mufti," announced the President of the Court, thereby letting us know only that at least one of them had been condemned to death. "The verdict will be rendered on June 7."

On June 7 the President announced the verdict. All eight were found guilty. All were sentenced to death.

Bedlam broke loose. The Enayat brothers nearly went berserk. "To death — my brother and I? Traitors! Liars!" one of them shouted. The elder of the two was in the worse state, continually screaming, "My brother to die? My brother to die?" The police had difficulty in dragging them out of the court.

Seven of the condemned, including both the Enayat brothers and Shafik, were duly executed. The sentence of the eighth was commuted to penal servitude for life.

Although to us this case was only one of many in which evidence from the medico-legal laboratories was of crucial importance, it became something of a landmark in the history of criminal investigation. We had shown that the identification of firearms was absolute and could not be shaken, and established quite definitely the value of the laboratory in the detection of crime. I wrote an article giving details of the investigation, which was published in the *British Medical Journal* in January 1926. It brought me a host of inquiries from police authorities throughout the world. I hope I may be pardoned for claiming that the scientific examination of firearms and projectiles in Great Britain had its beginning as a result of the publication of my report on this case.

The chief beneficiary in Egypt was the policeman who had been wounded in the shooting. It was unusual to find such valour in a political crime like this, and the High Commissioner, Lord

Allenby, visited the gallant officer in hospital and presented him with a medal and a cheque for £1000. The shock of receiving this fortune caused the onset of a high fever, and we nearly lost him.

I made a personal examination of the hero, including an X-ray photograph of his thigh, and when I had to see Lord Allenby shortly afterwards I was able to supply him with various details.

"An excellent fellow," said Lord Allenby. "Nearly lost his life defending the Sirdar and trying to arrest the assassins."

I had the photographs of the injury and the X-rays with me, and I let Lord Allenby see them. They showed that the excellent fellow had been shot in the behind, the bullet passing from back to front. He had obviously decided that discretion was the better part, and was accidentally winged in flight by a stray shot.

After scrutinizing the photographs Lord Allenby said, "I think this is a matter that we should keep to ourselves, Sydney Smith."

I agreed, of course, and my lips were sealed until I met Lord Allenby at lunch in Edinburgh many years later, when he had come to give his address as Rector of the University. I reminded him then of this brave policeman. He remembered him well, and was vastly amused, and as he laid no further embargo on its publication I now feel at liberty to tell the tale.

Before the assassins were executed some of them disclosed valuable information about other members of the gang. One of them was an official of the railway administration named Hag Ahmed Gadulla, and it was said that he had fired the shots in many of the earlier outrages — specifically those in which, according to our deductions, the assassins had used a ·45 Webley revolver and automatic ammunition.

The police searched his house, and dug up a wooden box that was found to contain a revolver and ammunition. They sent it to me for examination — and, sure enough, the revolver was a ·45 Webley, rifled with the characteristic seven right-handed grooves. I fired a number of rounds of automatic cartridges from it, and compared the bullets with one that I had taken from the body of a British official named Steele who had been murdered over three years before. Beyond all shadow of doubt Steele had been killed by this revolver.

I had previously established that the same weapon that had fired the Steele bullet had been used in four other cases; so it followed that this revolver had been used in these too.

The ammunition found with the revolver included ·45-calibre automatic cartridges of Eley manufacture identical with the bullets used in these five crimes. The box contained also revolver ammunition and a modern incendiary bomb.

The revolver was wrapped in a grey flannel bag, one side of which was machine-sewn and the other hand-sewn in a rough and clumsy way, from which I deduced that it had originally been part of a garment and had been made into a bag by someone not accustomed to sewing. The cartridges also were in a bag, this time composed of three different materials — plain white cotton, red-and-blue striped cotton, and plain blue cloth. Some seams were sewn by machine, others by hand, again in a rough and clumsy way. At my suggestion the house was searched again for clothes similar to these materials, and a number of such garments were found.

Shafik himself had not fired any of the shots when the attack on the Sirdar was made. His crime was inciting the others to murder, and he was not even with them at the time. For what it was worth, he had a cast-iron alibi. He was with the Minister of Education, Ahmed Maher, not very far away.

In one of his confessions Shafik said that Ahmed Maher and the Under-Secretary of the Interior, El Nokrashi, were both members of the council of the secret society responsible for the assassinations. Some more laboratory work was called for to help in the investigation of Shafik's story.

Several years earlier, he said, the society had been joined by a young man named Mustapha Hamdi, who had been a lieutenant in the police. He was dismissed owing to his political activities. About five years before the Sirdar trial he went out one day to practise bomb-throwing in the Mokattam Hills. According to Shafik, he was very efficient in making bombs and using them. He was apparently not so efficient on this occasion, as one exploded in his hands and killed him. The importance of the story was that Shafik said that Ahmed Maher was with Hamdi at the time.

My job was to try to find out whether Hamdi had been killed in the way Shafik said. I therefore went into the desert to the place where Shafik said the accident had occurred. Considering the time that had elapsed, we were very lucky to find quite a number of fragments of bones and clothing scattered in various parts of the desert, and also some bits of metal and glass. I examined them all where they lay, and then took them back to the laboratory for a closer examination.

The bones apparently all belonged to one person. They were all dry, bleached, and brittle, after obviously long exposure, but they still had a story to tell. They had belonged to a man of between twenty-five and thirty years, about five feet eight tall, and moderately well built. He had a rather narrow palate and a complete set of good teeth in the upper jaw. On the right side of his forehead was a hole about an inch in diameter, with some depressions and cracks round it and quite a lot of excavation on the inner side of the skull. I deduced that he was killed by the passage of an irregular-shaped projectile passing through his head. It could quite well have been caused by the explosion of a bomb.

The clothing, when put together, included a complete suit of heavy tweed, a shirt, collar and tie, thick underwear, socks with suspenders attached, two hemstitched handkerchiefs, and the remains of a tarboosh. From the condition of the sleeves and trouser-legs it seemed that the clothes had been removed from the body before burial. Two fragments of button and one complete button bore the name of a Cairo tailor, and a label sewn into one of the pocket bore the same name and a number written in ink. The tarboosh bore the name of the maker inside. Certain of the garments were identified as belonging to the missing man, and it was therefore assumed that the body was of Hamdi.

One of the handkerchiefs had been folded roughly in the form of a bandage, and on it I found fine traces of blood. There were other stains on the inner lining of the collar of the coat and the inside lining of the tarboosh. All these stains were very faint, and I could not get any reaction to the serum test to establish whether they were human or not. Nothing very definite, therefore, but all tending to corroborate the suggestion of death after an injury.

The fragments of metal and glass included pieces of an iron cylinder, a short piece of iron rod, a flat piece of tin, a tin cylinder, and the neck of a small glass bottle. I already knew the structure of the bombs that had been used in attempted political assassinations, and these fragments fitted perfectly with the theory of a bomb of a similar kind. It was an extremely dangerous type of bomb, as it did not explode on percussion but when thrown. It contained an uncorked bottle of sulphuric acid, and exploded

H

through the spilling of this on to a mixture of chlorate of potash and picric acid. If by chance the bomb was inverted accidentally a premature explosion would take place, and that was just what had happened to Hamdi.

Meanwhile the police had searched the house of an engraver named Yousef Taher, and found some eighteen bombs in his well. They were sent to me to examine. I compared them with the fragments of the bomb that had killed Hamdi, and found them identical. There was no doubt that they were of the same manufacture. What gave this added significance was the fact that Taher was Hamdi's uncle.

It seemed clear enough that Shafik's story of Hamdi's bomb-practice and its fatal conclusion was entirely true. Suspicion against Ahmed Maher was therefore strengthened, and he and El Nokrashi were arrested and committed for trial. This produced rather a delicate situation for me, as my senior colleague, Dr Mahmoud Maher, for whom I had the greatest respect, was the brother of one of the accused and was working in my laboratory all the time I was making those investigations. It must have been equally embarrassing for him, but throughout the whole proceedings his behaviour was impeccable.

Ahmed Maher and El Nokrashi were tried in May 1926 — and acquitted. The British member of the court, Judge Kershaw — who had also been on the Bench in the Sirdar murder trial — resigned in protest, on the ground that the verdict had been given by his two Egyptian colleagues in defiance of the evidence. The British Government sent the Egyptian Government a note declining to accept the verdict as establishing the innocence of the persons acquitted. The verdict aroused much indignation among British officials in Cairo, but personally I was comforted rather than aggrieved by the reflection that my investigations had not, after all, helped to send my senior assistant's brother to the gallows.

8

Bullets, Bones, and Fingerprints

IT WAS THE LONG SERIES OF POLITICAL CRIMES THAT PROVIDED us, quite literally, with ammunition for our researches into forensic ballistics; and the conviction of the murderers of the Sirdar was, in a sense, the triumphal climax. By then this part of our work had already proved its worth time and again in the investigation of ordinary crime.

Occasionally gun or rifle cartridges are ejected after firing, and these are just as valuable as the similar 'visiting-cards' invariably left by an automatic pistol. I had one such cartridge-case brought in from the desert.

Those who have never been in a desert generally imagine it as an expanse of sand stretching for miles in unbroken flatness. Actually it is not at all like that. Sometimes the surface may be flat, but more commonly it is undulating and interspersed with dunes and wadis. This limits the range of vision, and often causes the wanderer to lose himself. It also makes it relatively easy for an evil-doer to conceal himself while waiting for his intended victim. Further, because the desert is so lonely, a dead body can lie undiscovered for days or weeks, even when it is close to a village. Then identification is very difficult, for all the soft parts quickly disappear, and nothing is left but the skeleton; and even that may be partially destroyed by wild dogs. On the whole, the desert is a pretty good place for murder.

In this particular case the body was found soon enough for the relatives to identify it. The dead man was a postman who had been in the habit of walking across the desert between two villages. He had been killed by a bullet, which had passed through his head from right to left. No portion of the bullet was found in his brain or anywhere else. I did not see the body, but from the description of the wound in the post-mortem report I concluded that the bullet had come from a high-velocity weapon such as a ·303 rifle. That was as far as I could go; and meanwhile the police investigation also had come to a full stop. Although it was obviously a premeditated murder, no information that might suggest a motive could be gleaned from the postman's relatives or from anyone else.

At this point Bedouin trackers were called in.

Russel Pasha, the Commandant of the Cairo City Police, told me many stories of the remarkable skill of these men, among whom tracking was in its way a science. Children were taught from infancy to identify the tracks of their parents and the hoof-prints of the cattle and camels belonging to the tribe. Expert trackers developed an extremely fine sense by which they seemed to be able to visualize an individual from his tracks. They could without difficulty spot the tracks of different persons they knew, and could tell whether a person or animal was running or walking, whether loaded or free, and so on.

The police had, of course, already searched for traces that the murderer might have left at the scene of the crime. They had not found any; but the Bedouin found the footprints of a man — wearing sandals, they said — leading to the spot where the body was found. They traced the prints back to a place about forty yards away, where there were marks on the ground made by some one kneeling down. Within a few yards of these marks the Bedouin picked up a small metal object, which they handed to the police. It was an empty ·303 rifle cartridge.

The track made by the sandals showed that the murderer had walked to where the body fell; and there, said the Bedouin, he had taken off his sandals and had run along barefooted towards the road. They followed this trail, although there were other tracks as well — the marks of a motor-car, and the prints of four persons wearing boots — until they came to a fort where six members of the Camel Corps were encamped. Here the trail ended.

The next day all the members of the Camel Corps — and a number of other men — were marched barefooted across a prepared area of sand. The trackers examined all the prints, and immediately identified one set as the same as those they had seen leading from where the postman was killed. The test was repeated once, and then again; and each time the trackers picked out the same man's print. In the fourth test, from which the suspect was excluded, they said, correctly, that he had not taken part.

The police now thought they knew who had committed the murder, but they had not enough evidence for a conviction. The Parquet always hesitated to put a man on trial for murder on the evidence of trackers alone, and the courts were loath to accept such evidence unless it could be supported by other testimony. So all depended on the cartridge-case, which was sent on to me.

For comparison I obtained samples of cartridge-cases fired from each of the rifles of the men in the camp, and from all other ·303 rifles in the vicinity — of coastguards and so on — making a total of fifty-three in all. Six rounds were fired from each, and then one by one the cartridge-cases were put under the comparison microscope alongside the one retrieved by the trackers near the scene of the crime. From the marks of the firing-pin and its position, the marks of the bolt on the copper cap, and certain other marks on the cylindrical surface, it was easy to indicate the particular rifle from which the fatal shot had been fired. I reported accordingly; and the rifle I had identified as the crime weapon was found to belong to the soldier whose footprints had been identified by the Bedouin trackers.

The soldier was arrested, and, as usual, several other persons who had been withholding information now began to talk. The motive turned out to be a common one: the postman had had a guilty association with the soldier's sister, and in the East such a thing normally ended in either marriage or murder — usually the latter.

The case was interesting for the way in which two sciences, one very ancient and the other very modern, led to exactly the same conclusion.

Other cases involving firearms depended more on medical knowledge for their solution, and thus went some way to justifying the claim of forensic ballistics to be a branch of medical jurisprudence. Here is such a case, which began, like many others in Egypt, with the discovery of some bones in a disused well.

They comprised practically a complete skeleton, and they evidently all came from the same body. A hole in the top of the skull led the local authorities to think the deceased had fallen down the well and struck his head on a stone at the bottom, and on the strength of this theory the case was nearly closed, as an accident to some one unknown. However, it was decided to seek expert opinion, and the remains were sent to our laboratory for examination.

I was able to determine or estimate the usual basic facts needed for identification — sex, race, age, height, build, and so on — without difficulty. I found that the legs were abnormally flexed at the hip, which suggested that the body had been doubled up after death, and that it had stiffened and been artificially maintained in that position for a considerable time. It was conceivable that such a folding of the body could have resulted from its being wedged in that attitude by a fatal fall, but there was nothing in the structure of the well to support this idea. A factor that I thought might be significant was that some pieces of sacking, filthy and rotten, had been found with the bones. The abnormal flexion at the hip-joint could very well have been produced by thrusting the doubled-up corpse into a sack and leaving it there.

I did not think it was likely that the hole in the skull had been made by a fall on a stone. It was a circular hole, nearly three-quarters of an inch in diameter, on the left side of the crown, with a margin so regular and sharp as to give it a drilled-out appearance. On the inside of the skull the margins of this hole were bevelled. It looked as if the hole had been made by the passage of a projectile — in other words, a bullet. There were just two objections to this theory: the top of the head was an odd place for the entrance-hole; and, although the base of the skull was fractured, there was no trace of either an exit-hole or the bullet. In addition, the hole was much larger than any ordinary bullet would make. I still thought it probably was a bullet-wound, so I made a systematic search of the rest of the debris, bit by bit and bone by bone. When I picked up the breast-bone I noticed that it felt heavier than usual. I examined it closely, and found a small break in the upper rim — the bit you can feel in the neck between the two collar-bones. I put it under the X-rays — and saw a large home-made bullet embedded in the bone.

I extracted the bullet, which showed no evidence of grooving and had almost certainly been fired from a smooth-barrelled shotgun or pistol of large bore. The range was doubtful. The bullet had evidently struck the top of the head, passed through the brain, smashed the bones at the base of the skull, and then passed into the breast-bone. Therefore either the murderer had been almost directly above the victim, or — which seemed to me more likely — the victim had been shot while lying on the ground, possibly asleep. Immediately after death his body had been thrust in a doubled-up position into a sack and thrown into the well. I reckoned the murder had occurred about six months before.

The police changed the direction of their inquiries, and eventually the dead man was identified. Suspicion fell on a workmate; he was traced, and confessed to the crime, which he had committed exactly as I had surmised.

After Jehu had had Jezebel thrown from the walls, and after she had been trampled under foot, he said to his men, "Go, see now this cursed woman, and bury her: for she is a king's daughter." It is related that when they went to obey they found no more of her than "the skull, and the feet, and the palms of her hands," and were in some doubt as to her identity. Unwittingly they had found exactly those parts of the body on which an identification would now be based.

The value of fingerprints as a means of identification, because no two prints are identical, is common knowledge nowadays. What is not so commonly known is that individually distinctive markings do not exist on the finger-tips alone, but, on the contrary, are found on all friction skin covering, including the palms of the hands and the soles of the feet. They are specific to the individual, are present long before birth, and do not change with age. Any portion of this friction skin offers a means of absolute identification of a person if there is something to compare it with.

Another point that is not so generally known is that all these markings go deeper than the epidermis, or outer skin. It is from the dermis — the underlying, true skin — that the various ridges, loops, and whorls that form fingerprints develop. Dermal prints remain after the epidermis has been destroyed by putrefaction or other cause, and they are an equally certain form of identification.

Hassan Mohammed and his wife Halima spent the night in the house of a friend, and were never seen again. The friend said they had left the next morning and travelled to another town; but, as their disappearance was complete, relatives and friends of the missing couple began to fear foul play, and reported the matter to the police. Suspicion arose that they had been murdered by their host for the night. His house was searched, and some rather suspicious stains were found; but when tested for human blood their reaction was negative. Then the garden adjoining the house was dug up. In one part a putrefactive smell was noticed, and at a depth of a little over a foot the diggers found a piece of skin which appeared to be the complete epidermis of a hand. Near by they found a dead worm similar to a round worm that infests human intestines. That was all.

The investigation was continued. Information was obtained that the suspect had been seen digging at a certain spot on the banks of the canal about a quarter of a mile from his home a few days before the inquiry opened. This area was excavated, and two sacks containing bodies were found. In one there was a male body, doubled up. Although decomposed, it was identified by relatives, from the general appearance and clothes and a tattoo mark on the forearm, as being the body of the missing Hassan Mohammed. He had evidently been murdered, and the state of putrefaction was consistent with the period that had elapsed since the night he had disappeared. The skin of both hands was intact.

The other sack contained the body of a female, rather more decomposed, but identified by relatives as that of the missing woman Halima. She also had been murdered. The appearance of her body suggested that it had been partially eaten by wild animals, and her right hand and most of the right forearm had vanished. Her left arm and hand were still there, but the epidermis of the hand had disappeared.

Identification of the bodies was a simple matter, and so were cause of death and the time since death. The case was referred to me to try to find any evidence showing that either or both bodies had been buried in the garden of the house of the suspect and subsequently removed and buried in the canal bank where they were found.

First I submitted the worm to an expert helminthologist. He reported that it was in fact a round worm of a species that normally infests the human intestine. Worms of the same species were found in the body of Hassan Mohammed, and no doubt this one had escaped from his body into the soil.

The piece of skin found in the mud of the garden was carefully

washed and hardened in formalin, and, as skin withstands putrefaction fairly well, the ridge patterns and details on the fingers
and palm could readily be made out. Could this skin be the
actual epidermis that had become loosened and lost from the
woman's left hand? The question could be answered by comparing the markings with those on the exposed dermis of her
hand. I had photographs taken of each. The ridge patterns and
details appeared identical. I sent the photographs to the fingerprint department of the Ministry of Public Security, and the
identity was confirmed. Here was evidence that Halima, like her
husband, had been buried in the garden and afterwards dis-
interred and reburied on the bank of the canal.

As far as I know, this case, which occurred in 1920, was the
first on record in which the identical nature of the epidermal and
the dermal prints was made use of in a charge of murder. In the
Ruxton case in 1935 — of which more later — Lieutenant
Hammond of the Glasgow C.I.D. made an identification of one
of the victims by comparing her dermal prints with prints found
in Ruxton's house. There may have been other similar cases, but
I have not heard of them.

A less gruesome but equally interesting case began for me with
the delivery by the police of the tip of a finger. A man, they said,
had broken into a house at night with intent to rob. During his
wandering in the house he entered the bedroom of a woman,
who woke up and began to scream. He grasped her and placed
his hand across her mouth to keep her quiet, and she bit him with
sufficient force to remove a portion of a finger. Fortunately, she
did not swallow it, but handed it to the police when she made her
complaint the next morning. The burglar had escaped in the
darkness without being recognized. The finger-tip, therefore, was
the sole evidence by which he might be identified.

The portion consisted of the tip of a finger which had been
removed, not through the end joint but by breaking through the
bone near that joint. The nail was intact. It looked as if it belonged
to a person, probably a man, who had not been accustomed to
hard manual labour, but that was all I could deduce from it.
The ridges on the palmar surface were quite distinct and service-
able for comparison purposes.

Instructions were issued to the police and to hospitals to watch
for a man with a mutilated finger. Ten days later a man with his
right hand wrapped in a handkerchief was arrested on suspicion

at a railway station in the district. A portion of his right index finger was missing, and he was sent to me for examination. He said he had had an accident with a reaping machine. There was nothing improbable about that, but there were rather stronger grounds for thinking the finger-tip had been severed by a bite. I had the stump of his finger X-rayed, and compared the result with an X-ray photograph of the tip. The broken bones seemed to match. The raw end of the finger was roughly torn, and, though no teeth-marks could be seen, it looked as if it had been bitten through. The nail of the piece removed by the bite corresponded in appearance and size with the nail on the man's left index finger. On the whole there was at least a strong presumption that this was the man from whom the tip had been bitten.

Up till then the obvious thing had not been done, and it was the man himself who drew our attention to our lapse. In the course of his protests he mentioned that he had been arrested on a false charge once before, and had been put to a lot of trouble as a result. This made it easy for us, as his fingerprints were bound to have been taken when he was previously charged. We asked the Antecedents Bureau for the prints taken on that occasion, and then compared the prints of the right index finger with the ridge patterns on the tip that had been bitten off. They were found to be identical. This completed the absolute identification of the accused, who then pleaded guilty to the charge.

This case underlines an anomaly that was not peculiar to Egypt at that period but that is just as conspicuous in Britain today. This is that identification by comparison of fingerprints is possible only if the prints of the person concerned are filed in one of the fingerprint collections maintained by the police — in other words, if he has a criminal record.

If fingerprint identification is required — as it was in this case — to convict the person of another criminal offence, this obviously operates to the advantage of persons falling into the hands of the police for the first time, though not to the advantage of society. Often, however, the identification required is of persons who are suffering from loss of memory or who, as a result of some serious accident, are unconscious or dead. If such persons cannot be identified by the Fingerprint Department at Scotland Yard they have to pay the penalty for being so law-abiding.

There is a simple remedy for this unsatisfactory state of affairs. It is the establishment of a civil fingerprint register. Fingerprints could be taken of every child at the registration of birth, and then in less than a century there would be a record of the prints of everybody in the country. If the labour involved in classification were too great, the prints would still be of the utmost value in deciding the identity of unidentified bodies, of people who have lost their memory, of children claimed by two groups of parents —

The Title-page of our Text-book on Forensic Medicine in Arabic
[See p. 141]

often a difficult task when there are no prints available for comparison, as I know from experience — or of persons who claim to be heirs of property. The existence of such a record would therefore be of definite value even if the prints were unclassified.

I said all this in the first edition of my book *Forensic Medicine*, which was published in 1925. Others with experience of problems of identification have made similar suggestions. In 1937 the Home Secretary was asked to consider introducing compulsory national fingerprint registration. He refused, on the ground that there was no general desire on the part of the public for such a scheme. No doubt public opinion is still against it, and whenever the proposal is put forward there are usually loud protests against what is popularly regarded as a threat to the freedom of the individual; although compulsory registration has long been practised without any trouble in countries in what is commonly considered the free part of the world. The only persons whose freedom would be endangered are criminals who have not yet got a record. Those who would benefit include relations and friends of sufferers from amnesia and victims of accidents.

It would be wrong to think that the medico-legal section worked hand in glove with the police. On the contrary, the results of our investigations often demolished their theories and led them to redirect their inquiries. I always thought the reason why no one ever tried to assassinate me, although I probably sent more criminals to the scaffold than anyone else, was that I was also responsible for many of them being liberated after arrest.

Madame Karam was not a revolutionary, nor was she in custody; but the police made no secret of the fact that they suspected her of having taken part in the murder of her husband. She was young and beautiful, and was alleged to have a lover. Her husband was middle-aged and rich, and the police felt sure the murder was an inside job.

The scene of the crime was a very large and sumptuously furnished villa near Alexandria, standing in a garden of seven or eight acres. It was owned by a wealthy merchant named Karam, and occupied by himself and his wife together with his brother and his brother's wife. On the evening of January 14, 1923, the Karams had a party, which finished at about half-past eleven. According to her own story, Madame Karam went upstairs with her husband and stayed with him for about an hour, and then retired to her own room. The next morning she found the door of his bedroom open, and on the floor her husband dead.

He had definitely been murdered — shot from the side, the bullet entering behind his right ear and penetrating his skull to the brain. Also he had three contused wounds of the scalp and one under the eye, probably made by an iron bar which was lying near by. There had evidently been a struggle. The dead man was found beside the bed in a half-sitting posture with his legs stretched out in front and his body entangled in the mosquito-net. An electric lamp had fallen on the floor, and the commode had been knocked over.

Downstairs, in one of the outside doors, there was a hole, oval in shape — about six by four inches — that had been made by drilling a series of holes with a brace and bit and knocking out the piece of wood. The police found this piece of wood and a quantity of wood borings on the ground outside the door. The door was secured on the inside by two iron bolts fixed in the walls: to shut it fast the end of one bolt was passed into a ring on the end of the other, and then a chain on the door was attached to the ring. The hole was so placed that it would enable the intruder to put his hand in and raise the two bolts, and so open the door. As the bolting arrangement was an unusual one, it looked very much as if the hole had been made by some one who knew the premises. Inside, the bell-wires, which were not readily accessible, had been cut, as had been the telephone-wires. This also suggested a fairly intimate knowledge of the house.

Nothing of value had been taken away, although the key of a safe containing a large sum of money and valuable jewellery was in a bunch found lying in the middle of the bed where Karam was killed. Evidently it had been his habit to put this bunch of keys under his pillow when he retired. No one had heard a shot or any movements of intruders during the night. There were no fingerprints or other signs of intrusion except the hole in the door. The police inferred from the position of the panel and wood-borings that this hole had been made from inside, rather than from outside, the house. Because of all this the police not surprisingly took the view that it was an inside job.

They suspected a conspiracy between the wife and her alleged lover, who had been one of the guests at the party given the evening before the crime. But they were unable to find any other facts to support this theory, and eventually the medico-legal section was asked to investigate. With the request came the post-mortem and police reports, the bullet extracted from the dead man's brain, and the iron bar.

What first caught my attention was the bar. Pointed at one end and with a lever on the other, it was like a professional house-breaker's jemmy. It showed a number of brass marks and had been frequently used, and there were fragments of lime in the irregularities about the point. The pointed end was stained with human blood. It was not at all the sort of instrument one would expect to find in an ordinary household.

The description of the dead man's injuries also made me wonder. He had been shot from the side, almost at right angles, whereas the head injuries due to the blow from the iron bar had been made from the front.

I went to Alexandria and, with the local Parquet official and senior police-officer, set off to examine the scene of the crime.

The premises had been shut up since the murder, and even the hole in the door, the panel, and the wood borings had been left untouched. On examining these I spotted the first big flaw in the police theory: the drilling of the door had certainly not been done from within but from the outside.

It was a thoroughly workmanlike job, too. There were similar professional touches in the cutting of the bell and telephone wires, and, as I thought, in the total absence of fingerprints. Vases and other objects with smooth surfaces had apparently been handled without any prints being left, and this certainly pointed to a professional burglar wearing gloves.

The body had, of course, already been buried, but otherwise the room in which the murder had been committed was untouched. The mosquito-net was still there, torn from its fastening, contaminated with blood in one place, and showing traces of burning and blackening. These traces, and the relationship of the burnt area to the head wound, indicated that the revolver had been fired from close range, and that the victim was probably out of bed but behind the mosquito-net when he was shot. Even more illuminating was the evidence of the dead man's nightgown. There were clear signs of burning and blackening on the right sleeve round the elbow. From the relationship of these marks to the wound of the firearm it was obvious that Karam had raised his right arm to defend his head at the moment when he was shot, and that he had been facing away from the person who was doing the shooting. It could be safely assumed that he was facing the person who was striking him from the front, with the jemmy, at the moment when the shot was fired from the side. The conclusion was inevitable that two persons were implicated in the murder.

I could now offer a reconstruction of the crime.

"Two professional burglars," I suggested, "broke in by drilling through the door. Somehow they had obtained an intimate knowledge of the house, and they cut the telephone and bell connexions. Then they went to an antechamber and tried to open the safe. Unable to do this, they went to Karam's bedroom and tried to abstract the keys from under his pillow. He woke, jumped up, and tried to ring for help. One of the burglars struck him three or four times with the jemmy in an attempt to stun him. But he managed to jump out of bed, entangling himself in the mosquito-net, and probably yelled for help. At that moment, when he had raised his right arm to protect his head from the burglar with the jemmy, the other burglar shot him from the side at close range. Alarmed by the noise, both burglars ran away."

The local Parquet official and the senior police-officer looked doubtful.

"Why didn't anyone in the house hear the noise?" asked the Parquet.

"Why didn't anyone hear the shot?" asked the police-officer.

Karam's brother and sister-in-law occupied a separate wing some distance from his room, and I said it was unlikely that the noise would have reached them. The only persons who might have heard were Karam's wife and her maid.

"Haven't they already said they did hear a noise?" I asked.

"Madame Karam says she woke about four and heard a thud somewhere in the house, but did not pay any attention," answered the police-officer. "Katina, the maid, said she was awakened by a noise that sounded like a window-shutter banging in the wind. She reckoned it was about three o'clock." He was obviously sceptical; all along the police had suspected Katina of being a paid assistant in the conspiracy. "A shot does not sound like a thud, and anyone should be able to tell the difference between a shot and the noise of a window-shutter banging."

"I don't agree," I said. "Probably neither the mistress nor the maid had ever heard a shot in her life, and neither of them was expecting to hear one then. It is always difficult to identify a short, sharp noise that wakes you up."

"No one could mistake a shot for a banging window-shutter," said the police-officer doggedly. "That's my opinion, anyway."

"It's not mine," I countered. "So shall we put it to the test?"

They both agreed to this, and the three of us went into Madame Karam's room while another police-officer stayed in Karam's bedroom to fire a shot. We had no sooner gone in and shut the door than we heard the report.

"Well?" asked the police-officer, looking triumphant, as well he might.

"I'm afraid you're right," I conceded. "Even if Katina had never heard a shot in her life she could not have mistaken that sound for the banging of a window-shutter."

This was a mortal blow to my reconstruction, and I was dejected and distinctly puzzled when we returned to the scene of the crime. We found the other police-officer struggling with the pistol.

"It's jammed," he explained. "I'm sorry I haven't been able to fire a shot."

"But we heard one," said his superior.

"You couldn't have done."

"Then we heard something very like it," said the Parquet.

At that moment we heard it again, and knew it for what it was — a window-shutter with a loose hinge banging shut.

My reconstruction was accepted, after all.

Madame Karam, freed from suspicion, now offered a reward of £2,000 to any person giving information that would lead to the arrest of the criminals.

This advertisement was seen by a young Frenchwoman called Henriette, who was described as a lady without profession, but who undoubtedly belonged to the oldest profession in the world. She was living with a German, who was friendly with a compatriot known as Ferid Merkel. This Merkel had confided considerable information to Henriette's protector about a case he had been concerned with, which bore a very close resemblance to the Karam case. The German had discussed it with Henriette, just for interest, but she, after seeing the advertisement offering the reward, got as many facts as she could from him, and then — on February 4, three weeks after the crime — passed them on to the police.

From this information suspicion fell on two men who had been living together in one room of an apartment house but had since disappeared, leaving their belongings behind them. These were found when their room was searched, and gave us some clues to the men's identities. There was some clothing, of very mixed character, including a blue serge suit and a pair of tweed trousers that were much shorter in the leg than the serge ones. On the

tification from a Finger-tip removed by a Bite

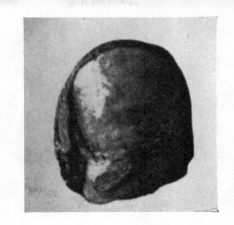

(*right*) Tip of finger with nail.

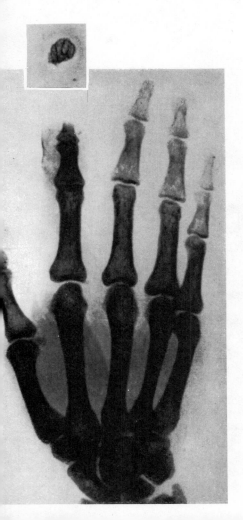

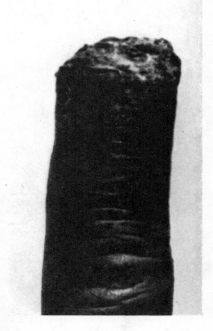

(*above*) Right index finger of accused.

(*left*) X-ray of accused's right hand. This shows the fracture of the end of the index finger. Inset is an X-ray of the finger-tip.

Index droit — العسبرة اليسرى

The Finger-tip Case

(*left*) The finger-tip removed by the bite; (*right*) The print of the right index finger of the accused.

Sir Bernard Spilsbury
Photo Topical Press

The Author in his Laboratory

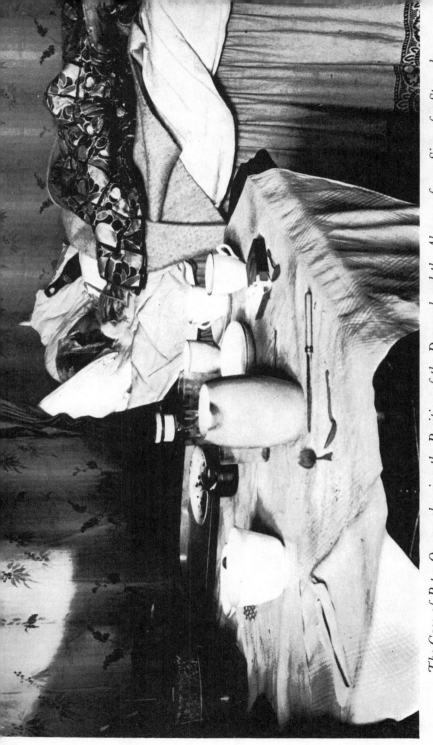

The Case of Peter Queen, showing the Position of the Deceased and the Absence of any Sign of a Struggle

The Aberdeen Sack Case (Mrs Donald)

The body of the child enclosed in a sack as found in the stair recess. Note the fold in the sack due to the body being carried on the arm.

By courtesy of the Aberdeen City Police

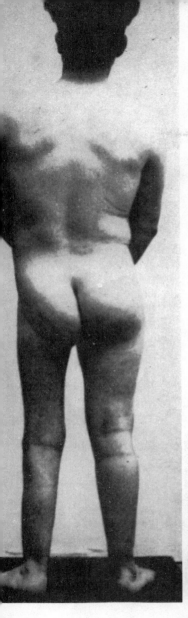

The Falkirk Cat-burglar

(*left*) Photograph of the accused. This shows the wasting of the left thigh and leg, and the spinal curvature.

(*below*) The feet of the accused. Note the difference in size, the apparent absence of a toe on the left foot, and the creasing of the skin on the left sole.

[*p.* 249]

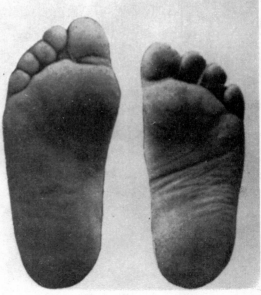

Right   Left

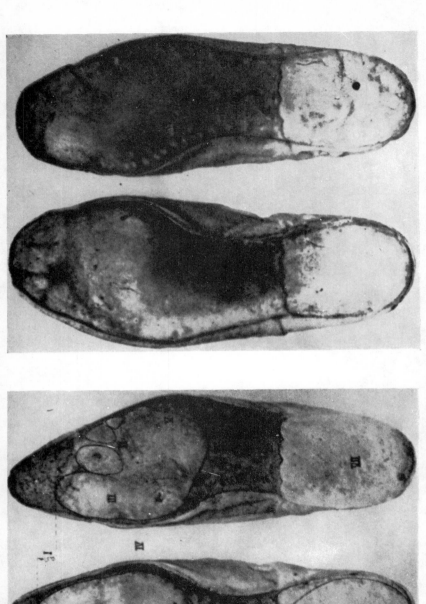

Identification of an Individual (the Falkirk Cat-burglar) from his Footwear: Casts from the Brown Boots (left) and the Black Boots (right)

In both pairs the right-hand shoe is shown at the left. The numbers denote differences in length, breadth, pressure-marks, etc. Note that in the left foot the only pressure of any importance is from the big toe.

The Ramensky Case : Reconstruction of an Envelope

One portion of the envelope was found in the possession of the accused, the others at the scene of the crime in Aberdeen.

[*p.* 242]

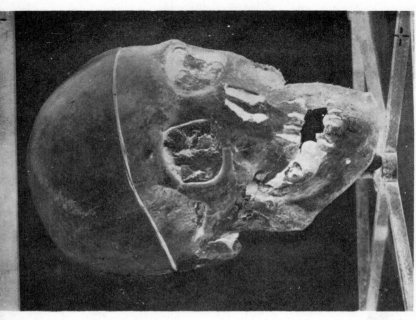

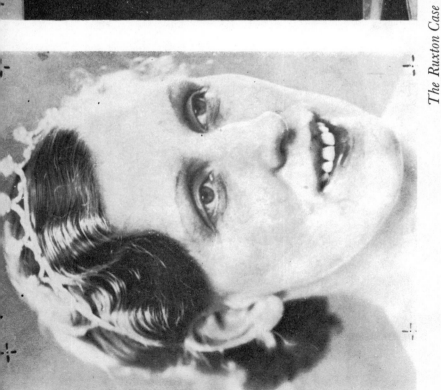

The Ruxton Case

(left) Studio portrait of Mrs Ruxton.

(right) The skull of one of the bodies found in the linn.

These plates and that opposite are from "Medico-Legal Aspects of the Ruxton Case," by Professors Glaister and Brash. Reproduced by permission of H. J. Vann, O.B.E., and of the Director of Public Prosecutions.

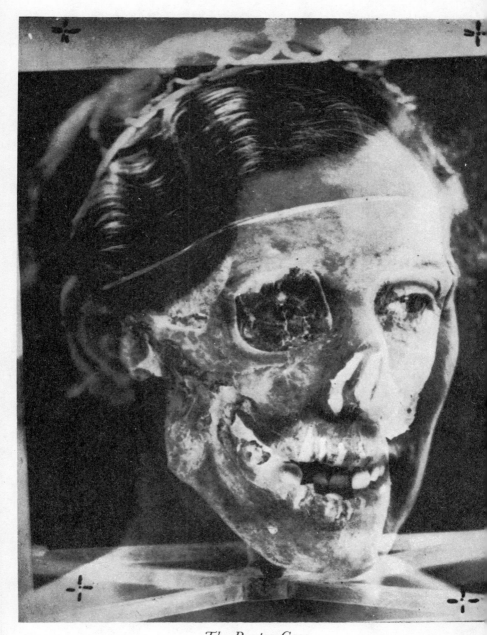

The Ruxton Case

The photograph of Mrs Ruxton with the photograph of the skull superimposed.

Murder in Ceylon

This shows the position of the body in the garage.

[*Chapter 20*]

collar of the suit and inside a felt hat there were some quite long dark hairs. Sticking to the bristles of a hair-brush were many fair hairs with their roots showing some atrophy, and also fragments of cotton and vaseline. From that evidence I deduced that the room had been occupied by two men, one about five feet ten in height and dark-haired, the other about five feet seven, slighter in build, with fair hair and going bald.

Among the other articles were some visiting-cards bearing the name "Klaus Chefer." There were some fragments of paper with writing in German. There were two photographs — one of a young girl, taken by Robert Hanneman of Leipzig, which had been in use for a considerable period, having at one time been tacked on the wall and afterwards placed in a frame; the other of a much older woman, taken in the London Studio, Cairo. There were a number of toothpicks, all from the Petrograd Restaurant, Cairo.

There was a writing-set with a seal bearing the initials "SC" or "SG," or these reversed: they did not, however, correspond with the initial of the name on the visiting-cards. The presence of this article of good quality, among belongings that were mostly of very poor quality, was suspicious. So were two velvet pads which had evidently been taken from a lady's jewel-case and bore marks of rings, brooches, bangles, and other articles of jewellery.

Even more suspicious were the tools found in the room. These comprised a brace and bit, a screwdriver, and some files and chisels. They were not likely to be the regular tools of a tradesman, nor were they such tools as anyone living in a furnished room would normally possess. The brace and bit was of the same kind as that which the burglars had used to drill the door. I compared the bit with the holes in the door, and found them the same size. On one of the files there was a trace of red-brown paint, similar to the paint on the Karam door. I had both paints analysed, and they proved chemically identical.

Among the articles of clothing was a pair of gloves of fairly good make which had been subjected to very rough usage. Many fragments had been torn off the surface of the leather, as if through rubbing against rough objects or in the handling of rough tools. These marks were of recent origin. There were fragments of plaster inside one finger — and in the pockets of the clothes, in addition to the usual debris, there were fragments of sand, limestone, plaster, iron rust, and a few fragments of wood which proved to be identical with the wood of the Karam door. This was of interest, but could not be given special consideration, as the wood was a fairly common kind; on the other hand, such fragments of wood are not as a rule found in the pockets of ordinary people, but if a brace and bit was used the bit might well be put in a pocket after use and leave fragments of wood there. Similarly, it is unusual to find limestone and plaster in the pockets of ordinary people, but they could very well have come from a jemmy which we knew to have plaster on its pointed end.

The German Embassy in Cairo was approached, and was good enough to furnish a report that it had received from two German seamen on January 31. They said that on January 18 they had met another German in Alexandria who told them that his name was Hermann Klauss and that he was living under the name of Klaus Chefer. They said they had stayed with him for a few days on board the steamer *Valtamery*, before it sailed for India. During that time they had gleaned some vague information about the Karam job, which he told them was carried out by himself and another seaman named Ferid Merkel.

This information enabled the police to trace Klauss to India. Acting on behalf of the Egyptian authorities, the Indian Police arrested a person named Magnus Klausen, and sent him to Egypt on April 13. Alas, when he arrived it turned out that he was the wrong man. However, the police sergeant who had accompanied him recognized the photograph of the wanted man, who, he said, had been detained at Calcutta on March 22 as a deserter, pending his return to his ship. The police in India were then asked to hold the real Klauss, and in due course he was sent to Egypt for trial.

The second suspect, Ferid Merkel, was said to have left on a steamer for Germany. The Secretary at the German Embassy in Cairo recognized his photograph as that of a person who had registered at the Consulate under the name of Fritz Doelitzsch, and who had left on board the German steamer *Georgia* on January 29. Wires were sent from Alexandria by the Italian Consul to the police at Trieste and by the German Consul to the German Consulate there, requesting his arrest on the arrival of his ship. He was duly arrested and brought back to Egypt for trial.

Klauss and Doelitzsch were arraigned on a charge of murder before a German court which sat at Cairo, presided over by judges of the High Court sent out from Germany specially for the trial. It was the first occasion since the War that the German Government were able to obtain this extra-territorial right, and they made rather a show-piece of it.

Klauss was tall and dark; Doelitzsch was short, fair, and slightly bald. When I examined them medically before the trial I asked one of them casually what he thought of the food at the Petrograd restaurant in Cairo. "Very good indeed," he said without thinking; then, seemingly alarmed, "How did you know we had been there?" I did not enlighten him.

My reconstruction of the case was carried out in detail in the court, with the actual bed, mosquito-net, and other exhibits. After this and all the other evidence both the accused confessed that they had been implicated in the crime, but their stories differed about their respective parts in it. According to German law, it was important to ascertain who actually killed the victim, even though the two were acting in concert.

Both men agreed that Klauss had the jemmy and Doelitzsch the revolver, and both admitted the facts as reconstructed until they went upstairs to Karam's bedroom to try to get the key of the safe. This was where their disagreement began.

Doelitzsch said that in the dressing-room he took the jemmy from Klauss and gave Klauss the revolver, and then entered the bedroom alone. He saw a man asleep in bed, and began to search under his pillow for the keys. Meanwhile Klauss, still in the dressing-room, accidently knocked over a vase and a chair. The noise woke Karam, who jumped up and tried to get out of bed. Doelitzsch struck him on the head with the jemmy more than once. Klauss, who by this time was also in the bedroom, on Karam's right, fired the revolver, and Karam fell to the floor. Frightened, Doelitzsch let the jemmy fall, and both men fled.

That was Doelitzsch's story. According to Klauss, however, Doelitzsch was responsible for all the violence himself. Doelitzsch wanted him to strike the sleeping man over the head with the jemmy, but he, Klauss, would not, saying that they had not come to kill. At this Doelitzsch seized the jemmy from Klauss and, still keeping the revolver, entered the bedroom alone. Presently Klauss heard a dull sound coming from the bedroom and, taking fright, fled, thinking that Doelitzsch was following. When at the bottom of the stairs he heard a revolver shot.

Our evidence was quite definite that the wounds from the iron bar and firearm wound were inflicted by two different persons. This opinion was accepted by the court. The Attorney-General charged Klauss with having fired the shot that killed Karam, and Doelitzsch with being an accomplice in the murder. He held that the murder was premeditated — otherwise, he said, the two men would have fled immediately Karam woke — and for this reason demanded that both should be sentenced to death.

The counsel for Doelitzsch agreed with the Attorney-General's accusation against Klauss, but strongly opposed the idea of a premeditated crime. He argued that both the blows from the jemmy and the revolver shot were sudden and unreflecting acts committed when the men were surprised in their search for the keys by the wakening of Karam.

Both men were found guilty of murder and condemned to penal servitude for life.

My work in Egypt was not exclusively devoted to the examination of the dead. Living persons also were brought to my laboratories for examination, usually for me to find out whether they really suffered from disabilities that they claimed. In criminal cases where there were personal injuries, damages could be awarded by the court as part of the judgment. Injured persons therefore had a strong incentive to make themselves out worse than they were, and malingering was rife. Sometimes the complainant was genuinely injured but was exaggerating in an attempt to increase the gravity of the case. Other cases were pure fakes.

One of the most ingenious was of a woman who claimed that she had been assaulted while pregnant, and, as a result of the violence, had aborted. In such a case the penalty was very much heavier than if there had been no abortion, and the complainant became eligible for higher damages. This woman was admitted to hospital, and the products of the alleged abortion followed in a bottle of preservative. I sent one of my assistants to investigate the case. He found nothing much to observe in the patient, but asked me to look at the fœtus, which, he said, seemed to be rather peculiar about the legs. I examined it and agreed, and asked him whether he meant the forelegs or the hind-legs. I was not joking, for the 'fœtus' was a fœtal dog. The forelegs and tail had been clipped off and the remains bottled. Crude though the attempted imposture may seem, it had completely deceived the hospital authorities. Indeed, the doctor in charge had spent quite a time waiting for the after-birth.

Another unusual case of faking was that of a young woman who was sent to me to see if she was a virgin. It was quite a common thing to be asked to examine a girl before marriage for this purpose, for in the East, and particularly among Mohammedans, virginity was considered a very important matter. Pre-marital sexual adventures often led to the sudden death of the woman, sometimes to a particularly unpleasant death for her paramour too, and whenever the body of a young woman was found in the Nile it was a routine measure to see if she was pregnant. But this was an examination for virginity, and I thought at first that it was established. Further investigation, however, revealed the presence of a suture which stitched up the torn hymen — a reconstructed virgin, as it were.

A quite unexpected fake was brought before me in connexion with dog-bites. Hydrophobia, or rabies, was prevalent in Egypt, and anyone bitten by a dog could obtain prophylactic treatment at the Pasteur Institute in Cairo. I knew the Institute fairly well, having recently had to undergo the treatment myself.

A trip up the Nile in a *dahabiyeh* — a large sailing-boat — is a delightful experience, and when a legal colleague asked me to accompany him on an inspection of Parquets I jumped at the chance. We passed up the river in easy stages, and eventually tied up for the night a few miles from Luxor. The sunset was particularly lovely that evening, and we went ashore to observe it over the palm-trees. Before we had gone far we were attacked by a group of wild dogs. These dogs are extremely dangerous animals, and have been known to attack and kill strangers. We had successfully fended them off with walking-sticks and were slowly making our way back to the boat when one of them sneaked behind me and bit me just above the ankle. I put my hand down and felt blood. I knew then that my boating trip was over, since there was a good deal of rabies in that district. So I had to return to Cairo immediately to begin the routine course of daily anti-rabic inoculations. I suffered little inconvenience beyond a sharp attack of nettlerash and the psychological disturbance resulting from the remarks of my friends, caninely suggestive in their nature, when I entered the club.

It was shortly after this association of mine with the Pasteur Institute that the Director noticed an extraordinarily large number of cases of dog-bite from a particular province and asked me to have a look at them. They were nearly all youngish men, and all had been bitten in the leg about the same place. I examined the bites closely — and found that they were all identical in appearance. This was too much of a coincidence, and it was not difficult to obtain confirmation that the "bites" had all come from the same skeleton of a dog's jaws.

The object of the faking was simple: two or three weeks' holiday in Cairo at the expense of the Government. But one of the patients, an older man, had another motive. He told me it was generally believed that the Pasteur treatment would cure addiction to drugs, and as a chronic hashish-smoker he took the chance to try his luck.

Malingering for the sake of damages usually took the form of feigned deafness or blindness. Malingerers who feigned defects of hearing or vision usually pretended a unilateral disability, for this was much easier to sustain than complete deafness or blindness. Unmasking malingerers, however, was reasonably simple and always amusing. After a careful examination to detect any real damage that might be present, a series of tests was applied. The object of these was to induce the patient to see with the blind eye, hear with the deaf ear, make movements with the paralysed or disabled limb, and so on without his knowing that he was doing it.

It was comparatively easy so to alter the vision in the sound eye by means of lenses, prisms, and combinations of colour that the patient, if he could read at all, had to do it with the eye which he alleged to be blind.

Feigned deafness, also, was not difficult to expose. After making sure there was no pathological condition present, I used in the early days to fix a tube to each of the person's ears so that I could speak into either or to both at will. After alternating from one tube to the other, asking part of a question in one ear and the rest in the other, I soon reduced a malingerer to a state of confusion. If I felt sure he was malingering I then used to play on him a trick that never failed. After ostentatiously plugging up his good ear, so that no sound could enter, I spoke into the other ear in a confidential tone, saying, "Now that your good ear is plugged, can you hear anything that I am saying, or do you hear just a confused buzzing noise?" Invariably the malingerer replied, "Just a confused buzzing noise," and that concluded the unmasking.

Later I invented a device which the telephone department made for me. It was really the forerunner of the modern audiometer, and it enabled me to keep a more careful check on the sounds going to one ear or the other. No malingerer could cope with this. It led to rather a humorous interlude in one case.

A young woman had received an injury to her head, and had complained of deafness in one ear as a result. She was examined by two reputable ear specialists, both of whom certified that she was malingering. She was sent to me in the ordinary way, and I came to the conclusion that her complaint was genuine.

At the court the Judge said he could not just throw out certificates from two well-known consultants, and asked me what I thought should be done. I suggested that he should adjourn the court for an hour and ask the consultants to confer with him and me in the chambers. He agreed, and I brought my home-made audiometer.

"This machine," I said, "cannot fail to unmask a malingerer." I showed exactly how anyone feigning deafness could be tricked into hearing with his alleged deaf ear. Then I proposed that the doctors should in turn submit themselves to examination, assuming that they were feigning deafness in one ear. I guaranteed to prove their claims to be false within a minute. They agreed to take the test.

"Now," I said to the first, "you are an experienced surgeon and, of course, it must be much more difficult for me to unmask you than an ignorant peasant girl." He said he thought so too. Then I said, "The test starts now. You are supposed to be quite deaf in the left ear." He agreed. I carefully plugged the right ear and said, "Is that comfortable?"

"Yes," he said. "Quite comfortable."

"Then there is no need for a test," I remarked. "You heard my question in your deaf ear."

"Oh, I wasn't quite ready," he said. "Start again."

Then I said, "Let us be precise. You are now unable to hear in the left ear. Since your right ear is plugged you cannot hear through that, so if you hear anything at all it is through your left or deaf ear. Is that right?"

"Yes," he said.

I said, "You have proved that you are malingering."

I then quite openly spoke by the audiometer into the left and right ears by turn, and had him answering questions that he heard with the ear he was trying to pretend was deaf. In the end he gave it up and admitted that the deceit could not be sustained. The young woman thereupon got her verdict and her compensation, and I got complete freedom from counter expert evidence in these matters.

When paralysis of a limb was claimed it was usually necessary to have an assistant who would keep the patient engaged in making certain movements with one limb while I moved the paralysed limb sufficiently to demonstrate to the malingerer the falseness of his claim. I found that most malingerers took a sporting attitude, and when they were obviously unmasked they made no further fuss.   Feigning loss of sensation in a limb or over half the body was very common after head or back injuries. After the usual test for sensation it was surprising how often the malingerer fell for a simple trick. After bandaging his eyes I would tell him that I was going to prick him with a needle to test the extent of the damage. I would then ask him simply to say "Yes" when he felt the prick and "No" when he didn't. I would prick him a few times on the sound side, to get him used to saying "Yes," then I would prick him on each side in turn. If he was malingering I almost always got the reply "No" when I pricked the side he said was insensitive.

Faked cases of shooting, stabbing, and cutting were everyday affairs. Firearm injuries were often self-inflicted to get an enemy into trouble. Usually a weapon was discharged through the clothing only; occasionally injuries such as cigarette burns or punctures in the skin were made to look like firearm wounds, while in some cases shots were actually fired through the skin. In the latter the marks on the clothing rarely fitted in with the wounds on the body, for as a general rule no malingerer was prepared to shoot himself while clothed. Very often he would forget to make any mark on the clothes at all.

Personal gain and revenge were not the only motives for faking injuries. I well remember one case when I was called out late at night to examine a newspaper editor who had complained to the police that he had been attacked and wounded by two British soldiers with bayonets. The editor was a man of some influence, and the policy of the newspaper was strongly nationalist and anti-British. I found a number of high officials awaiting my report with great concern.

I examined the man, and saw that he had wounds of some sort

in the front of the chest, coated with blood. When I washed the blood away they turned out to be a series of rather fine cuts, never penetrating below the outer skin, running neatly parallel with one another, and apparently inflicted with great care. The clothing above them was not cut at all. The cuts had undoubtedly been

Menu Cover of Farewell Dinner given
at the Turf Club, Cairo, 1928
[See p. 148]

self-inflicted with a razor-blade or some other small, sharp instrument. I reported to this effect, and the editor was at once arrested and charged with making a false accusation against the soldiers. So ended the political importance of the case, but it is easy to understand the trouble that could have arisen without this medico-legal evidence.

9

Return to Edinburgh

BRIBERY, OF COURSE, WAS RAMPANT IN EGYPT, BUT THIS WILL not be looked upon as a grave defect in character if we remember that morals are largely a matter of geography, and that honesty depends to a great extent on one's financial situation and general upbringing. It was generally accepted that merit was not necessarily the first requisite for an appointment in Government service, and that patronage and influence could be much more effective. Very reprehensible, no doubt, but it is not so long ago that such principles obtained in our own country — and, in a certain way, they still do.

Many amusing instances of attempts to obtain recommendations came before me, one of which I think is worth telling. A Coptic clerk in the department, whose post was a long distance from Cairo, badly wanted to get transferred to the capital where there were openings for his family of five, which, he said, consisted of "three adults and two adultresses." After a heart-rending account of his troubles and difficulties, his letter finished as follows:

> I know, sir, that you have great influence with Mr Hughes and can thus help the unfortunate who now places his future in your hands. As you know, honoured sir, I am a Copt — a Christian like yourself — and I ask this favour in the name of our mutual friend J. Christ Esq., whom your excellency so strongly resembles.

Now, could there be any more convincing flattery than this? Of course, I immediately put this cogent appeal before Hughes, the Inspector of Parquets, for it was too good to withhold. But I never learnt whether my co-religionist obtained his transfer or not.

Knowing that bribery was rampant, I asked my confidential

secretary how it was that none ever came my way, since obviously a report from an official in my particular position might mean all the difference between liberty and imprisonment, or even between life and death.

"Ah," he replied, "no English official can be bribed, that is well known. Besides, they would have to bribe me first."

Whatever the reason, I was never once approached during my eleven years there.

But Egyptians were not the only ones who indulged in bribery. A foreign acquaintance of mine once asked me if I knew Mr X, who was a judge in the mixed courts. I said I knew him quite well. "Do you think," my acquaintance then asked, "that it would be helpful if I sent him a case of champagne? I have a plea down for hearing before him." Judge X was a highly austere man, and I replied that I could think of no better way for him to lose his case. He thanked me for my advice and went away thoughtfully. A week or so later he told me that a decision had been given in his favour. "No doubt the champagne helped," he added. "You don't mean to tell me you had the impertinence to send it to Judge X?" I said. "Yes," he replied. "I sent it all right — in the name of my opponent."

A minor case of bribery came to my notice in the medico-legal section. The culprit was the mortuary attendant — a humble post that did not seem to offer much chance of outside profit. I found out, however, that he had developed a nice little side-line. Autopsies are anathema to the Mohammedan, and often this enterprising servitor used to inform relatives that for a small consideration he would use his influence with me to secure a death certificate without the body being touched. As he was apparently successful — not surprisingly, for he knew pretty well the kind of case in which I would or would not require a full post-mortem examination — he probably acquired quite a reputation for influence with the "Hakeem Basha" until he was stopped. This fellow, by the way, had another source of income which I discovered only after we had put him on the mat. Gold-filled teeth were popular among those who could afford them, and I found that our friend was in the habit, after the post-mortem was completed, of drawing any teeth that were gold-filled and, as it were, cashing them. I believe he made quite a bit out of this. He was an arrant rascal, but a cheerful one, and we did not sack him.

A much more important case of bribery had to go to the courts.

One of my chemists was charged with accepting bribes for giving false certificates in connexion with alleged narcotic drugs. I had learnt to trust him over several years of work, and, although he was convicted, I never really felt that he could have been guilty.

While I was in Cairo I indulged for the first time in a commodity speculation.

A great friend of mine and an astute businessman, William Delaney, asked me, shortly before the summer vacation, whether I would like to have a flutter in beans. It had come to his knowledge that the bean crop in Egypt was likely to be a partial failure, and there was every ground to believe that there would be a substantial rise in price. I agreed to join him in the venture, and we bought a large quantity of beans — many, many tons — which we stored in the *shoonas* of the Bank through which we operated. We both went on leave shortly afterwards, but left instructions with the bank to sell our holding if the price rose to a certain level, or alternatively if it should decline below a lower level.

During the holiday in Britain I closely followed the market quotations for beans, and was delighted to note a regular rise in price. When it rose above our upper selling limit I said gleefully to my wife, "We are having a holiday entirely on the house." On arrival back in Cairo a couple of months later I rang up Delaney, congratulating him on his business acumen. "We have made quite a pot of money," I said. A gloomy Delaney at the other end of the wire said, "Not so fast — the bank hasn't sold out." We were, he thought, the victims of a ring of regular dealers who disliked outsiders butting into their business.

I went over to the *shoonas* to look at the beans. I had never seen so many beans in my life. There were tons and tons of them, and at least half were mine. My wife said, "It looks as if we'll be eating beans for the rest of our lives without making much of a hole in that lot." I noticed on my visit that the *shoonas* were in rather a bad hygienic state, and that the beans on the floor-level were already beginning to sprout.

Back in Cairo I interviewed the manager of the bank. He admitted that the price had gone well above our limit, and that there were a number of sales at that advanced figure; but, he said, his agent could not get a buyer for our beans. It seemed to me that he had not exerted himself on our behalf, but was in-

fluenced by our opponents. I therefore tried my hand at their own
game. I told him what I had observed about the conditions in
which the beans were stored, and I said I would have to consider
reporting their unsatisfactory state to the proper authority. This
was pure blackmail, but it had the expected effect. Our beans
were sold the same day at a reasonable profit. But that was the
first and last time I speculated in commodities.

In Cairo also I engaged for the only time in my life in the
notoriously speculative business of publishing. This was to bring
out my first book on forensic medicine, which was in Arabic: I
had the active collaboration of my Egyptian assistant, Dr Ahmer
Bey, in turning the material into that language, which I could
never have done by myself. There were no publishing houses in
Cairo at that time (1924), and we had to arrange the whole
business ourselves — purchase of paper, making blocks for the
illustrations, contracts for printing and binding, and so on. Fortunately, little or no advertising was required, for the book filled
a long-felt want, there being no other book in Arabic on the subject. It was a surprising financial success, and it struck me at the
time that I had entered the wrong calling, since publishing
offered such excellent rewards. My fellow-author and I were
honoured by an invitation from King Fuad to attend Abdine
Palace to receive his congratulations. We prepared for presentation to him a specially bound volume in green morocco
leather, with the royal coat of arms in gold. His Majesty was
graciously pleased to accept this for the royal library.

My first edition in English of *Forensic Medicine and Toxicology*
was published by Messrs. J. and A. Churchill in 1925. This was
probably the first really well-illustrated work on the subject in
Great Britain, and it also was an immediate success. It is now in
its tenth edition. Harvey Littlejohn helped me considerably in
preparing the book, and wrote a generous foreword commending
it. It was extremely unfortunate that this act of kindness to me
should have caused him so much trouble when he appeared
as an expert witness in the celebrated trial of Donald Merrett.

John Donald Merrett, like me, was born in New Zealand and
went to Edinburgh University; but there, I hope, the resemblance
ends. His University record was highly unsatisfactory, and he
occupied the time supposed to be devoted to his studies in dancing
and associated diversions with many young ladies. He required

a good deal of money for his adventures, and he supplemented the generous allowance from his mother by forging cheques in her name. All this came out later, after her death.

He was in his eighteenth year when she was taken to the Royal Infirmary suffering from a bullet wound of the head. The police, having questioned her son and a servant, were convinced she had attempted to commit suicide. So sure of this were they that they neglected to take a deposition from her when she recovered consciousness, although there was ample time to obtain one, and it was known that she had made several important statements to the hospital staff.

Mrs Merrett died a fortnight after the shooting, on April 1, 1926. On April 5 Littlejohn performed a post-mortem examination. In his report he stated that there was a wound in the right ear which had been caused by the entrance of a bullet. He described the path taken by the bullet, but said there was nothing to indicate the distance from which it had been fired. He concluded that "*as far as the position of the wound is concerned* the case is consistent with suicide." He added that there was some difficulty in attributing it to accident although such a view could not be wholly excluded.

I was in Edinburgh on vacation that summer, and Littlejohn consulted me about the case. He told me that he was worried about it, and by then, no doubt, the police were too.

According to what Mrs Merrett had said to the doctors and nurses at the infirmary, she was writing a letter at her desk, with Donald standing beside her, when "suddenly something burst in my head, just like a pistol-shot." She appeared to know nothing about any firearm, and the evidence of the doctors in the infirmary was by no means in favour of suicide. The doctor in the outpatient department, who examined Mrs Merrett when she was admitted, saw no sign of blackening or burning, and did not detect any smell of burnt powder. He also noted the absence of any tearing about the entrance-wound, which is common in suicidal injuries. The house surgeon who dressed the wound confirmed these observations. Both doctors had made a careful examination specifically for the purpose of deciding whether there was any evidence of a close discharge — and there was none.

"What do you think?" Littlejohn asked me when I had gone through all the evidence.

"It looks to me like murder," I said. I hesitated to advise my old teacher but it seemed to me that there was one obvious course to be taken. "Why don't you make some experiments with the weapon that killed her?" I suggested. "Find out if a discharge close to the skin would cause powder-marks."

Using the same kind of ammunition, Littlejohn carried out a series of tests in August. First he fired the weapon — a six cartridge ·25 Spanish automatic — at cardboard targets, carefully measuring the distances between the barrel and the cardboard. Then he repeated the experiment, using as his target a sheet of skin taken from the freshly amputated leg of an accident victim.

Anybody firing a pistol at his own head is inclined to hold the barrel close to the skull — certainly not more than three inches away. And at three inches the Spanish automatic left very definite powder and burning marks round the wound in the skin area. It left marks at six inches. What was more, the discolorations could not readily be washed off. Littlejohn had to go to nine inches before the gun left no marks — and nobody would shoot himself with the barrel nine inches from the head.

There were no powder or burning marks at all on Mrs Merrett's head. So somebody else must have fired the fatal shot.

Littlejohn readily admitted his mistake. He wrote a second report in which he said that accident was inconceivable, that suicide was in the highest degree improbable, and that all the circumstances pointed to the conclusion that the weapon had been fired by another party.

By some queer chance Littlejohn did not issue this report until January 13, 1927 — five months after his experiments, and over a month after Merrett had been arrested and charged with the murder of his mother.

The trial was held in February, and of course Littlejohn was called by the Crown. He repeated that in his opinion both accident and suicide were inconceivable, but naturally the fact that he had changed his mind after issuing his first report was made much of by the defence. This was in the able hands of Mr Craigie Aitchison, who discomfited Littlejohn by quoting a passage from my book. In this I had devoted a good deal of space to a discussion of firearms and firearm injuries, of which I had had considerable experience, and concerning which I had carried out an enormous number of experiments. In discussing bullet-wounds I had written: "Although automatic pistols produce wounds identical with wounds from revolvers, it should be remembered that automatic ammunition is always charged with smokeless powder and that absence of blackening and burning in close discharges is relatively common." This was the passage quoted by the defence counsel, who held that because of his foreword it had Littlejohn's approval — a suggestion, incidentally, which Littlejohn immediately denied. In the same section I had also mentioned that if the actual weapon was found the question should be decided by experiment, but the defence did not allude to that passage.

To counter Littlejohn's expert evidence they put up Sir Bernard Spilsbury, the Home Office pathologist, who was very brilliant and very famous, but fallible like the rest of us — and very, very obstinate. In England, where he always appeared for the Crown, many murderers were justly convicted on his evidence. Now he was making one of his rare appearances for the defence.

With him was Robert Churchill, often described as the expert on ballistics. Robert Churchill was famous, too, and I am sure he was an excellent gunsmith. He also was stubborn and dogmatic. He and Spilsbury often appeared together in shooting cases, and they were indeed a formidable team — terrifying when they made a mistake, as they did here.

They also had carried out some experiments, on the same lines as Littlejohn's, but with exactly opposite results! They claimed that their experiments proved that marks need not have been left round the wound, and so that Mrs Merrett could have shot herself. Spilsbury said he thought she had.

This difference of opinion between experts is less startling than it may seem. The reason was that Spilsbury and Churchill used, not the pistol she had been killed with, but an entirely different weapon and different ammunition.

In the circumstances their experiment was worthless, and the judge warned the jury of this, but a clash of experts always makes a jury sceptical about the whole scientific evidence, although the point was especially important here because of the poor quality of the police evidence.

When they first questioned Merrett the police were so convinced that they did not doubt it was a case of suicide. This was an error of judgment, but it did not excuse their neglect to carry out ordinary routine procedures.

They failed to make any record of the position of the body when it was found. They failed to note the position of the weapon that had fired the fatal shot. They did not even test it for fingerprints. They knew Mrs Merrett was writing a letter when she was shot, but failed to produce it in court. I think they had lost it.

The judge said of the police conduct, "the position seems to be unsatisfactory, inconclusive, and perfunctory." That was putting it mildly, and Mr Craigie Aitchison cut the case for the Crown to pieces. He called the failure of the police to take a dying deposition "an almost criminal defect of an obvious and imperative duty," and said he thought that if it had been taken "the accused would never have been put upon his trial." In point of fact it would probably have hanged his client.

As it was Merrett did not miss the rope by much. The evidence of the nurses who had looked after his dying mother was nearly enough. "Did Donald do it? He is such a naughty boy," she had said to one of them; to another, "I said, 'Go away, Donald, and don't annoy me.' The next I heard was a kind of explosion." But the slackness of the police and the credit given to the misleading evidence of Spilsbury and Churchill, who had made a mistake and were too stubborn to admit it, allowed Merrett to live — and to kill again. A worthless life was saved, and two innocent women were thereby condemned to die.

On the murder charge the jury returned the Scottish verdict of "not proven." On a second charge — of uttering forged cheques — Merrett was convicted and sentenced to twelve months' imprisonment.

I had no doubt about his guilt. "That is not the last we'll hear of young Merrett," I said when Littlejohn told me how he had escaped conviction on the murder charge. It certainly was not. Discharged from prison in October 1927, Merrett's subsequent history was that of an outlaw against society — smuggling, gunrunning, gambling, and so on. During the War he joined the Navy under the name of Ronald Chesney, obtained a commission, and was finally promoted to the rank of Lieutenant-Commander. He had charge of a gunboat in the Mediterranean, and as far as I know had quite a good record, although suggestions have been made that even there he could never resist making a bit of money on the side. After the War he joined the Control Commission in Germany, and continued his nefarious practices. He served more than one term of imprisonment, and became 'known to the police' in many countries. Finally, in 1954, he conceived a plot to murder his wife, and thus obtain a sum of money he had settled on her many years before when he inherited his mother's estate.

His plan was in keeping with his flamboyant personality. He was living in Germany at the time. One day he took the boat to England, using his own passport in the name of Chesney. He visited his wife, contacted enough people to establish the fact of his presence there, and then returned to Germany, making himself sufficiently conspicuous at the port of departure to secure evidence that he had left on that particular day. While in England he had stolen a passport from a man he had met in a public-house, and immediately after his arrival back in Germany he returned to England under the stolen passport in order to kill his wife.

He reached the house without being seen, entered through a window, killed his wife, and immersed her body in a bath to simulate death by accident. Unfortunately for him, his wife's mother saw him as he was making his escape. He therefore had to kill her too. The old lady apparently resisted, so that he had to use a certain amount of violence. This completely destroyed his plan to make his wife's death appear accidental. He got away, however, without being detected, and returned to his lodgings in Germany.

Step by step the police unravelled the crime. They became convinced that it must have been Chesney who had committed it. They discovered that a passport had been stolen from a certain man, and that it had been used on the night of the murder by some one else who had crossed from Germany to England. Chesney, who apparently knew that arrest was imminent, walked out into the night and shot himself. Thus ended a life colourful and adventurous enough, but without a gleam of normal decent behaviour.

The Merrett case caused Harvey Littlejohn a great deal of worry and anxiety, and was, I feel certain, a contributory factor in his relatively early death. This occurred the same year (1927), and it came as a great shock to me. I had visited him in hospital a week or two before, and though he was in a very weak state I never expected him to die so soon.

In the last talk we had before I left Edinburgh he had asked me whether I would return and take his Chair when he died. I told him that I hoped to see him in his Chair for many years to come.

With that testiness which was part of his personality he said, "Don't be a sentimental fool, Smith — you've seen, and I've seen, hundreds of cases like mine. You know perfectly well that one of these mornings soon the nurse will come in and find me dead. Will you come back and take my place?" I said that of course if such a contingency arose I would consider it very carefully, but I would not allow him to discuss it further. Within about ten days, just as I was returning to Egypt, I heard of his death.

The Chair of Forensic Medicine in Edinburgh is a Regius Chair — that is to say, appointments are made by the Crown and not by the University, although the University is usually asked to advise the Crown about it. Shortly after my arrival back in Egypt I received a letter from the Dean of the Faculty of Medicine in Edinburgh asking me whether I would apply for the post. A later letter from the Secretary of State for Scotland offered me the appointment. As the senior Chair of Forensic Medicine in Great Britain, it was obviously most attractive.

Hardly, if at all, less attractive was my position in Cairo, which had improved since the British recognition of Egypt's independence. The Egyptian Government had then decided to terminate the employment of all foreigners as permanent officials, and it had gone about this in a very gentlemanly way. The question of compensation for loss of employment and prospects was placed in the hands of the Society of Actuaries, who worked out a scheme taking into consideration age, length of service, salary, and so on. Those wizards of the world of figures produced a scale of compensation which, though not erring on the side of too prodigal generosity, yet was not of unseemly proportions. It seemed a truly Oriental procedure that I should receive on the one hand a cheque for loss of employment and prospects, and on the other hand a contract for further employment at an enhanced salary. Truly all things work together for good. This was the only time I have ever been sacked, and a most remunerative sacking I found it.

Now I had to decide whether or not to return to Edinburgh. It was a matter for careful thought. I had spent eleven happy years in Egypt. I had a job that kept me interested and busy. I liked it, and did not want to leave. I had a multitude of friends, both Egyptians and Europeans, who made life pleasant. The Government were appreciative of my work, and had honoured me by awarding me the decoration of Commander of the Order of the Nile. My department was about to expand into other areas. Upon hearing that the Chair in Edinburgh was likely to attract me they offered me a considerable increase in salary to remain. The salary offered in Edinburgh was a good bit less than half my Egyptian salary, which at that time was tax free.

But we had two children who had to be educated, which meant that my wife had to spend a good part of her time in Great Britain, and that I saw comparatively little of the children at their mos formative period. A divided home is no good to anybody, and so I decided to accept the Edinburgh job — not without much heart-searching. Farewell to the sunlit days of Egypt, which appeared all the more delightful in retrospect when we came back to a cold and cheerless Edinburgh, a University in vacation, and an apparently moribund department. It seemed not inappropriate that I should have arrived on April the first.

I returned to Britain at the time of the Gutteridge case, which was of exceptional interest to me. I have mentioned that the paper on the identification of firearms which I wrote after the Sirdar murder case aroused much interest among police authorities: the Gutteridge case was the first in Britain in which the methods of identification that I described there were used.

P.C. Gutteridge, on his beat in a country village in Essex, stopped a motor-car, apparently to get particulars. The two occupants were car-thieves, and they shot the constable in the face, and followed this up by shooting out both his eyes. They then drove off, and eventually abandoned the car. It was badly bloodstained, and in it was a cartridge-case which later proved to be their undoing.

Despite all the efforts of the police, the men were not traced until three months later, when, after a lucky observation in connexion with a car-theft, the authorities at Scotland Yard were informed of the names of the assailants. Browne was arrested at a garage in Battersea, and Kennedy in Liverpool. A weapon in their possession was seized, and the ballistics experts at Scotland Yard proved conclusively that it was from this weapon that the shots that killed P.C. Gutteridge had been fired. The men were found guilty, and executed on May 31, 1928. Since then, of course, the scientific examination of firearms has been a feature of importance in many shooting cases; but this was the first time the British police had used the technique that, by trial and error over the years, we had evolved in Cairo, and I followed the case with an almost proprietary interest.

After I had been back in Edinburgh a couple of years the Medical Faculty elected me their Dean, a post which I held for about twenty-five years. I found this part of the work — dealing with students and their difficulties, and with the general administration of the Faculty — highly diverting in its way, and, of course, it brought me into contact with all the other departments of University life.

Being Dean also reminded me that it was not only in the East that attempts were made to influence officials. Admission to the medical school was much sought after, and I dealt personally with applications. One day a letter arrived for me marked "Strictly Private." It was from a gentleman who suggested that he would like to place a fairly large sum in dollars at my absolute disposal "to help deserving Scottish students who were unable to pay their own way." He added as a postscript that his son, who was apparently a remarkably clever young man likely to be a credit to any university, was desirous of taking a degree in medicine. After considering the whole field, as it were, he had decided that Edinburgh had the most famous school of medicine in the world, and, therefore, he would prefer his son to take his degree there.

I replied accepting his generous offer, and suggested that he should send the cheque to the secretary of the University, and thereafter we could arrange the management of the fund. In a postscript I told him we could not take his son, as our lists were full. I heard no more from him, and have wondered since whether he was possibly trying to bribe me.

Although I succeeded Harvey Littlejohn in the Chair, I did not take over his appointment as Chief Surgeon to the Edinburgh Police. During the period between the death of Littlejohn and my arrival this appointment had been given to Littlejohn's assistant, Dr Douglas Kerr, who had been acting for him, and whom the police knew and liked. This division persisted until I retired and was succeeded in the Chair by Dr Kerr, who retained his appointment of Chief Surgeon to the Police. Although the loss of this appointment cut off a great deal of routine medico-legal work, I was always asked by the Crown to take part in the more important cases.

There were numbers of interesting cases, and I developed the laboratory side of the work on the lines of my section in Cairo. This proved very successful as a help with the investigation of all types of police work, including house-breaking, safe-breaking, and forgery, for example, as well as cases of unnatural death. I shall describe a few typical cases of this nature in later chapters. The police were interested and co-operative. Officers of the C.I.D. were always welcome to visit the laboratory, talk over their cases, and have all the help I could give them in their investigations, official or otherwise.

Of course, there was nothing like the number or variety of cases that I had been used to in Cairo, nor the staff or equipment to cope with them if there had been. But there was one important new experience in store for me. That was appearing as expert witness for the defence.

The first case in which I appeared in that capacity was one of the *causes célèbres* of the century. The expert witness appearing for the Crown was Sir Bernard Spilsbury. The stage was set for our first major clash in court.

10

The Case of Sidney Fox

SIDNEY HARRY FOX WAS NOT A GOOD CITIZEN. HE WAS IN THE hands of the police before he was twelve, and in prison at nineteen; and he was in and out of gaol throughout the remaining eleven years of his life.

He was a forger, a blackmailer, a swindler, and a thief. He was also a homosexual, although when he appeared at his last trial he had just been cited as a co-respondent in an action for divorce. He admitted the adultery but denied any pleasure in it. He was proud of his inversion, and claimed that he had never been with a woman except as a means to get her money.

Clever and plausible, and something of a charmer, he had lived by his wits all his life. Yet as a criminal he had not been a success. At the time of his final arrest, when he was thirty, he possessed nothing in the world but a long record of convictions and a number of debts. He had even been hard put to it to find two shillings for the premium on an accident insurance he took out on his mother's life.

They made a pretty picture, the dear old lady with the shuffling gait — she suffered from paralysis agitans — and the devoted son. She was undoubtedly fond of him, although hardly a model parent. Her husband was probably not Sidney's father, and she was a confederate in most of her son's crimes. When he was not in prison they lived mainly in hotels, moving round the country and leaving a trail of unpaid bills and dud cheques. It was a hand-to-mouth existence, and they had no luggage at all when they arrived at the Hotel Metropole, Margate, on October 16, 1929. Six days later Fox went to London and arranged for two accident insurances that he had taken out on his mother's life to be extended until midnight the following day. At 11.40 p.m. that day Mrs Fox was dead.

Fox himself had raised the alarm about ten minutes earlier. He ran down the hotel stairs, wearing only a shirt and shouting that there was a fire. It was in his mother's bedroom. A commercial traveller ran up with him, and succeeded in dragging her out of the smoke-filled room. Artificial respiration was applied, and two doctors were called. By the time the first of them — Dr Austin — arrived Mrs Fox was already dead. Dr Austin examined her, and certified her death as due to shock and suffocation. His colleague, Dr Nichol, arrived soon after, and did not question Dr Austin's opinion.

An inquest was held the next day. The proceedings were brief, and the expected verdict of accidental death was returned. Five days later Mrs Fox was buried in her native village of Great Fransham, in Norfolk. So far as the police were concerned the case was closed.

Fox put in for the insurance. His claims were investigated. An official of one of the insurance companies wired his head office, "Extremely muddy water in this business." Scotland Yard was informed. The case was re-opened, and eleven days after the funeral the body of Mrs Fox was exhumed. A post-mortem examination was performed by Sir Bernard Spilsbury, who said she had been strangled. Fox was charged with murder, and eventually committed for trial. I was asked by his solicitor to give evidence in his defence. After examining the medical part of the case for the Crown, I agreed to appear in the role of expert witness.

I had, of course, given evidence in this role hundreds of times before, but always for the prosecution. I was always available to the Crown in cases occurring in and around Edinburgh, and was commonly asked by them to investigate cases in other parts of the country; but I could also give expert evidence for the defence in cases outside Edinburgh.

It is, I think, to the credit of the British legal system that expert witnesses are made available to the defence by the Crown, and paid by them in cases in which the defendant is without means. Apart from this, I believe that any expert witness should be prepared at any time to place his special knowledge at the disposal of the defence, whether it is in a position to pay him a fee or not. The Crown has all possible resources at its disposal; it can afford to call in as many experts as it wishes, it has access to all records, and has control of the whole machinery of the police, including the Criminal Investigation Department and the police laboratories. The defence usually has only limited resources, is often short or entirely devoid of funds, and must depend to a great extent on a critical appraisement of the evidence produced by the Crown.

The attitude of a scientific witness should be the same whether he is called in by the Crown or by the defence. It is not for him to concern himself with the previous character of the accused or with other evidence in the case. As a scientist he should be completely detached: he must not let himself be influenced in any way by emotional considerations such as sympathy or antipathy. His sole function is to examine the facts which come to his knowledge in his special capacity, to decide what is the true or the most probable interpretation of them, and to indicate to the court that interpretation, along with the grounds on which it is based.

I have often been asked why I have given evidence for the defence in cases in which the accused seemed to be guilty or in which he seemed to be a scoundrel who was not worth saving. In a particular instance the life of the accused may not be worth saving, but the principles of justice always are. Once concede the possibility of conviction on insufficient evidence because the accused is a worthless scamp, and you open the way to flouting the fundamental proposition of our law that every man is innocent until he is proved guilty.

Fox was a bad hat, and he would be in every way, as an eminent Scottish judge said of another rogue, "nane the waur o' a hangin'." It was clear from the start of the case that the circumstantial evidence, especially that relating to the fire and to the insurance policies, might be strong enough to earn him one. That was no concern of mine. My interest was limited to the medical evidence, which I found remarkable.

It depended almost entirely on Spilsbury's post-mortem report. The surprising thing about this came at the end — "Cause of death: asphyxia due to manual strangulation."

A person being strangled fights like mad. Even if the victim is a feeble old woman, Nature will supply her with unsuspected additional strength to help her in her fight for life. She will struggle furiously to wrench the strangler's hands away from her throat. She may fail, but some marks of the struggle will remain. Nearly always there will be scratches about the neck.

There were none here. According to Spilsbury's report, there was no trace of external injury at all — no sign of injury about the mouth or nose or in the skin of the neck, no marks left by the indentation of finger-nails or pressure of finger-tips.

Nor were there any of the usual signs of manual strangulation under the skin or in the tissues, such as bruises in the muscles surrounding the neck and in the larynx where the fingers would grip. Most remarkable of all, there was no fracture of either the thyroid cartilage or the hyoid bone. In elderly persons the hyoid becomes brittle and is easily broken, and this is one of the most characteristic marks of strangling. Yet Mrs Fox's hyoid was unbroken — until Spilsbury broke it himself unintentionally while taking it out. For all his care he could not avoid breaking it in two places. It was as brittle as that.

A strangler's victim is usually not a pretty sight. Bluish or purple lips and ears, change of colour of the nails, froth and possibly blood-staining about the nose or mouth, the tongue forced outward, the hands clenched — these are the typical signs of death from asphyxia.

There were none on Mrs Fox.

There were none of the usual internal signs of asphyxia, either. Instead Spilsbury found, on opening the body, natural disorders that pointed to a different conclusion. Her kidneys were cirrhosed, her arteries diseased, and her heart was in an advanced state of degeneration. The state of the heart alone, as described in Spilsbury's report, seemed to me to have been bad enough to cause death at any time.

Spilsbury himself emphatically rejected this possibility. "Cause of death: asphyxia due to manual strangulation." The oracle had spoken. There was nothing more to be said.

At the trial, under cross-examination, Spilsbury agreed that he had never known of a case of strangulation with fewer signs. He agreed cheerfully, for by then the point was immaterial to him. Spilsbury, like the rest of us, could make mistakes. He was unique, I think, in that he never admitted a mistake. Once he had committed himself to an opinion he would never change it.

"The injuries could, in my opinion, only have been produced by strangulation by the hand." That was Spilsbury's opinion at the beginning and the end, in spite of all that went between.

This opinion was based on four signs. These were hæmorrhage

in the epiglottis and three bruises — one on the tongue, one at the back of the larynx, and the third on the thyroid gland. On these he based his theory of strangulation, which he subsequently outlined to the court. Firm pressure, he said, between the thumb and fingers applied to the larynx could have produced the bruise on the thyroid and the hæmorrhage in the epiglottis; the bruise on the larynx might have been caused by forcibly pressing that organ upward; and this pressure could also have closed the victim's jaws and forced her to bite and thus bruise her tongue. With his use of tentative verbs like 'could' and 'might' the theory sounded so plausible that the unwary could forget it was only a theory, not hard fact.

Spilsbury gave evidence at the proceedings before the Margate magistrates, which began on January 9, 1930. As is usual in such cases, the defence was reserved and no witnesses were called, but Fox's solicitor, George Hindle, cross-examined the Crown witnesses very thoroughly. His purpose was to get them to commit themselves as far as possible — to make definite statements of which they might be reminded, if necessary, at the trial; and also to try to find out as much as possible about the prosecution's line without giving away any clue to the line of the defence.

Thus Hindle sent me an account of Dr Nichol's evidence with a request for any observations that might help him in cross-examination. In fact there was not much that could be asked, as Dr Nichol had neither examined Mrs Fox nor noticed anything special about her appearance. I advised Hindle to ask Nichol to confirm that he saw no signs of death from asphyxia, no marks of violence of any kind, no signs of froth or blood-staining at the mouth or nose; and that the appearances were quite consistent with death from heart-failure. Hindle followed my advice, and in cross-examining Dr Austin also he asked the same questions and received similar answers; but while Dr Nichol thought the appearances were not consistent with heart failure, Dr Austin thought they were.

Spilsbury gave his evidence in his usual clear and definite way, and he was too experienced in being cross-examined for Hindle to get much out of him.

"Is it not extraordinary that there were no marks of violence on the neck?" Hindle asked.

"It is not," Spilsbury replied. "It is unusual in a case of manual strangulation, but that is another matter."

The case was transferred from Kent to the Sussex Assizes, and the trial was fixed to begin at Lewes on Wednesday, March 12. On the preceding Saturday I went to Spilsbury's laboratory at the University College Hospital in London to look at the various specimens he had removed at the exhumation.

It was my first professional encounter with the Honorary Pathologist to the Home Office, a prelude to our first conflict in court. He could not have been more courteous or helpful. He showed me the whole of the exhibits.

Among the parts he had preserved was the larynx, which I was particularly interested to see. Spilsbury regarded the bruise on this as the main prop of his strangulation theory. I was inclined to think it was the only prop, and not a very good one at that, for I regarded the whole theory as flimsy. At the same time I was intrigued by this bruise. Spilsbury had said in his report that it was behind the larynx and about the size of a half-crown. I could not imagine how such a large bruise could have been inflicted there without damage to the tissues on the side of the larynx or the neck.

Spilsbury said nothing while I examined the larynx. He just stood beside me silently, while I looked — not at, but for, the bruise.

There was none to be seen.

Putrefactive discoloration, yes. No doubt about that. But not even a sixpenny bruise, let alone one the size of half a crown.

With me in the laboratory was Dr R. M. Brontë, formerly Crown Pathologist for All Ireland, who had also been asked to appear for the defence. He had crossed swords with Spilsbury in court before. He also examined the larynx, and finally shook his head.

"I can't see any sign of a bruise, Spilsbury," I said at length.

"Nor can I," said Brontë.

"No," agreed Spilsbury. "You can't see it now. But it was there when I exhumed the body."

That fairly staggered me. The larynx had been preserved in formalin ever since the exhumation.

"Where's the bruise gone, then?" I asked.

"It became obscure," said Spilsbury, "before I put the larynx in formalin. That is why I did not take a section."

A microscopical section would have been of inestimable value in showing whether the patch of discoloration Spilsbury had seen was a bruise or not. Personally I was pretty sure it was not. A bruise is caused by the breaking of small vessels which allows blood to be forced out of the vessels into the tissues, where it clots. To get a bruise the size of a half-crown quite a lot of blood would have to be extruded. The blood remains in the tissues, and cannot be removed by post-mortem changes.

"I don't see how a bruise of that size could have just disappeared," I said.

"It became obscure," he repeated. "It was there. I saw it myself."

"Spilsbury, I don't doubt that you saw something," I said. "But I put it to you that it might not have been a bruise. It could have been a patch of discoloration from post-mortem staining or putrefaction." Brontë nodded agreement. "We all know how difficult it is to diagnose a bruise with the naked eye after partial putrefaction has occurred."

Spilsbury listened attentively and was very polite, but he would not argue the point. I had the feeling that nothing I said would make any difference, that his mind was closed. Had I known him then as well as I came to later I would have realized why I was wasting my time. He could not change his opinion now because he had already given it. He had described the alleged bruise in his report and given evidence about it before the magistrates. His belief in himself was so strong that he could not conceive the possibility of error either in his observation or interpretation.

We looked at the other signs of alleged injury. The hæmorrhage in the epiglottis was there—a spot the size of the head of a pin, such as might be found on five out of six cases of death from natural causes. There was the bruise on the side of the tongue, which might well have been caused during strangulation — and, just as easily, by the old lady biting her tongue, as she could so easily have done with the badly fitting dentures she wore. Finally there was the alleged bruise on the thyroid gland, and this led to another difference of opinion. It consisted of a few stray red blood corpuscles such as might be found in a section of any ordinary thyroid.

"I cannot accept that as a bruise," I said emphatically.

"Nor can I," said Brontë.

Spilsbury said nothing, but we found an ally in Dr Henry Weir, a pathologist of standing whom the Crown had engaged to support

Spilsbury's evidence for the prosecution. He also said it was not a bruise.

The four of us discussed it in the laboratory, and I thought Spilsbury yielded to our view. He said little himself, but I went away with the definite impression that he accepted that on this relatively small point we were right and he was wrong.

Brontë knew him better than I did.

"Not Spilsbury," he said as we left. "You wait till we're in court."

The case for the Crown was that Fox had strangled his mother and then set fire to the room to cover up his crime. Spilsbury had looked for soot on the linings of the air passages, and had tested the blood for carbon monoxide, with negative results in each case. He was therefore satisfied that Mrs Fox had not died through suffocation by smoke. So was I. In my opinion she had not died of asphyxia at all. I thought she might very well have died of heart failure brought on by sudden exertion or fright. The shock of waking up and finding the room full of smoke, and the effort to get out of bed and escape, might well have put a fatal additional strain on her already weakened heart.

One would have thought that any pathologist would have agreed that this was a possibility, but though Weir agreed Spilsbury would not.

The prosecution of Fox was led by the Attorney-General, Sir William (later Lord) Jowitt, and he seemed determined to hang Fox. It is, of course, not the proper function of the Crown counsel to press the case against the accused. An eminent authority, Mr Justice Crompton, once said that the duty of prosecuting counsel was to acquit themselves as ministers of justice, aiding in the administration of the criminal law, and not as advocates attempting to secure a conviction.

Jowitt's attitude was anything but judicial. His treatment of the medical evidence in his opening speech was open to criticism, especially the part dealing with the half-crown bruise. "It will be said, how could the inside bruise be done without an outside bruise? This much is plain: the inside bruise is there. It is there — "

It was not there. Spilsbury himself was to testify that it had vanished from sight four months before.

The first five days of the trial were taken up mainly with non-medical evidence, which was heavy against Fox. Of course, nothing was said about his criminal record, and when Chief-Inspector Hambrook of Scotland Yard gave evidence on his conduct of the case the jury had no inkling that he had arrested Fox for forgery thirteen years before. The evidence that could properly be brought, however, made it pretty clear how he normally obtained his living. There was adequate evidence of motive in the insurances he had taken out on his mother's life. His conduct on the night of her death was at least suspicious.

Dr Austin was the first medical witness. He repeated the evidence he had given at the proceedings before magistrates. Cross-examining for the defence, Mr J. D. Cassels asked him if he saw any signs of death by asphyxia.

"No, except that the face was very flushed, which you find in a case of asphyxia."

"Did you see any marks of violence?"

"No."

"Or appearances consistent with death by heart-failure?"

"Well, I should hardly think so."

Cassels's next question brought out the value of Hindle's careful cross-examination at the preliminary hearing.

"Did you say, in examination at the police court, 'I saw no signs of death from asphyxiation and no marks of violence. As far as I was able to see, the appearances were consistent with heart-failure'?"

"If I am reported to have done so I must have done," Dr Austin replied. "It is five months ago."

Dr Nichol also was cross-examined to good effect. He said that after death Mrs Fox's face was composed, pale, and presented no special significance, that he saw no marks of violence, and that "the woman did not give me the impression of having died from asphyxia."

But all this was of little consequence compared with Spilsbury's evidence, which was given clearly and with great sincerity — and complete conviction.

To explain his theory of how Mrs Fox died, Spilsbury produced a porcelain model of the human mouth and neck.

"At the back of the larynx," he said, pointing to the spot, "I found a large, recent bruise about the size of half a crown. It was then that I had the first indication of the conclusions to which I finally came, that death was due to strangulation."

Spilsbury repeated his previous evidence about the bruise on the tongue and the very small hæmorrhages on the epiglottis. Then he came to the alleged bruise on the thyroid gland.

"I found a small dark area just on the surface which I thought might be a bruise," he said. "I made microscopical preparations of it which in my view confirmed the presence of a little bruising. I showed the preparations to Dr Weir, Professor Smith, and Dr Brontë, who, however, did not take the same view, and for that reason I prefer that the bruise shall not be considered as a possible injury caused at that time."

"Apart from the thyroid gland," he was then asked, "are we, in your view, outside the region of doubt?"

"Yes."

This answer implied that Spilsbury accepted that there was doubt about the bruise he claimed to have seen on the thyroid gland. With Weir against him as well as us he could hardly do otherwise. But when he was cross-examined he made it clear that he still thought that he was right and the rest of us wrong.

"Is your opinion upon this part of the case as definite as it is on the other parts of the case?" Cassels asked.

"Yes."

The judge asked, "Your opinion is still that the thyroid gland was bruised?"

"That is so."

Since he was still so sure of this, it was not surprising that he refused to admit even the possibility of doubt in the matter of the alleged bruise on the larynx, which only he had seen or would ever see.

Cassels suggested it might have been a mark of putrefaction.

"It was a bruise and nothing else," Spilsbury answered shortly. "There are no two opinions about it."

Certainly only he had seen it. This sort of thing is a common handicap to medical expert witnesses appearing for the defence. The Crown's experts are there from the start, and often there is nothing left to see when the experts for the defence come in. Spilsbury was scrupulously careful and painstaking in his work, but once he had given an opinion nothing would make him change it. The supposed bruise on the thyroid gland was a case in point. No doubt if he alone had seen it he would have put that also outside the region of doubt.

He was an excellent witness, especially for the Crown. I listened attentively while he gave evidence, making notes and passing them to Cassels whenever a fresh line of questioning occurred to me. But there was very little to be got out of Spilsbury, and as usual he made a good impression on the jury. Even the admission that this was the first exhumation he had done in a case of what he thought was manual strangulation did not detract from the effect of his undoubted reputation and complete assurance.

Spilsbury was followed by Dr Weir, who was pathologist to the National Hospital for Diseases of the Heart. He had not seen any more of the remains than I had, but he accepted Spilsbury's statement about the half-crown bruise. However, he did not share Spilsbury's view that death was caused by asphyxia, but agreed with us that it was due to heart-failure, and he was an expert on diseases of the heart. He attributed it to commencing strangulation — but "in my opinion, except for the bruises, there was sufficient disease in the heart to account for death from natural causes."

So the conflict of medical evidence was not only between the prosecution and the defence.

Weir was the last witness called by the Crown. Fox himself was the first witness for the defence, and probably he did himself much more harm than good. He made what was considered his worst mistake when Jowitt questioned him about his actions after discovering the fire in his mother's room.

"Can you explain to me why it was that you closed the door instead of flinging it wide open?" Jowitt asked.

"My explanation for that now is that the smoke should not spread into the hotel."

"Rather that your mother should suffocate in that room than that smoke should get about in the hotel?"

"Most certainly not, sir" — and then, realizing the implication of his answer, Fox half-denied that he had closed the door. But by then the damage was done.

I was called later the same day.

In the course of the years I had learnt a number of lessons about giving evidence in court. One was to confine one's answers to the questions asked; another was not to try to score off counsel. I had also found that it pays to be reticent, and to keep back a few odds and ends to release under cross-examination; this makes the opposing advocate more careful in his approach.

Until this case I had always been treated with consideration and courtesy, and my evidence had not been seriously challenged. Over many years and in many different courts I had always tried to give my evidence on the facts as I saw them without any regard as to whether my opinions were helpful to the prosecution or the defence. This was my first experience of the clashes between counsel and expert witness that are a feature of British criminal courts.

In my examination-in-chief I gave my opinion that there was not sufficient medical evidence to support a charge of strangulation.

Jowitt began his cross-examination the next morning.

"You stated in your evidence-in-chief that you had a very long experience in cases involving manual strangulation?"

"Yes."

"Were they cases of strangulation by a young man of an old woman as the old woman lay in bed?"

"I have had many cases of strangulation of elderly men and elderly women."

"Will you try to answer my question?"

"I will think of the special conditions for one moment. Yes, I have had."

"Do you mean to tell us you had not considered that question before you came to give evidence in this case?"

"I have considered the question."

"Then I take it you have brought your notes of a person being strangled in bed."

"No, I have not."

"Was there one case, or more than one case?"

"I have had many cases of a somewhat similar nature. May I explain?"

"Please answer my question. It may be difficult for a gentleman who gives lectures to answer questions, but I want you to answer mine."

So it began, and so it went on: sharp, harsh, and somewhat blustering. Jowitt had been well briefed. After a series of questions about the signs of asphyxia he read out a passage from Taylor's *Medical Jurisprudence* and asked me if I agreed. As my name was on the title-page of the book as the current editor I could not have easily disowned it. In fact, however, it was not in conflict with the opinions I had expressed in evidence, as I was able to explain.

Jowitt continued to press his questions in a rather hectoring way.

"Do you think that is being quite candid with me?" he asked once. Then, "If the answer is 'No' say 'No.' You are not trying to make it difficult for me, are you? I want you to try to help."

"I am, to the best of my ability," I replied, "but you won't give me an opportunity of putting you right. If I begin to explain you say, 'Please answer my question.' It makes it very difficult."

Jowitt went on to the matter of the half-crown bruise.

"You said yesterday that in training assistants you had to be careful in distinguishing in post-mortem examination between bruises and discoloration marks. Do you put Sir Bernard Spilsbury on a par with one of your assistants?"

This was a catch-question. Jowitt was trying to make me belittle Spilsbury.

"Do you suggest Sir Bernard would not know the difference between the two?" he persisted.

"Nobody can tell merely by looking," I replied. "I do not think anyone should say a bruise is a bruise until it has been proved that it is."

"Do you say that you would not say a bruise was a bruise until you put it under a microscope?"

"No, I should cut into it."

"If you saw a fellow with a black eye would you say, 'Let me put it under a microscope before I say it is a black eye'?"

This question surprised me. It was not the sort of thing I would have expected from the Attorney-General.

"Sir Bernard says there can be no two opinions about it," he went on.

"It is very obvious there can be," I pointed out.

"You are bound to accept the evidence of the man who saw the bruise?"

"I do not think so."

"How can you say there was not a bruise there?"

"Because if there was a bruise there it should be there now. It should be there for ever. The larynx is there to be examined by anybody."

With that Jowitt left the half-crown bruise, and the rest of his cross-examination was in a slightly milder tone.

He began pressing again when he cross-examined Brontë, who confirmed my evidence and went on to give the opinion that putrefactive changes "would magnify the bruise and make it easier to detect." He quoted a case in which Spilsbury himself had said the same thing.

Jowitt asked more pointed questions about Spilsbury and the half-crown bruise.

"Are you suggesting Sir Bernard did not see what he said he saw?"

"Far be it from me to make such a suggestion."

"Did you suggest that Sir Bernard Spilsbury was wrong, and that it was a post-mortem change? If Sir Bernard made this mistake it would be a very elementary mistake to make? It is a sort of mistake that every laboratory assistant is warned against?"

Cassels put the matter back into perspective in his closing speech. He recalled the two bruises on which Spilsbury based his theory of strangulation.

"There was, of course, another at one time," he reminded the jury. "Another pinpoint mark, which under a microscope was said to be a sign of bruising upon the thyroid gland — that mark which Sir Bernard Spilsbury still retains his opinion about, but does not desire to have as much importance attached to it as to the other two, because Dr Weir, Professor Smith, and Dr Brontë did not agree with him. If Sir Bernard Spilsbury is wrong about one thing might he not be wrong about something else? No one can say that an individual, whatever his position and skill, is never likely to be mistaken. No one can claim for anybody infallibility."

Mr Justice Rowlatt summed up with perfect fairness.

"There were no external indications of asphyxia. There were no external marks on the throat. Sir Bernard Spilsbury has said it was quite possible there would be none, but you and I might think it difficult to believe it. As regards the brittle bone in the throat known as the hyoid, it is a very curious coincidence that that bone was not broken in this case. That is a very strong point in favour of the accused. As to the mark at the back of the larynx, alleged by the prosecution to be a bruise, there is no doubt that Sir Bernard Spilsbury saw some object there. It is unfortunate that those tissues could not have been preserved for others to see. The defence have said — and are justified in saying it — that that point rests on the testimony of what one skilled man observed, and observed at one moment only . . ."

Perhaps the judge did not quite appreciate the dangerously

high esteem in which that one skilled man was held. Perhaps Spilsbury did not fully realize that fame brings responsibility as well as honour. I do not think the jury would have returned the verdict they did if his evidence had been given by anyone else but Spilsbury.

One hour and ten minutes was all they needed to find Fox guilty.

"My lord," he whispered, "I did not murder my mother. I am innocent."

I believe he was.

I certainly would not have put it past him to murder his mother. He was bad enough for any crime, and the evidence about the renewal of the insurances was heavy against him.

There were many suspicious circumstances in the case, but Fox was specifically charged with and was hanged for strangling his mother. I thought then — and I still think now — that he was innocent of that.

I I

The Case of Annie Hearn

ARSENIC WAS THE POISON MOST COMMONLY USED FOR MURDER when I was in Egypt, as it has been in every country, from remote periods. It is almost an ideal poison, since it has no colour, no smell, and no taste. It can be used in powder form or in solution, and can be given in any form of food or drink without making any alteration that could be detected by the victim. As a rule, there is a time-lag of about half an hour or even more between the taking of the poison and the onset of symptoms, and this tends to divert attention from the true cause. The main symptoms — vomiting and diarrhœa — are such as might just as well be produced by an infection or any other irritant in the digestive system.

Arsenic has, however, one characteristic that prevents it from being the perfect poison; it is the most easily detected of them all. It becomes stored in chemical combination in the hair and nails and also in the bones, and remains there for months in the living person. If death should occur as a result of taking arsenic the analyst can isolate the poison from these tissues after burial for practically any length of time.

This should be a grave deterrent to the use of arsenic. It seems, however, that poisoning as a fine art has almost disappeared. In spite of the many better poisons that modern research has brought to light, arsenic continues to be used in most murders by poisoning; or rather it is the poison most frequently discovered. There is, of course, the possibility that other poisons are used so successfully that the murders are never found out.

Arsenic was not always easy to detect. Until less than a century and a half ago, indeed, it was often practically impossible to prove that it had been used. With the improvement in chemical knowledge and methods of analysis, and particularly with the discovery of the Marsh Test in 1836, it became possible to prove the presence of arsenic in infinitesimal quantities. This test was used in a criminal trial for the first time in 1840, in the celebrated case of Marie Lafarge; and perhaps justice would have been better served on that occasion without it.

Orfila, the leading expert on poisons in France at the time, found a trace of arsenic by the new test after former analyses had failed, and he testified that arsenic was the cause of death. This evidence was decisive, and Marie was convicted and sentenced to imprisonment for life. It has been said that Raspail, another French chemist of repute, traced the zinc that Orfila had used in his test and found it was contaminated with arsenic, but for some reason was prevented from testifying to this effect at the trial. Knowing as we do now the danger of contamination of test agents with arsenic, we are entitled to wonder whether the unfortunate and tragic Marie would have been convicted at the present time on the slender evidence produced.

I wonder also how many other persons may have been convicted in those early days for murders they did not commit on evidence derived from the Marsh test.

Which brings me to the case of Annie Hearn.

Annie Hearn disappeared six days after Alice Thomas died. She wrote a letter before she went. It ran:

Dear Mr Thomas,
Goodbye. I'm going out if I can. I cannot forget that awful man and the things he said. I am *innocent, innocent*, but she is dead and it was my lunch she eat. I cannot bear it. When I'm dead they will be sure I am guilty and you at least will be cleared. May your own dear wife's presence guard and comfort you still.
Yours,
A. H.
My life is not a great thing anyhow, now dear Minnie's gone. I should be glad if you would send my love to Bessie and tell her not to worry about me. I'll be all right, my conscience is clear so I'm not afraid of afterwards.

William Thomas, the dead woman's husband, took the letter to the police. They traced Annie Hearn as far as the cliffs at Looe, on the Cornish coast. There they found the check coat she had been wearing; that was all.

A fortnight later — on November 24, 1930 — the inquest on Alice Thomas was held. She had died of arsenical poisoning. The verdict was homicide by some person or persons unknown.

Annie Hearn was still missing.

Her married sister, Bessie, lived in Doncaster, and could not throw any light on the affair. Her other sister, her dear Minnie, had died four months before. She had died of chronic gastric catarrh with colitis, Dr Gibson certified, and she was buried in Lewannick churchyard on July 24.

On December 9 her body was exhumed. Dr Eric Wordley, a pathologist, performed a post-mortem examination in the churchyard. He removed certain organs, and sent them to Dr Roche Lynch, the Home Office analyst.

Lynch found arsenic in all the organs. Most of it was in the muscles, nails, and hair.

He took the longest lock of hair he could find, and found arsenic in it from root to tip. It was four and a half inches long. Reckoning the growth of hair at half an inch per month, he deduced that arsenic must have been absorbed for at least seven months before death.

He cut the lock into three equal portions, and calculated the approximate amount of arsenic in each. His estimate, in parts per million, was 10 in the portion farthest from the scalp, 15 in the middle portion, and 23 in the portion nearest the scalp. From the last figure he inferred that the dose had been increased in frequency or in amount, or in both, in the two or three months immediately before death.

His conclusion was that Minnie had not died of chronic gastric catarrh, but of arsenical poisoning administered over a period of several months.

The police stepped up the search for Annie Hearn. They found her at last, working as a housekeeper under an assumed name, in Torquay. She was arrested on January 18, 1931, and charged with murdering both Alice Thomas and her sister Minnie.

At her trial she gave her age as just over forty, although she was not certain to a year. She said she looked upon herself as a widow, as she had not heard of her husband since they parted a few days after their wedding in 1919. For the next eleven years she lived with her unmarried elder sister, Lydia Everard — called

Minnie — a chronic sufferer from gastric trouble. In 1921 the two sisters moved from the Midlands to Cornwall for the sake of Minnie's health. In the autumn of 1925 they went to live at Trenhorne House, Lewannick. The house was about two hundred yards from Trenhorne Farm. The farmer and his wife, William and Alice Thomas, were both in their forties and had been married for nearly twenty years. They became quite friendly with the two sisters, and sometimes they all went out for drives in William Thomas's car. When Minnie was ill, as she often was, Mrs Thomas used to send her junkets and other home-made delicacies.

So matters went on for nearly five years.

In February 1930 the other sister, Bessie, came to Lewannick from her home in Doncaster and stayed at Trenhorne House for a month. Minnie had two or three bad attacks while she was there. She was attended by two doctors who were in partnership, Dr Gibson and Dr Galbraith. Both had first treated her in 1922, and she already had a long history of gastric trouble then. Now she was getting worse; and on July 21, 1930, she died.

Mrs Hearn, who had nursed her sister throughout her last illness, stayed at Trenhorne House and continued to see the Thomases as before. On October 18 they invited her to drive with them to Bude for the afternoon. As her contribution to the outing she made some sandwiches, filling them with tinned salmon as she had often done before on similar occasions.

They set off about 3 p.m., and arrived at Bude an hour later. At five they went to a café and ordered tea and cakes. While the waitress was in the kitchen getting their order Mrs Hearn opened the packet of sandwiches and put them on the table. The waitress saw them there when she returned with the tea-tray. She said the three stayed in the café for about half an hour, and did not leave any of the sandwiches behind.

At about a quarter to seven they began their return journey. After a short while Mrs Thomas felt ill, and vomited several times in the car. Neither her husband nor Mrs Hearn was sick, although both said later that they had felt a bit queer. When they got back to Trenhorne Farm Mrs Hearn helped Thomas to put his wife to bed. She was now suffering from diarrhœa as well as vomiting, and had abdominal pain and cramp in her legs. Her husband therefore fetched Dr Graham Saunders from Launceston, and he arrived at about half-past nine.

He had not attended her before — Mrs Thomas had not been

ill for many years — and he did not consider that she was seriously ill. Her husband told him about the tinned-salmon sandwiches, her symptoms were consistent with food-poisoning, and he prescribed accordingly. Mrs Hearn agreed to stay at the farm to do the cooking and act as nurse.

The next day Dr Saunders called again, and found Mrs Thomas a little better after more vomiting and diarrhœa. She continued to improve, and after a few days the cramp disappeared. She seemed much better on October 29, when the news of her illness reached her mother, Mrs Parsons, who lived about five miles away. Thomas said afterwards that he had not told her before as he did not want to worry her, and in fact she learned of her daughter's illness from another source. She then moved to the farm and took over the nursing and invalid cookery from Mrs Hearn, who had been looking after Mrs Thomas continuously since she was taken ill. Mrs Hearn stayed at the farm after Mrs Parson's arrival, running the house and doing the general cooking.

Alice Thomas continued to make progress. Dr Saunders put her on a fuller diet, and on Sunday, November 2, he omitted his usual daily call. But the next day when he called he found her critically ill. She was delirious and unable to move her legs, and her reflexes had gone. The doctor began to suspect arsenical poisoning, and advised that a consultant should be called in. As a result Dr Lister from Plymouth arrived in the evening. He diagnosed arsenical poisoning and recommended that the patient should be transferred to Plymouth City Hospital. She was taken there about midnight, but died shortly after admission, on the morning of November 4. The death was reported to the coroner, who ordered a post-mortem examination. This was performed by Dr Eric Wordley, who sent certain organs to the city analyst. These were found to contain a total of 0·85 grains of white arsenic.

Naturally, the results of these post-mortem investigations were not made public, but William Thomas was told something of what was going on. He mentioned it to Mrs Hearn, saying that there would be police inquiries and an inquest. Meanwhile there was much local gossip, and on the day of the funeral — November 8 — matters came to a head. A brother of the dead woman, Percy Parsons, questioned Mrs Hearn about the tinned-salmon sandwiches and then said, "This looks serious and will have to be seen into." He had not met Mrs Hearn before, but he said in court later that he had heard a rumour that she and his brother-in-law had been too friendly.

Two days later Mrs Hearn disappeared.

I came into the Annie Hearn case when her solicitor, Walter West of Grimsby, asked me to look at the medical evidence. He sent me all the documents, and after reading them I was convinced that the case against her was not good enough from a medical point of view.

Alice Thomas had died from arsenic poisoning — there was no doubt about that, and I told West so. How and when the poison was administered was quite a different matter. It seemed to me highly improbable that there was any in the sandwiches she had eaten in the café on October 18.

All the doctors in the case agreed that food-poisoning could have accounted for her symptoms after that meal, and it was for food-poisoning that Dr Saunders had treated her for the next sixteen days. There was no evidence that she had taken arsenic on that day at all. Nor did anyone suggest that a single dose in the sandwiches had killed her. On the contrary, the analyst's findings made it clear that she had taken arsenic much nearer the date of her death. We were asked to believe that Annie Hearn had poisoned her friend first with the sandwiches and then again during her illness.

The case of Minnie, or Lydia Everard, was even less conclusive. The doctors' reports showed her symptoms during her long illness were mainly gastric upsets, bowel trouble, and chronic constipation; yet arsenical poisoning usually causes diarrhœa. There had been some suggestion of peripheral neuritis, but most of the other classic signs of chronic arsenical poisoning were lacking. The doctor attending her had certified that her death was due to natural causes.

I thought — and I still think — that he was right.

I did not doubt that Roche Lynch had found arsenic in Miss Everard's muscles, nails, and hair.

I did not doubt that its presence would have pointed to poisoning — if she had been buried in almost any other county of England.

Cornwall is famous for its tin, and where there is tin in the ground there is usually arsenic too. In Cornish soil the arsenic content is exceptionally high. In Lewannick — in that particular churchyard — the soil was fairly impregnated with it.

On the coroner's instructions samples of earth had been taken from above and below the coffin, and sent to Lynch for analysis. He found that the soil from above the coffin contained 125 parts per million — and the soil below, 62 parts. A finding of signal importance. So too was the fact that Wordley had performed the post-mortem in the open churchyard. I wondered what, if any, precautions he had taken against contamination by dust from the arsenic-laden soil.

It would not have needed a large speck of dust, although Lynch's report had put the total amount of arsenic found in the body as 0·776 of a grain. This estimate was, of course, based on calculation as well as analysis. He had followed the normal practice of analysing small parts of the organs and then multiplying by the appropriate factor.

Here I found reason to disagree with Lynch.

Most of the arsenic — 0·64 of a grain — was said to be in the muscles. Lynch had reached this figure by analysing a sample of muscle weighing one-eighth of an ounce — in which he found 1/6400 of a grain of arsenic — and then multiplying on the assumption that the muscles accounted for 40 per cent. of the total weight of the body. The body weight had been estimated at eighty pounds, and Lynch had therefore assumed the total weight of the muscles was about thirty-two pounds.

I thought the assumption was quite unwarrantable. An adult weighing only eighty pounds is obviously in a very emaciated condition, and in a badly nourished body the muscles are the first to lose weight. I thought the proportion in this case could not have been more than 15 per cent. at the most, and probably it was less. It seemed to me that Lynch had made a very serious error.

Merely by examining the documents on which the case against Annie Hearn was based, I formed the opinion that she was probably innocent.

Her trial was fixed to begin on Monday, June 15, and was expected to last a week. When I sent West my report on the documents I told him I would not be able to attend. I was fully engaged with my University work, and I could not afford to be away from my classes at that time. However, on June 11 I received this telegram:

BIRKETT THINKS IT VITAL YOU SHOULD BE AT BODMIN ON
SUNDAY FOR CONSULTATION ABOUT SIX EVENING. I THINK

SO TOO AND MOST EARNESTLY BESEECH YOU TO COME.
WIRE REPLY AT ONCE. WEST.

My impulse was to refuse, on the grounds that my first duty
was to my students. Then I thought it would be the negation of
all my teaching if it meant that an innocent woman might be
convicted and hanged. So I went.

It was my first meeting with Lord Birkett — Mr Norman
Birkett he was then — whom West had briefed for the defence.
I had never known anyone quite like him. He grasped the technicalities of the evidence with extraordinary speed, and saw the
implications of my points at once.

"Will you be here to give evidence if it is needed?" he asked,
at the end of our Sunday-evening conference.

Having come so far, I said I was willing to see it through.

"I don't know if I shall call you," said Birkett. "I hope it won't
be necessary, but I would like to have you beside me in the court."
If he called the accused and no other witness he would gain the
right to address the jury last before the judge's summing up.
To do this he would need to get all the evidence he needed from
his cross-examination of the Crown medical witnesses.

This he did.

In a sense the Crown played into our hands. The Crown
counsel made it clear from the start that he attached great importance to the theory that Lydia Everard had died of arsenical
poisoning as well as Mrs Thomas, as this seemed to strengthen
the case against Mrs Hearn. "If," he said to the jury in his
opening address, "you are satisfied that there was arsenic in the
sandwiches and that it might have been put there by somebody
other than Mrs Hearn, you are entitled to consider the circumstances of the death of Miss Everard. Mrs Hearn was the person
in contact with both of these. In each case arsenic was the cause
of death, and you will have to consider whether this does not
take the case far beyond the region of suspicion."

It seemed to me more likely to have the opposite effect. The
medical evidence was definitely weaker in the case of Miss
Everard; if this charge could be destroyed the charge in respect
of Mrs Thomas would be badly shaken. Birkett agreed, and

proceeded with the demolition. While he was cross-examining I passed notes to him from time to time, drawing his attention to particular points arising from the witness's replies, and he made full use of these notes.

He quickly disposed of the clinical evidence in Miss Everard's case. He drew from each of the Crown witnesses an admission that the symptoms might have been due to natural causes, and that was that. This charge now depended solely on the laboratory evidence, and this in turn he seriously damaged.

Dr Wordley had to admit that no special precautions against contamination had been taken at the post-mortem. The grave-digger who opened the coffin agreed that soil might have got inside. When the organs for analysis were removed they were left in uncovered glass jars in the churchyard for an hour or more, exposed to contamination by dust raised from the arsenic-impregnated ground. Birkett had got all this on the record before Roche Lynch was called.

The chief witness for the Crown in the case of Minnie Everard was a quiet, unassuming man of considerable eminence. Although never as famous as Spilsbury — with whom he often appeared for the Crown — Lynch was firmly established as the leading analyst in the public mind. He was neither as brilliant nor as stubborn as Spilsbury, but he shared his dislike of admitting an error. This seems to be a weakness of experts, whether medical or scientific.

A sound chemist and a good witness, Lynch was accustomed to having his evidence treated by juries with great respect. He had little clinical experience, but that did not stop him from beginning with a detailed account of the symptoms and signs likely to be found in a person suffering from arsenic poisoning at different stages. I scribbled an obvious note for Birkett. I wrote another soon after, when Lynch testified to the quantity of arsenic he had found in Miss Everard's remains.

"What was the total amount of arsenic in the organs?" the Crown counsel asked him.

"0·776 of a grain."

I do not think that Lynch was trying deliberately to mislead the jury into thinking he had actually found three-quarters of a grain of arsenic, but that is probably the impression that any body of laymen would have received.

All these replies of Lynch were duly noted by Birkett, and

there was an expectant hush as he rose. The court seemed to have sensed that this was to be the decisive phase of the trial.

Birkett's first question was deadly.

"Have you ever," he asked, "attended a patient suffering from arsenical poisoning?"

Lynch had to admit that he had not. Gently pressed by Birkett, he conceded that all the information in his learned exposition on this subject had been derived from reading.

In fact, of course, this did not make it any the less valid; but Lynch's admission made an unfavourable impression on the jury, who were mostly practical men. Lynch could have felt aggrieved, but he had left himself open to this criticism.

Birkett then asked him about the arsenical content of the churchyard soil. Lynch admitted he had never had experience of a body exhumed from soil impregnated with so much arsenic. At the same time, he remained quite definite that this could not account for the presence of all the arsenic he had found in Miss Everard's body.

Birkett led him on, and then asked him about the figure he had given for the amount of arsenic in the remains.

"Was this quantity not arrived at by a process of multiplication?" he asked.

"Yes."

"Can you give the amount that you actually found in the muscle?"

"It was 1/6400 of a grain."

If Lynch had been trying to mislead the jury it had certainly rebounded now, and there was more to come. Birkett was questioning the correctness of the multiplication factor Lynch had used.

"Should not the weight of the muscle have been 12 or 15 per cent. of the weight of the body, instead of 40 per cent.?"

"I am afraid not," Lynch answered. If the muscle wasted, he went on, so would the other parts of the body in proportion; so that the 40 per cent. would still apply.

"But is it not a fact," Birkett persisted, "that after seven months of weakness and illness there is a natural waste?"

"Some muscles waste."

Again he looked as if he had lost his point.

The factor Lynch had used in multiplication was over 4000. Birkett suggested that the slightest error would have been multiplied 4000 times. Lynch had to agree. It followed that one speck of arsenical dust on the material that had been left exposed in the churchyard for over an hour could have accounted for all the arsenic the analyst had found.

Birkett then questioned Lynch about another possible form of contamination — the percolation of water through the soil into the coffin. Lynch denied that this was possible at all, saying that the arsenic in the soil was mostly in insoluble form. He had tested this experimentally by percolating water five times through a tube a foot long filled with soil from the churchyard which, he said, would represent percolation through five feet of soil. He performed this experiment first with soil from above and then with soil from below the coffin, and estimated the arsenic content of the liquid in each case.

The figures were 0·11 and 0·08 parts per million respectively. Lynch assumed that all the soluble arsenic was removed in his percolation experiments, and therefore practically the whole of the arsenic in the soil was in an insoluble state. Birkett suggested that arsenic was constantly being rendered soluble, and asked, "Is it not the case that every time there has been a shower of rain over thousands of years your experiment has been repeated, and you still find arsenic in your percolating fluid?" This, of course, was a telling point, and naturally threw some doubt on the deductions drawn from the analytical results.

Another weakness in the Crown case was that the coffin itself was not examined for arsenic. Lynch admitted that if he had known he was going to find arsenic in the soil he would have asked for a bit of timber of the coffin.

"It was a matter of surprise to you to find arsenic in the soil after all?" asked Birkett.

"Yes, it was."

"And when you found it in these quantities your surprise was the greater?"

"It is there."

"If the hair had been in contact with arsenic either inside or outside the coffin it might have absorbed it?"

"If in contact with soluble arsenic."

"On the possibility of contamination of the hair and organs by diffusion, it is a possibility that cannot be excluded from this case, is it not?"

"It is a possibility, but I also put it as being extremely unlikely."

Lynch maintained that the amount of arsenic found in the hair and nails was too great to have been absorbed from such a weak fluid, and at that time I was not able to provide the defence with a complete answer to this. I knew that in absorption from external contamination the hair and nails take up arsenic preferentially and hold it in chemical combination. What I was not sure of was whether the amount thus absorbed might attain a much higher concentration in the hair and nails than was found in the arsenical fluid in which they were immersed. This gap in my knowledge I remedied later, and the knowledge was to prove useful in another case.

In spite of this defect in my assistance Birkett shook the analytical evidence so badly that, as I had hoped, Miss Everard's case did not strengthen the Crown case but greatly weakened it.

The case of Mrs Thomas was, on the face of it, medically much stronger, because there was not the slightest doubt that she had died of arsenical poisoning. However, the prosecution based its case on the charge that the arsenic had been administered in the sandwiches, and there seemed to be room for much doubt about that.

They said the arsenic had been given in the form of a weed-killer that Mrs Hearn had bought four years before. Roche Lynch had estimated that ten grains of arsenic were taken in the fatal sandwich, and he thought that for this about 14·3 grains of the weed-killer would have had to be used. It was implied that Mrs Hearn had added the weed-killer to the tinned salmon when she prepared the sandwiches, some hours before they were eaten. This seemed to me unlikely, because all weed-killers containing arsenic are coloured with a purple dye. Surely, I thought, if this amount of weed-killer was put inside a moist sandwich the bread would soon be badly stained?

This, at least, was something that could be taken out of the region of doubt. After the first day of the trial, when the prosecution made its line on the sandwiches clear, I put it to the test. I mixed 14·3 grains of the same weed-killer with tinned salmon of the same brand as Mrs Hearn had used, and prepared some sandwiches.

Within half an hour they were stained a bluish-purple.

It was ridiculous to imagine that anyone would have touched them with a barge-pole, let alone eaten them.

Naturally, we took care not to let the prosecution know of our experiments, and Norman Birkett's cross-examination of Roche

Lynch on this point was much more deadly than the court knew.

"You say that in your opinion the weed-killer was used in solid form?" he asked.

"That is what I suggested."

"Have you taken sandwiches and put 14·3 grains of weed-killer on them?"

"No."

"You have shown that when put in Benger's food the weed-killer discolours the white fluid?"

"It changes the colour."

"That is with two grains."

"Yes."

"Seven times as much would discolour it very much more?"

"Yes."

"If you put fourteen grains on a moist sandwich and carried it for hours," Birkett asked, in his most guileless tone, "is it not inevitable that the sandwich would be discoloured and blue?"

"I have not tried it," said Roche Lynch, "but my opinion, for what it is worth, is that it would not."

The celebrated analyst little knew how easily Birkett could have proved his opinion worthless. His rather pompous statement escaped deflation only because Birkett wanted to avoid having to call me as a witness if he could. The non-medical evidence concerning the sandwiches seemed likely to help him further in this aim, for there was nothing in it to show that any attempt had been made to juggle with the sandwiches after they had been unpacked in the café in order that Mrs Thomas should get a particular one.

Birkett was quick to expose the weakness in the Crown evidence about the alleged second dose.

The analyst's findings had proved that Mrs Thomas had received arsenic some days after she had eaten the sandwiches in the café, but it was impossible to know exactly when. The prosecution, however, made the surprising statement that it could not have been less than five days before death.

"The expert analyst will tell you that although in all probability another dose was given after the 18th of October, none was given after the 29th," said counsel for the Crown in his opening address. Then he explained the significance of the second date. "It was on that day that Mrs Parsons took charge and did all the nursing and most of the cooking."

This was, to say the least, disingenuous. The implication was obvious and most sinister, and it was based on an untruth. The expert analyst never had said that no arsenic was given after the 29th, and the Crown counsel had no reason to think that he ever would. When the Crown counsel examined the expert analyst on the point he said, as he had said before, that he thought the second dose of arsenic had been taken "not within three or four days before death." Mrs Thomas had died on November 4. In cross-examination Birkett picked the point up.

"Do you say that in your view there was arsenic taken into the body of Mrs Thomas on or about October 30?" he asked.

"I cannot fix the date, but somewhere about that time."

This was a very different story from the Crown counsel's definite and damning "no arsenic after the 29th." The other Crown witness on this point, Dr Wordley, was no more helpful, but suggested that the dose was administered "three to five days before death."

My own opinion, based on the same analytical findings, was that it could have been given less than forty-eight hours before death. Every one is entitled to his own opinion, of course, but I did not think the Crown had the right to distort the evidence of its own witness.

Norman Birkett's cross-examination of the expert witnesses lasted several hours, and as we walked away from the court he said to me, "That has been a very exhausting business for me. It has taken months off my life."

"Possibly," I said, "but it has added a good many years to your client's."

The Crown case closed. Annie Hearn was called for the defence. She gave evidence in a clear, firm voice, and never once faltered under cross-examination.

Now Birkett had to decide whether to call me or not. If he did he could reveal the test we had made with weed-killer and the sandwiches. He could ask me to give the court my opinion of when Mrs Thomas received the last lethal dose of arsenic. He could show that, because arsenical poisoning was rare in England but commonplace in Egypt, my experience in this matter was vastly greater than that of Lynch and all the other Crown medical witnesses together. But he would lose the right to address the jury after the Crown counsel's final speech.

He decided not to call me. I think his decision was correct. He had obtained nearly all the information the defence needed from cross-examination of the Crown witnesses, and having the last word before the summing-up was a considerable advantage. Especially in the hands of Birkett.

The Crown counsel, in going over the medical evidence, reminded the jury of the eminence of Roche Lynch.

Birkett countered that with a reference to his opening questions to Lynch and the replies.

"Dr Roche Lynch has never attended one person suffering from arsenical poisoning, yet he spoke of symptoms with the same confidence as he spoke of other matters. Let the cobbler stick to his last."

It was good rhetoric, and probably the jury took more notice of it than was due; but that seems fair enough when there is an infallibility legend to be destroyed.

Any medical witness would, in his own interests, do well to take this piece of advice from Birkett. Personally I have always tried to confine myself to my own subject and not express opinions on matters outside it. Too often I have seen an expert witness discomfited by being lured gently along the broad path that almost inevitably ends in destruction. Often a man of high scientific standing in his own field, he has been led into expressing opinions on matters outside his practical experience. The bringing out of this in cross-examination has undoubtedly caused the jury to give less than the proper weight to the scientific opinions that the witness was qualified to express.

If that happened in the case of Annie Hearn it was, paradoxically, in the interests of justice. Roche Lynch was eminently qualified to express opinions as an analyst; but he was human, and therefore fallible, and on this occasion his opinions were wrong.

During the process of the trial of Annie Hearn the diary of her sister Minnie had been in evidence, and in it were references to the habit of holding a little religious service in her bedroom during her illness. It was usual for the two sisters and a neighbour to read a chapter from the Bible and sing a hymn. Towards the end it described how on one occasion the fourteenth chapter of St John was selected, and no doubt it gave some comfort to the very sick sister: "Let not your heart be troubled: ye believe in God, believe also in me. In my Father's house are many mansions . . . I go to prepare a place for you."

On the Sunday before the closing speeches we held a meeting at which the various scientific details were carefully vetted. It was at this conference that Birkett said, "The Cornish are very religious people, and I intend in my speech to draw the attention of the jury to the difficulty of reconciling the loving care which the accused lavished on her sister with the fiendish project of slowly poisoning her with arsenic." And he said, "I will read the fourteenth chapter of St John, which, I think, will be most effective."

At that moment Walter West arrived with the information that the jury, when asked whether they would prefer to go to church or for a drive to one of the beaches, had unanimously elected to go for a drive. At this Birkett threw up his hands and exclaimed dramatically, "Ah! There go my Father's mansions!"

In his address he did not include a reference to the Scriptures, but he did have a most dramatic closing sentence. The sun was streaming through the windows of the court on to the accused. Now, Mrs Hearn had been in prison for nearly six months awaiting trial, and Birkett, pointing to her in the sunlight, said, "Members of the jury, this poor woman has dwelt in the shadows, and with the shadows over her, for many months. I ask you by your verdict to send her back into the sunlight, away from the shadows which have haunted her for so long."

The judge summed up, and the jury retired. They came back after fifty-four minutes with a verdict of "Not Guilty."

Three weeks after the trial ended I received this moving letter:

Doncaster
July 15th, 1931.

PROFFESSOR SMITH.
DEAR SIR,

I have only just got your address, and I want to thank you *so much* for all you have done for me, but for you I dare not think what the end might have been. I had no idea all those long lonely months, how much, how very much was being done for me. Mr West has told me how you put aside important engagements to come to Bodmin and help to save a life, my life.

I am convinced no one else could have done what you did there, it was wonderful. I feel that I owe my life to you, and I do want to thank you, but it feels too big a thing to put into words, but please accept my heartfelt gratitude and sincere thanks — I shall never forget.

Yours very sincerely,
ANNIE HEARN

She was a foolish woman but not a murderess. I am ready to stake my reputation on that. If she had not bolted I doubt if she would have been charged.

Who, then, killed Alice Thomas?

She was poisoned by a dose of arsenic given to her many days after eating the sandwiches which first made her ill — while she was recovering in bed at home.

Apart from the doctors, and her mother at the end, only one person besides Annie had access to her. That was her husband.

We are unlikely to know the truth now, because on December 14, 1949, William Thomas died on the remote farm at Broadoak, Cornwall, where he had led a lonely life after Alice's death.

So far as I know Annie Hearn is still alive. I do not think she has any more secrets to tell.

12

The Strangling of Chrissie Gall

CHRISSIE GALL WAS STRANGLED AS SURELY AS ALICE THOMAS was poisoned, but who did it was just as hard to say. I think it still is.

The whole case turned on a single word.

According to Peter Queen, who said it, the word was "Don't." According to the police, who heard it, the word was "I."

Just the difference between one word and another — but a world of difference in its effect.

If Queen was to be believed, he was innocent. If the police were right, he was a killer.

For both he and they agreed on the text of the remaining five words of the sentence he uttered when he rushed into a Glasgow police-station and threw some keys on the counter at about three o'clock in the morning of November 21, 1931.

"Go to 539 Dumbarton Road," he said in great agitation. "I think you will find my wife dead."

And then, according to his own version:

"Don't think I have killed her."

But according to the two police-officers who heard him it was:

"I think I have killed her."

You would think they would have recorded a statement like that. Yet they never wrote it down.

Which was one of the things that inclined me to believe Peter Queen.

Chrissie Gall was not his wife, and that may be why she died.

Peter Queen was the son of a Glasgow bookmaker, and he worked in his father's office as a clerk. At eighteen he married. His wife became an alcoholic, and two years later she was put in a home. They never lived together again.

When Peter was about twenty-four his father engaged a nurse-maid, and this was Chrissie Gall. One of six children of a shoe-maker, she had left school at fourteen and been in domestic service ever since. She was three years younger than Peter Queen, and she lived and worked in his father's house for a little over a year. Then she took other jobs, worked in a factory for a while, and finally returned to her own home to nurse her mother, who was seriously ill. Peter Queen saw her from time to time, and began to take her out regularly in his car. They fell in love.

Mrs Gall died, and Chrissie stayed to keep house for her father. Most of her brothers and sisters had married and left home. Peter Queen called more frequently than ever. Her father discovered Peter was married, and was not very happy about the association, but did nothing to break it off. They were very much attached to each other, and Peter was always gentle and kind. Chrissie was an attractive, pleasant, cheerful girl, but she had a weakness for drink. Peter himself was a temperate man, and tried to break her of the habit, but it gradually became worse.

About three years after the death of her mother Chrissie suddenly had to leave home. Her father decided to move in with a married daughter, and he put Chrissie out of his house. Peter arranged lodgings for her in the house of a friend of his, a tram conductor named James Burns. Chrissie was drunk when she arrived there, and continued to be drunk for much of the time during the next three months. Then — at Christmas 1930 — Peter Queen moved in with her. He was now thirty, and she was twenty-seven; and from that time they lived together as man and wife.

Burns and his wife, Fay, both tried all they could to help Peter over Chrissie's drinking. Mrs Burns had heart-to-heart talks with her about it, and when she found bottles that Chrissie had hidden she poured their contents down the sink. Chrissie did not resent this, but was penitent and continually promised to try to mend her ways. At the same time she began to have moods of depression after her drinking-bouts, and twice she threatened to commit suicide.

The first time she was sitting in her room talking to Mrs Burns when she suddenly said she was going to "make a hole in the Clyde" and rushed for the door. Mrs Burns ran after her, pulled her back, helped her to undress, and put her to bed. She then made her a cup of tea, and extracted a promise from her that she would not touch drink any more. She kept the promise for about a week. Then she appeared the worse for drink again, and Mrs Burns reminded her of the promise.

"It's all very fine for you to speak, but you don't understand," Chrissie replied. Then she made a second suicide threat. "Some day some of you will come in and find me strung up."

What Mrs Burns did not understand was that Chrissie was tormented by the fear that people would find out that she was living in sin. She was especially worried that the knowledge would reach her relations. She had told them all that she was still in domestic service, and she used to visit one of her sisters regularly on Wednesday afternoon under the pretence that it was half-day off.

Another time, at about eleven at night, Chrissie went into the kitchen, turned on the gas under the kettle, and, by accident or design, omitted to light it and went up to her room. Mrs Burns fortunately woke up and smelt the gas. Later she complained to Peter, who told her that he had been going round after Chrissie all night turning off gases, and that at one point she had locked herself in the lavatory with the gas turned on.

This occurred in the summer of 1931. In August Peter and Chrissie left the Burnses' house and took a house of their own in Dumbarton Road. They lived there also as man and wife, but towards her family Chrissie maintained the fiction that she was still in domestic service. The deceit preyed more than ever on her mind, and there were more heavy bouts of drinking followed by fits of depression. Mrs Helen Johnston, a sister of Mrs Burns, tried to persuade her to stop drinking, and Chrissie threatened suicide again more than once. Sometimes she told Mrs Johnston she would take a double dose, at other times that Peter would find her hanging behind the door some night.

James and Fay Burns also called a few times at 539 Dumbarton Road, and on Thursday, November 12, they were invited there to tea. On entering the house Burns took off his coat and went to hang it behind the kitchen door, but found that the peg was broken.

"Who has been breaking up the happy little home?" he asked jokingly.

"What is it?" asked Peter Queen.

"About the peg," Burns explained.

"That must have happened during the night," said Peter. "Chrissie tried to do herself in."

He said this in the hearing of both Mr and Mrs Burns and of Chrissie herself, whose only reaction was to say that she had been a damned fool, and was going to make an effort to stop her drinking. She was quite sober at the time, and very quiet. No drinks were consumed during the evening.

At his trial Peter Queen said that Chrissie had tried to hang herself from the peg on the kitchen door during the previous night. The noise woke him up, and he went and saw her sagging at the knees near the door with the free end of the clothes-pulley rope twisted round her neck. He got her up, removed the rope, and put her back in bed. The next morning she was very sorry, and promised to keep from drink. Peter then suggested that she should have a holiday in Aberdeen. She was not enthusiastic, but agreed to go, and he wrote to arrange accommodation for her.

Two days after the visit of Mr and Mrs Burns, Leonard Johnston, Fay's brother-in-law, paid a call. Chrissie was in the house alone: very sober, Johnston said later, and very depressed.

"Chrissie," he said, "why not try to stop this drink? It is doing you harm."

"Don't I know that!" she replied. "But do you understand the position I am in? Do you understand the pretension [sic] of it all? You know, I am fed up with life, I have to tell lies wherever I go. I cannot go home to my own people but I have got to tell lies." She added, "Some day Peter will find me behind the door."

It was arranged that Chrissie should go to Aberdeen just over a week after this, on Monday, November 23. She was to take her young niece Nessie, who had not been very well; Peter thought that if she had the child to look after she was more likely to look after herself. Meanwhile, on Thursday, November 19, she went to see her father at work and told him of these arrangements. He was too busy to talk, and they agreed to meet the next evening at the house of Mrs Walker, one of Chrissie's sisters; but she was not to keep the appointment, and this was the last time he saw his daughter alive.

After leaving her father Chrissie went to Mrs Walker's house, arriving there about a quarter to three in the afternoon. There she met her brother Bert, a grocer, whom she had not seen since August. She produced some beer and whisky, and sat drinking for quite a while. Two or three times Chrissie said she would have to be going, as she had to meet Peter at a quarter-past five.

Eventually she and Bert left together just before five, and he thought she was then getting rather drunk. They went into a public-house near by, where they both drank more whisky and beer, and Chrissie had a large port as well. She also bought a gill of whisky to take away. Then they took a bus to Dumbarton Road, where they went into another public-house. The barman refused to serve Chrissie, saying she had had enough. Eventually Chrissie agreed to leave, and she and Bert arrived at 539 Dumbarton Road at about 9 p.m. to find Peter Queen waiting and looking very upset.

"Where have you been, Chrissie?" he asked.

She and her brother replied that they had been at Mrs Walker's, and he seemed satisfied. Seeing that Chrissie's feet were wet, he lit the fire and took off her shoes. Then he helped her over to the fire, saying, "You will need to get your feet dried, and I will give you a cup of tea. Then you will be all right."

This was the first time Chrissie had ever brought any of her relatives to the house in Dumbarton Road, and as she sobered up a little she quickly repented her rashness. So she asked Peter for a pencil and paper, and then wrote him a note asking him to pretend that it was his aunt's house. Peter caught on quickly. Putting the note in his pocket, he said, "You see, Bert, this is my aunt's house. Now I will have to get a move on, as, Chris, you have a good bit to go to get home."

Instead of making tea he gave Bert a glass of whisky, and offered a small one to Chrissie, which she refused. Then he went out with Bert and walked with him to the tram-stop, and that was the last time Bert saw his sister alive.

The next day — Friday, November 20 — Mrs Johnston called at Dumbarton Road at half-past two in the afternoon. Chrissie was there, alone, and very drunk. Ten minutes later Peter Queen came in. Mrs Johnston advised him to get a doctor, and then left. At four o'clock she returned with her husband, and found Chrissie asleep in bed. They went away, but came back later, and spent most of the evening talking with Peter.

Chrissie woke up at about half-past eight and asked for a drink. Mrs Johnston gave her some ginger ale, and then hot water and sugar, and she slept again until about ten. Then she had tea and sandwiches in bed. She was still awake when the Johnstons left, at a quarter to eleven.

Peter had been unable to get a doctor, but had arranged for

one to call and see her in the morning. Just over four hours after the Johnstons had left, however, Peter was telling the police his wife was dead.

They found her body in bed with the bedclothes pulled up over her chest. Her head was facing to the left; her left arm was at right angles to it, stretched along the pillow outside the bed-clothes; her right arm was lying alongside her body under the clothes. A thin rope encircled her neck low down below the Adam's apple. It was tied in a half-knot — the first twist of a reef knot — and the knot was slightly to the right of the middle line. Her tongue was protruding a little; her upper teeth, which were artificial, were in position. She was dressed in her night-clothes, with a boudoir cap.

A police-constable loosened the knot. He found it had been tied quite tightly. The rope was part of a clothes-line, and it had been cut from the pulley.

Everything in the room was remarkably tidy. There was no disturbance of her night-clothes or of the bedclothes. Furniture — much of it quite close to the bed — had not been moved. There was not the faintest sign of struggle anywhere in the room.

Yet Chrissie Gall had been strangled to death.

At half-past five the same morning Peter Queen was formally charged with murder. His only remark was, "I have nothing to say."

He had already said too much. Or the police had heard too much.

Two pathologists performed an autopsy. They found that the groove from the rope completely encircled the neck, that there were only slight signs of hæmorrhage under it, but that the cricoid cartilage — a ring-shaped cartilage below the voice-box — was cracked. .Her internal organs showed signs of asphyxia, but were otherwise healthy. They said that death was due to strangulation, and there could be no two opinions about that. They said it was homicidal; what else could it have been?

It could have been suicide, of a particularly difficult and grue-some kind. She could have strangled herself.

Unusual? Very. Unlikely? Well, Spilsbury said he was sure she had.

He was appearing for the defence.

So was I.

It was the first time we had been colleagues in a case — and it was also the last.

"It was suicide," said Spilsbury after we had carefully inspected the premises and tried some experiments with the rope.

"Certainly there isn't much to suggest murder," I said. I had never seen a case of homicide by strangulation in an adult in which there were so few signs.

Together we went over the points in favour of suicide. There was the undisturbed state of the room, the natural position of the body, the tidiness of the clothes — including even the boudoir cap. There was the fact that the upper denture was in place.

There was the absence of hæmorrhage and bruising in the deeper parts of the neck and in the thyroid. This showed that relatively little force had been used — for normally a strangler pulls the cord very tight and keeps the pressure up. Especially if he made only a half-knot, which was all there was here; and that also spoke for suicide. A murderer would have been unlikely to run the risk of the knot slipping. Then there was the position of the noose — low down in the neck, with the knot just to the right of the middle line. In murder the noose would tend to be high up on the neck, with the knot more on the right, because the murderer would have to bend over the bed to tie it.

All this favoured the theory of suicide, and yet I did not think it could exclude the possibility of murder. The absence of any struggle could conceivably have been due to the fact that the woman was very drunk. Yet the circumstantial evidence was against this, and so was the medical evidence as far as it went. At the autopsy some fluid was found in the stomach, and it was free from any smell of alcohol. Unfortunately, it was not examined chemically, and neither was the blood. This was a great pity, because the murder theory depended on the idea that she had been too drunk to resist.

There was still one thing that disturbed me about the possibility of suicide.

"Would a rope tied only with a half-knot," I asked, "keep tight enough to cause asphyxia after she had lost consciousness and her hands had let go of the ends?"

"Yes," said Spilsbury after examining the cord under a microscope. "Definitely yes. Look how the fibres bite into one another where they cross. They would hold the knot tight enough after her grip had relaxed."

I was by no means convinced, and I warned the defence to this effect. The police were bound to say they had found the noose tight after death, and Spilsbury would say that he was satisfied that the noose would have remained tight. That seemed to me as far as we could go. The defence would certainly have to make the point without me. I said that if I were asked I would have to express doubt.

The trial of Peter Queen was held in Glasgow, and began on January 5, 1932. The police evidence was given first, and it was by no means satisfactory. Queen's alleged statement "I think I have killed her" was tantamount to a confession of murder and should, of course, have been recorded in writing. The police witnesses were evasive under cross-examination, and only after close questioning by the judge, Lord Alness, was it brought out that no record had been made.

After the police witnesses came the relatives and acquaintances of the deceased. One after another these Crown witnesses went into the box and freely and unhesitatingly testified first to Peter Queen's love and kindness towards Chrissie, and secondly to her depressions and suicide threats and attempts. No wonder the judge, in his summing up, was to describe the evidence of the Crown case of what preceded the tragedy as "scanty and unconvincing in so far as it supports the theory of homicide by the accused."

The evidence of the Johnstons was exceptionally important, as they had been the last persons apart from the accused to see Chrissie alive.

On most points they supported each other, but on one matter they were in disagreement. That was Chrissie Gall's condition when they left her for the last time. Mrs Johnston said she was still stupid with drink and in a helpless condition. Her husband, on the other hand, said that, although she was not sober, she talked sensibly and he thought she could have walked all right.

The two pathologists who had performed the autopsy — and neglected to examine the stomach-contents or blood for alcohol — explained why they were sure it was not suicide but murder. Their opinion was supported by Professor John Glaister, who had for many years held the Chair of Forensic Medicine at Glasgow University and who, incidentally, had examined me in 1913 for my Diploma in Public Health. That ended the case of the Crown.

Peter Queen elected to give evidence in his own defence.

He said that a good while after the Johnstons left he spoke to Chrissie about her proposed holiday in Aberdeen. She told him she had not packed anything, and he had the impression that she was not keen on the holiday at all. Then she asked if he thought her brother Bert had really believed that the house belonged to Peter's aunt, and she began to worry that Bert might tell all the rest of the family about her true way of life. Queen told her not to worry, and then mentioned that the doctor would be calling the next morning. Chrissie asked him to get out the best pillow-slips for the doctor's visit.

"I tried to find them," he said, "but couldn't, and when I told Chrissie she did not reply. I thought she was asleep, and I sat on a chair and smoked a cigarette. Later I prepared to go to bed, and then I saw that she had a rope round her neck and that her face was swollen.

"I called out 'Chris! Chris! Chris!' and shook her — I was shocked and completely knocked out — I don't know what I did for some time. When I came to my senses the first thing I thought of was to go to the police."

He did not loosen the cord round her neck or feel her pulse or call the doctor — all points that told heavily against him at his trial. So, of course, did his alleged statement at the police-station, to which the Crown counsel, Mr John (now Lord) Cameron attached great weight.

"When you were asked what was the matter what did you say?"

"I said, 'My wife is dead. Don't think I have killed her.' "

"What gave you the idea that there was any question of killing?"

"They kept on asking me what was the matter. I thought I might be blamed. That is why I said, 'Don't think I have killed her.' "

Another piece of evidence that was to Queen's disadvantage was his reply when charged with murder, "I have nothing to say." An innocent man might be expected to deny the charge vigorously and say that she had killed herself, but Queen did nothing of the sort.

The only other witnesses for the defence were Spilsbury and myself. This was the first time I had seen him appearing for the defence, and he was as uncompromising as ever. Cameron put him through a severe cross-examination, and he never budged an inch. I had the impression that he would have gone on saying it was suicide even if Queen had suddenly confessed to murder. Indeed, when pressed Spilsbury as good as said so.

"If you found a boy strangled in a position and under conditions which were consistent with either homicide or suicide," asked Cameron finally, "the true conclusion of the issue might be radically altered by the fact that a man had given himself up and had admitted that he had caused it?"

Without a moment's hesitation Spilsbury replied:

"I do not think it would affect my opinion that it might be either suicidal or homicidal."

The answer was characteristic of the man. It took my breath away.

The case worried me. The medical experts for the Crown seemed quite certain that it was a case of murder; my colleague Spilsbury was equally certain that it was a case of suicide.

The facts did not warrant a definite opinion either way. My evidence was at least balanced with a slight leaning towards the defence.

I fully expected the jury to bring in a verdict, not of Guilty or of Not Guilty, but that convenient Scottish verdict Not Proven. "Surely," I said to myself, "with this conflict of opinion and complete absence of direct proof they will be unable to decide positively between homicide and suicide, especially in view of the previous history of the pair, and in particular the psychological state of the girl?" After a bout of drinking she was always seized with remorse. When Omar Khayyam wrote:

> Indeed, indeed, Repentance oft before
> I swore, but was I sober when I swore?
> And then and then came Spring, and Rose-in-hand
> My threadbare Penitence apieces tore —

he was, for once, uttering bad psychology. Repentance, I think, always comes with sobriety, for sinners do not repent when drunk. Nor in Chrissie's case was it rose-handed spring which came to tear her penitence, but her own searing conscience. Her religious scruples would not let her forget that her relationship with Peter was sinful in the eyes of God.

This ever-present sense of guilt does give some reason to suggest that on the fatal night it may well have been her hand that pulled tight the cord round her neck. Did she suddenly decide, when Peter was looking for the pillow-slips, to get that ease from her conscience which she had so often vainly sought in drinking? Possibly. Could she have cut the rope from the pulley without his being aware of it? I think not. Maybe, goaded by her incessant talk of suicide, he had cut the rope and thrown it to her with the remark, "Well, if you want to die, take this and get on with it," not expecting for one moment that she would. Who knows? Nobody but Peter Queen, but there was no time in their history when anybody had noticed the slightest sign in him of irritation or impatience towards her, or of anything but loving care and attention. Could his hand have tied the cord round her neck and held it tight for some minutes while he watched her slowly die? I cannot believe that possible. We shall never know, and in any case those two paid a heavy penalty for loving so unwisely.

In his charge to the jury his Lordship dealt with the medical evidence in some detail. It was clear that the opposing views had afforded him little on which he could advise the jury. The case therefore rested more on the general evidence than on the scientific, and he directed the attention of the jury to the importance of the circumstantial evidence.

"Remember," he said, "that circumstantial evidence is often the best evidence. Better than direct evidence in some cases. Conduct can be a more eloquent and a more reliable guide in many cases than speech."

He thereupon discussed the conduct of the accused when he found his "wife" dead, his action in going to the police before finding out whether she was alive or not, without loosening the ligature and without calling the doctor; his words when he arrived at the police-station — "I think I have killed my wife" — and his reply that he had nothing to say when charged with her murder.

His Lordship dealt with the absence of motive as follows: "No doubt it is very helpful to be able to establish a motive, but the springs of the mind and emotions are so obscure that it is not always possible to discover, far less to establish, the motive which animates human conduct."

After two hours' absence the jury returned a majority verdict of guilty. So, in the only case where Spilsbury and I were in pretty complete agreement, the jury believed neither of us.

Yet they added a unanimous recommendation for mercy, and four hundred leading citizens of Glasgow — including M.P.'s, former Lord Provosts, and councillors — petitioned for his reprieve. The Secretary of State for Scotland interviewed the judges and lawyers in the case, and three days after he heard the death sentence Peter Queen was told it had been commuted to penal servitude for life.

A few years ago he was released. He stayed in Glasgow, and got a job as a bookmaker's clerk. He made friends and became well liked in his circle, which knew nothing of his past. In May 1958 he died.

Did he kill her? Probably not. I would still not be as dogmatic about it as Spilsbury was at the time, but I think that there was insufficient evidence to justify a conviction.

When a person is found strangled there is a strong presumption in favour of murder. Suicide by strangulation or by suffocation is rare. Though I had seen many hundreds of cases of homicidal strangulation, my own experience of suicide by strangling was extremely limited. On the other hand, since cases of undoubted suicide are rarely the subject of investigation by the courts, details are not published, and there is a general ignorance of the subject. I made this point at Peter Queen's trial, and about a year later I was given startling proof of it.

It came in a communication from Dr Hinks of Westcliff, and I would not have heard of it otherwise. The case was of a spinster of forty-five, and she had seemed in good spirits when she went to bed the night before. In the morning the maid taking her breakfast was unable to open the door of the room. She summoned Dr Hinks, who eventually broke the door down. It had been locked, and the key left on the inside.

The woman was dead. She was in bed, lying on her back, covered by the bedclothes but with both arms outside. Over her mouth, but not completely covering it, was a scarf. It was folded to about the width of four inches, and tied at the back slightly to the left side in a granny-knot. There was another scarf of about the same width round her neck, and tied in front just tightly enough to impress the skin. When Hinks pulled away the scarf over her mouth he found a small handkerchief inside, tightly pushed into the back of the throat. There was very little alteration in the colour of her face and lips.

Clearly death was due to asphyxia by strangulation and

smothering, and, but for the attendant circumstances, the case might easily have led to a criminal charge. But it was undoubtedly suicidal. The woman had suffered from attacks of severe depression ever since the death of her mother three years before, and she had often threatened to take her life. She had tried to do so more than once by tying a stocking or handkerchief round her neck. These attempts were always made in front of other people, who thought they were put on to excite sympathy. Her depression had got worse, however, and in the end, quietly and privately, she had killed herself in this unusual way.

Unusual, yes — as I said in the case of Chrissie Gall. She also had been depressed, and had threatened suicide more than once. If the Westcliff case had occurred a year earlier, and been quoted at Peter Queen's trial, it might well have tipped the balance in his favour.

13

The Jersey Abortion Case

THE NEXT TIME I MET SPILSBURY WE WERE AGAIN ON OPPOSITE sides of the fence, and after the trial he refused to speak to me.

It was the type of case commonly called unsavoury, and none the less grave for the undoubted prevalence of this crime. Dr Marie Stopes once said at a meeting of the Medico-Legal Society that after the publication of one of her books 10,000 women wrote to her openly asking for advice about abortion, and asking the amount of her fee. The evidence from birth-control and similar clinics is to the effect that contrived abortion is an everyday occurrence, and there are probably few women with an unwanted pregnancy who have not contemplated the possibility of getting rid of it.

There must also be few doctors who have not, at one time or another, been asked to help some girl or woman to terminate a pregnancy.

On grounds of friendship, of compassion, or for social or economic reasons a doctor may be tempted to comply with the wishes of a patient or of the parents of an unmarried prospective mother, with possibly disastrous results to himself. Ordinarily, however, doctors steadfastly refuse to interfere with a pregnancy unless it is considered necessary to conserve the mother's health. Ethical standards of professional conduct laid down by Hippocrates about two thousand five hundred years ago are still observed. To the doctor life, including embryonic life, is sacred.

In their relationship to one another doctors form a true brotherhood. They loyally stand together, and refuse to make any public criticism of the conduct or practice of any of their fellows. When, therefore, one medical practitioner expresses an opinion that another is open to a charge of criminal abortion, and when that opinion seems to be held by other colleagues in the profession, the probability is that there is something in it.

It was for this reason that I felt little sympathy for Dr Avarne when he came from Jersey to ask my advice and help in his case. However, after I had heard his story I agreed to look into it without binding myself in any way.

Dr Avarne came to see me in Edinburgh on October 4, 1933. He was then forty-two years of age. A native of South Wales, he had qualified in 1913, served in the Navy during the War, and then specialized in obstetrics, first in London and afterwards in Jersey. For ten years he was on the surgical staff of the General Hospital at St Helier, for much of the time as Senior Medical Officer. This appointment had ended eighteen months before.

The woman in the case was an unmarried domestic servant of twenty-eight. She was the mistress of a retired hotel-proprietor, who had known her for ten years: in fact, their association had begun when she was employed as a chambermaid at his hotel. She had been pregnant before, in 1926; and although he said there was some doubt whether he was responsible, he gave her enough money to go to Southampton and have her baby there. She returned to her job at his hotel, and later went into private service. In May 1933 she informed him that she was pregnant again. He denied paternity, but told her to see Dr Avarne. The two men were personal friends, and used to go fishing together, and Avarne readily consented to see the woman. At this point agreement about the facts came to an end.

The doctor said he was asked to perform an illegal operation and refused. The man said Avarne performed an illegal operation without being asked. The woman said that she thought Avarne would help her to end her pregnancy, but had no idea that this would mean such drastic treatment as an operation. The only thing that all three agreed on was that none of them ever mentioned the question of a fee.

Avarne saw her first on May 27, when she was two and a half months pregnant. About a month later he prescribed a bromide which would have a sedative effect. It was never suggested that he gave her any other drug or took any action that might be construed as an attempt to interfere with the pregnancy before she entered a nursing-home in the fifth month.

She was admitted on Friday, July 21, after Dr Avarne had explained the case to Sister Le Feuvre, who kept the home. The patient told Sister she was four and a half months pregnant, and complained of hæmorrhage and pains. She said the father of the child would pay the nursing-home fee.

Dr Avarne said he would examine the woman under an anæsthetic and, if necessary, operate, and the next morning Sister Le Feuvre prepared the theatre. Dr Avarne had not said at what time he would call. Sister tried to ring him up, but the exchange told her he was not on the phone. The patient said that Dr Avarne had told her that Dr Mattas would administer the anæsthetic, and so Sister telephoned him. Dr Mattas told her he had nothing to do with the case. The anæsthetist proved to be Dr Wallis, who arrived about half-past eleven. Avarne came a few minutes later, examined the patient under anæsthesia, and performed an operation with the object of inducing abortion. There was no consultation between the two doctors, Wallis acting only as an anæsthetist.

Nothing happened to the woman, and so three days later — on July 25 — the doctor performed another operation, this time attempting the removal of the child with instruments. Again Dr Wallis gave the anæsthetic. This operation also was unsuccessful, and Avarne told Sister to have everything prepared, as he might need to operate again that evening or the next morning.

When he telephoned the nursing-home the same evening Sister Le Feuvre said the patient had no hæmorrhage or pain and her general condition was good. Avarne phoned again the next morning, and was given a similar report. But on the following morning — Thursday, July 27 — the news was more serious. The patient had had a rigor at 2 a.m., and her temperature was 104·8. Dr Avarne called between 10 and 10.30, examined the patient, and went to fetch another doctor for consultation. He returned with Dr Mattas, who thought the patient was seriously ill but would recover. The two doctors had a consultation in the presence of Sister Le Feuvre, and agreed on the treatment to be given. Sister said later that Dr Avarne promised to call again at 2 p.m. but failed to do so.

At 8.30 p.m. the baby was born dead. At 9.45 the patient had a severe rigor, and at 10 the placenta was expelled. The rigor continued, she vomited twice, and her temperature rose to 107. Sister Le Feuvre tried to get Dr Avarne, but failed, and then rang up Dr Mattas. He was out, but she was told he would return any moment. She then phoned Dr Wallis, but he was also out. Sister asked if anyone knew where Dr Avarne could be found, and was told he was out of the island. Then she tried Dr Mattas again, and as he was still out she left a message for him to phone her without fail on his return.

Sister could have only just put the phone down — the time was about 10.15 — when another doctor arrived.

This was Dr Bentlif, and he brought a patient. Sister Le Feuvre told him her dilemma, and he asked if he could help. She said she would be very pleased if he would. He saw the patient and approved Sister's treatment after she had told him the history of the case. The patient, who had been unconscious when Dr Bentlif arrived, was puzzled when on recovering she saw it was not Dr Avarne. When the doctor and Sister went out to confer, fearing that she was being left without any medical attention at all, she rang the bell and said to Dr Bentlif, "If you will help me I shall tell you the whole truth." Then she said that she had not had any pain or hæmorrhage before admission to the nursing-home, but had complained of these symptoms on Dr Avarne's instructions. She said she had gone to him with a view to having her pregnancy terminated.

On hearing this Dr Bentlif without contacting Dr Avarne telephoned Centenier Foster, of the Honorary Police Force.

Centenier Foster went to the nursing-home and asked the patient if she wished to make a statement. She said she did. He thought she expected to die.

"As a matter of fact," he said afterwards, "the girl could hardly speak."

In the presence of Dr Bentlif and Sister Le Feuvre she repeated what she had already said, and the statement was duly signed and witnessed.

Centenier Foster summoned Dr Blampied, the police surgeon, who arrived soon after midnight. By then the patient had improved. She confirmed her statement verbally to the police surgeon. In the presence of Sister Le Feuvre he and Dr Bentlif placed the fœtus and placenta in jars. On the following day Dr Halliwell, a physician from the General Hospital, examined the patient at the request of the Attorney-General. All three doctors examined the remains of the child and the afterbirth, and all agreed that there were no signs of maceration — that is, a softening of the tissues which occurs when death has taken place some time before the birth.

The patient made a complete recovery. Dr Avarne was arrested and charged with criminal abortion.

The Crown called Sir Bernard Spilsbury into consultation. He examined the fœtus and placenta, agreed that there was no maceration, and concluded that a criminal abortion had taken place.

Dr Avarne, however, held that the fœtus was dead when he sent the patient into the nursing-home, and that the clearing out of the uterus was essential to save her life. This, if true, was of course a complete answer to the charge; but with the evidence of three experienced colleagues against him, plus the supporting evidence of Spilsbury, the case against him looked pretty black. Yet Avarne seemed confident of being able to prove his innocence. When he came to see me in Edinburgh he brought me certain sealed specimens that Spilsbury had taken from the fœtus and placenta.

Professor Murray Drennan, of the Pathology Department of Edinburgh University, made microscopic sections from these, and he and I examined them together. We came to the conclusion that all the specimens showed distinct signs of maceration due to the retention of the child in the uterus after it had died. This conclusion was supported by the microscopic examination of certain macerated fœtuses obtained from the hospital, and by the examination of infants which had been born dead and kept in preservative in my laboratory. There were also signs of degeneration in the blood-vessels in the placenta, and evidence of a hæmorrhage into its substance. These findings and other experimental work convinced us that Avarne was correct in his diagnosis that the child was dead before he sent the patient into the hospital.

I agreed to give evidence for the defence, provided that supporting evidence on the clinical side could be obtained from a recognized consultant in gynæcology. I had no wish to be drawn into any argument about treatment, since I had very little practical experience in those matters, which are the province of practising clinicians. The defence was fortunate in securing the help of Dr Aleck Bourne, one of the leading consultants in midwifery and gynæcology in London.

The trial was fixed to begin on November 6, 1933. Bourne and I went across a day before and obtained permission to examine the remains of the child and the placenta, which had been kept in preservative solution. Spilsbury and the police surgeon were present at this examination, which confirmed the opinion of Bourne and myself that the child had been dead for several days before the birth took place. The afterbirth, as we suspected from the conditions seen in the microscopic sections, was the seat of successive hæmorrhages which formed layers of blood clot in the organ. These hæmorrhages must have taken place over a long period.

The results of our examination definitely proved that this was a genuine case of fœtal death. Although we demonstrated these conditions to Spilsbury in detail, together with the sections I had made in Edinburgh, they had no effect on him. He had already made up his mind and given his opinion, and nothing could shake it.

Legal procedure in Jersey differs from that in England, Scotland, or France. It is, I think, a relic of Norman French.

There was a jury of twenty-four composed of both English-speaking and French-speaking members, not all of whom could understand both languages. The right of challenge was exercised after the jury had been called. A two-thirds majority was sufficient to convict.

The Bailiff of Jersey sat as the judge with ten jurats, or magistrates, who, if they had any function, successfully concealed it. The witnesses were all called to the bar and sworn in together. The Attorney-General, who led for the Crown, did not make an opening speech but immediately began examining witnesses. The rules of evidence were lenient by our standards: statements made in the absence of the accused were admitted, and leading questions were common.

Centenier Foster gave evidence first, followed by Sister Le Feuvre and the patient herself: when continuing her evidence on the second day of the trial she broke down in the box and burst out, "I can't bear it any longer. Let me go, let me go — I have told you all I have to say."

But she recovered her composure, and under cross-examination she did not retreat at all from the statement she had made in the nursing-home. A much sorrier figure was cut by the man she named as father of the dead child, a prominent citizen of St Helier, married, and, ironically, himself a Centenier of Police.

A point to which the Crown attached much importance was the undeniable fact that Dr Avarne had given his patient a certificate saying that she was suffering from a cyst on the groin and needed seven days' rest. He had given her this to show to her employer before going into the nursing-home: an irregular act, of course, but probably merely done out of kindness to save her from losing her job. As it happened, it did her no good, for her employer tracked her down to the nursing-home and went to see her. She arrived just when Dr Avarne was operating, as Sister Le Feuvre told her on opening the door.

"To remove the cyst?"

"It's not a cyst. It's a baby."

Besides Spilsbury, Bourne, and me from the mainland, the witnesses included twelve of the most prominent medical men on the island.

Bentlif, Blampied, and Halliwell testified that the foetus and placenta showed no sign of maceration. On the third day of the trial this vital point had the authoritative backing of Sir Bernard Spilsbury. He gave evidence in his usual clear, lucid style, didactic and convincing, and, of course, conceded nothing to the defence. He said positively that there was no hæmorrhage before the woman entered the nursing-home, and that the foetus died in the course of the second operation. He was led into expressing definite opinions about symptoms and clinical signs, the indications that might warrant therapeutic abortion, and into committing himself as to whether certain treatment was advisable or not. He said that Avarne had failed to give her the right treatment before her admission to hospital, and that the first operation was not the proper kind to perform. Like Roche Lynch in the case of Mrs Hearn, he went outside his own subject; and, not surprisingly, the first question put to him in cross-examination was when he had last treated a case of abortion himself. He had to admit that he had no clinical experience of pregnancy for the past twenty years.

Not all the other medical witnesses for the Crown shared Spilsbury's views on Avarne's professional ability. Dr Wallis, the anæsthetist in the case, called him a very clever surgeon, whom he had never known to perform an operation unless it was necessary. Dr Mattas, the consultant, who gave his evidence in French, said he had assisted Avarne in operations, and considered him a first-class surgeon. This witness said also that Avarne had not tried to hide anything, and he pointed out that if there had been anything suspicious about the case their consultation would hardly have been held in front of Sister Le Feuvre. He declared that he would not be prepared to accept a statement from a person in such a state of fever as the patient in the case. "She could not possible be fully aware of what she was saying."

So much for the case for the prosecution. The first witness for the defence was the Matron of the General Hospital, who said that but for the skill of Dr Avarne many patients would have gone out in their coffins. Then came four local doctors, all full of praise for Avarne. "I say emphatically there are hundreds of people in this island to-day who thank God that Dr Avarne came to Jersey," said one. They all thought his handling of the case was perfectly correct, and expressed their conviction that no criminal abortion had been performed.

Other evidence for the defence revealed bitter personal animosities among the medical profession in Jersey, but as this was irrelevant the Bailiff instructed the jury to ignore it.

The last two witnesses for the defence were Bourne and myself. I gave my opinion on the microscopic sections we had prepared, and on my experimental work on children born several days after their death in the uterus of the mother. These observations proved conclusively that the child was dead before Avarne operated.

Bourne was a magnificent witness, and the star turn of the trial. He had no doubt whatever that the patient had been treated properly, and said it was "asking one to believe an almost impossible thing that Dr Avarne would have attempted to perform a criminal abortion at the period he had." Asked whether he thought that the evidence of Sir Bernard, whose reputation was world-wide, was to be considered unreliable in this case, he answered unhesitatingly, "I have the greatest respect and admiration for Sir Bernard when he speaks as a pathologist, but when he dares to give an opinion about the treatment of a living woman I would regard it with contempt." Blunt words, but Bourne was highly critical of any clinical evidence given by pathologists.

After a very short retiral the jury gave a verdict of "Not Guilty." Cheering broke out in the public gallery, and the Bailiff cleared the court. A crowd of about seven thousand waited outside, and when Avarne left the court his supporters tried to carry him shoulder-high. A bonfire had been built in the Town Square in expectation of an acquittal, and the general air of rejoicing left no doubt about the popularity of the doctor with the people of the island.

Spilsbury, Bourne, and I had travelled in the same boat across to Jersey for the trial, and we had all slept at the same hotel. There was nothing odd about that. It was not remarkable, either, that from the beginning Spilsbury had held himself more or less aloof, because he was naturally reserved and never seemed able to relax or enjoy himself. I think he was too deeply immersed in his work. Perhaps that made him over-sensitive to criticism and defeat. At any rate, he refused to speak to Bourne and me when the three of us travelled in the same boat back to the mainland.

Spilsbury is dead now, and his death was tragic. At the inquest on his last case of suicide — and there was no room for doubt this time — he was the deceased. I mourned him sincerely, for we had lost a man of outstanding brilliance and complete integrity. He was so often right that he could almost be forgiven for being so stubborn when he was wrong. One might almost hope that there will never be another Bernard Spilsbury.

14

Child-murder in Aberdeen

HELEN PRIESTLY WAS EIGHT YEARS OLD, AN ONLY CHILD, AND she lived with her parents in Aberdeen. At about half-past one on the afternoon of Friday, April 20, 1934, her mother sent her to the local Co-operative Stores to buy a loaf of bread. The shop was a hundred yards along the road. Trade at that time of the day was usually slack, and Helen could be expected back in five minutes. When she had not returned after ten minutes her mother began to get worried. Helen was normally punctual, and was always anxious to be back on time at school, where she was due at five minutes to two.

Mrs Priestly went to the front window and looked along the street. There was no sign of Helen. She asked the neighbours, but none had seen the girl come back. Then Mrs Priestly went out to look for her.

Helen had been to the shop and bought the bread. She had gone out with the loaf and the store voucher slip recording the sale: that was all the shop assistants knew.

After making further inquiries, and returning home again, Mrs Priestly went to the school, which was three minutes' walk away. The children were just going in. Among the girls in the playground Mrs Priestly recognized one, Jeannie Donald, who lived in the same tenement, in the flat immediately below her own. Mrs Priestly was not on speaking terms with Jeannie's mother, but at that moment she would have spoken to anyone who might help her to find Helen.

Jeannie had not seen Helen, but she went into the school to see if she was there. She returned to tell Mrs Priestly that Helen had not arrived. Mrs Priestly went back home again, searched the flat, became thoroughly alarmed, and raised a hue and cry.

The police were informed, inquiries were made at hospitals, and Helen's father, a painter and decorator, left his work and started a search of his own.

About six o'clock a boy named Richard Sutton reported that he had seen Helen taken away by a man.

Richard was a schoolfellow and playmate of Helen's and was nine years old. He said he had seen Helen, carrying a loaf, dragged up the street by this man, who took her on a tramcar going towards the post-office. He was middle-aged, said Richard, about five feet ten in height, and wore a dark coat with a tear in the back.

A small girl had been abducted in Aberdeen in just this way some months before; so the police were on their toes. Descriptions of the man and the girl were broadcast, messages were flashed on cinema screens, asylums were asked to report if any patients had escaped, and a search was begun of the whole city and its surroundings.

It was a wet and blustery night, and heavy rain fell from about eight o'clock, but most of the Priestlys' friends and neighbours took part in the search. A pause was called at midnight, and Helen's father, who had been driven round in a friend's car, returned home for a few hours. At half-past four he went back to the police-station, where there was still no news of the girl or of the middle-aged man with the torn coat. A few hours later police-officers asked Richard Sutton for a more detailed description of the man. The young rascal lost his nerve and confessed that he had not seen Helen at all the previous day, but had made the whole story up.

By this time, however, the search had already been called off. The body of Helen Priestly had been found.

It was found in a sack lying on the floor in the tenement where she lived.

This tenement was a building of four floors, with two flats — or houses, as they are called in Scotland — on each floor. All the houses above the ground floor were entered from a common stair. The street door, which was used by all the tenants, opened directly from the pavement. Inside, a passage led to a back yard that was also common to the whole tenement. Near the back door there was a water-closet shared by the two houses on the ground floor. Opposite the door of the water-closet was a cupboard under the stairs. Between the two doors was a recess, and it was here that the body of Helen Priestly was found.

The discovery was made accidentally by a neighbour who entered the tenement at about 5 a.m. He had come to resume the search. Part of the sack protruded into the passage, and he went to see what it was. When he saw a child's foot projecting from the sack he immediately raised the alarm.

There was a great deal of shouting and screaming and banging of doors. There was no reply from either of the two houses on the ground floor. William Topp, the tenant of the house on the left of the passage, had gone out to resume the search half an hour earlier, just after Helen's father. His wife was awakened by the screams but fainted: later she became ill and had a miscarriage. The house on the right of the passage — which was immediately under the Priestlys' house on the first floor — was occupied by Alexander Donald and his wife and their nine-year-old daughter Jeannie, the girl whom Mrs Priestly had asked about Helen at the school. Mrs Donald said afterwards that when she heard the screams she wanted to go out, but her husband said the people outside were hysterical, and joining them would do no good. Mrs Donald also said afterwards that among the shouts and screams she heard a woman say, "She's been used"; but nobody else could remember either uttering or hearing those words.

The police were called and photographs were taken, and the body was examined on the spot by Dr Richards, police surgeon for the city and lecturer in forensic medicine at Aberdeen University. After inspecting the sack he removed the body, which was fully clothed except for the knickers and beret. On her right palm was printed the number of the store voucher, which she had evidently held in her hand. There were some cinders in the sack, a small piece of cinder between the girl's teeth, and three more in her hair; and there were signs of vomiting on her dress and round her mouth. The body was lying on its right side in the sack, but post-mortem lividity showed that she had lain on her left side for several hours after death. The body was completely rigid. There were bloodstains on her thighs and combinations, and very serious injuries to her private parts.

At five past seven the body was taken to the mortuary for identification and a full post-mortem examination. Meanwhile the police began to look for the murderer in the tenement where Helen had lived.

From the moment the body was found it seemed extremely unlikely that the crime had been committed anywhere else. The sack, a jute bag, had a depression at the level of the child's abdomen, as if it had been carried over the arm, but was not wrinkled as it would have been if carried any distance. Both the sack and the girl's clothing were dry. There was a pool of water outside the back door, and in the yard the ground was soft: there were no footprints there or on the doorstep or the passage floor. In the street in front of the house, in spite of the weather, people had been walking or standing about all night. No suspicious person had been seen — no one carrying a parcel or bundle.

There had been a great deal of coming and going throughout the night. The police had called at about 11 p.m., and searched the back yard and all the coal-cellars. Priestly had been in and out several times after midnight. William Topp had used the ground-floor water-closet at half-past one, and the body was not there then. Probably it was still not there at half-past four, when first Priestly and a friend and then Topp left the house to resume the search.

It was therefore reasonably certain that the murder had been committed in the tenement, and the question was which of the eight houses had been the scene of the crime. Because of the injuries to the girl's private parts the police concentrated on accounting for the movements of all the men, and they took statements in each house in the tenement.

The post-mortem examination was performed the same day by Dr Richards and Professor Shennan, Professor of Pathology at Aberdeen University.

They found marks of strangulation on the neck. When the body was opened vomited matter was found in the wind-pipe and the smaller air-tubes, and bruises were found in the muscles in front of the voice-box and wind-pipe. The condition of the other tissues was consistent with asphyxia from strangulation, which Dr Richards and Professor Shennan gave as the cause of death.

They were able to assess the time of death with some degree of precision.

The stomach contained meat and potatoes which Helen was known to have eaten at half-past twelve; and since only the early changes of digestion could be seen, they reckoned that death had taken place within between one and two hours of the meal. Later, the possible period was narrowed to a maximum of an hour and a half after the meal — that is, to not later than 2 p.m.

All the male inhabitants of the tenement had alibis for this period, being out at work. But the post-mortem brought to light another factor that changed the direction of the police investigation. From the examination of the child's private parts it was clear that the injuries had been inflicted before death, but there was nothing to show that they had been caused by a male. They had probably been made by some kind of sharpened instrument, such as a poker or porridge stick, which could have been used by a person of either sex. The theory of sexual assault therefore had to be abandoned, and it was succeeded by a strong suspicion that the injury to the private parts was inflicted in order to lead the police to think it was a case of rape. Obviously the more likely person to do this was a woman, for, if successful, the subterfuge would divert — as, indeed, it had at first diverted — investigation from the whole of her sex. The police obtained two more pieces of evidence that might have saved them trouble had they known of them earlier in the case. First, a girl reported having seen Helen walking home with the bread, and indeed actually passing the tenement next door, at about a quarter to two; while the evidence of other persons in the street showed that she had not walked past her own tenement and along the street. There was no reason to doubt that she had gone into her own stair.

The other piece of evidence was supplied by a slater working in the back yard next door, who said he had heard a sound like the scream of a frightened child at about two o'clock, coming from the direction of the tenement where Helen lived. No one else had heard the scream, and this evidence was not very favourably regarded at the trial. The slater had not mentioned it to anyone at the time, even after learning that a child had disappeared.

He reported it to the police on the Monday after the murder, April 23.

On Wednesday, April 25, the police visited the Donalds.

They called at eleven in the morning, and stayed for thirteen hours. They did not leave alone.

Of all the families living in the tenement only the Donalds had not helped in the search. A dour and taciturn couple, they generally kept themselves to themselves. Priestly said he always used to speak to them when passing, although they had never visited each other's homes. Mrs Priestly said she had not been on speaking terms with them for four years. Mrs Donald said it was one year. Their respective daughters had been more friendly, and sometimes played together. Once they had quarrelled, and Jeannie, who was the elder, hit Helen. Her mother told her not to do that again.

Mrs Donald, whose Christian name was also Jeannie, was a good-looking woman of thirty-eight. She took a large part in church activities, and went regularly to the weekly mothers' meetings at the Salvation Army Citadel. Her main interest, however, was her daughter, of whom she was extremely proud. Young Jeannie showed great promise as a dancer, and her mother made and cared for all her dresses. Indeed, on the day Helen Priestly disappeared she spent nearly two hours — from about a quarter-past two till four in the afternoon — ironing at least five frocks for her daughter to wear at a dancing rehearsal the same evening. She had finished by the time the child returned home from school, and at twenty-past five they went together to the Beach Pavilion at the Links. The rehearsal lasted until eleven, when Alexander Donald collected them and took them home.

Mrs Donald related all this to the police when they asked her to describe her movements on the day Helen was killed. She answered their questions freely, did not get any more confused than most people under questioning, and was outwardly calm and composed; although her hands drummed incessantly on the table. For their part the police were just making a routine call, as they had made at the other houses in the tenement. They did not go to see the Donalds with any idea of arresting anybody. At the same time, they had been watching them more closely than the others.

At first there was only Mrs Donald in the house. Her husband, a hairdresser, was at work; her daughter was at school. They both came in at midday, and she prepared their dinner. Young Jeannie returned to school. Her father stayed. So did the police.

Mrs Donald gave them a clear and precise account of her actions about the time Helen was killed. She said she left the house at about ten or fifteen minutes past one, and went to the weekly market at the Green. She bought some eggs and oranges, and then went to Raggy Morrison's shop to try to get some material to make a new frock for her daughter, but found none suitable. When she came back home, she said, she saw several people she knew standing at the street-corner, including Mrs Priestly, who was wiping her eyes. Just after she entered the tenement, she continued, Mrs Topp came in through the back door from cleaning windows. They exchanged some words, and then Mrs Donald went into her own house and began ironing her daughter's frocks. She looked at the clock, and it was then ten or fifteen minutes past two. She said she did not hear that Helen was missing until another neighbour told her at four o'clock.

This was all very plausible, but the police were still not satisfied. At 9 p.m. they asked the Donalds for permission to search the house. Consent was given at once. The police found nothing suspicious except some stains at the bottom of a cupboard that they thought might be blood.

They sent for Dr Richards, who made preliminary tests and said the stains were blood. On this the police arrested both the Donalds on a charge of murdering Helen Priestly.

"I did not do that," said Mrs Donald.

"Not guilty," said her husband.

It was then a quarter-past midnight, but a crowd was waiting for them in the street. Press cameras flashed, and there were cries for vengeance as the Donalds boarded the police-van and were taken to the cells.

The next day Dr Richards examined scrapings from the stains in his laboratory. He found that they were not blood after all.

But the Donalds stayed in their cells.

Alexander Donald remained in custody for over six weeks. He was released on June 11, when the police were satisfied that at the time of the murder he had definitely been in the hairdressing saloon where he worked. It was impossible to dispute that his alibi was genuine.

His wife's alibi was not so easily confirmed. On the contrary, it could be broken.

The women were at the street-corner as she had said, although none remembered seeing her, and she could just as well have seen them through her front window. Mrs Topp agreed that when she came in from the back she saw Mrs Donald standing near the street door, but she thought the time was half-past instead of a quarter-past two, and she neither saw nor heard Mrs Donald come in from the street. So these points were neither proved nor disproved. The account of the visit to the market at the Green did not stand up so well to investigation. The prices Mrs Donald said she had paid for the eggs and oranges were not those of the day; instead, they were accurate for the previous Friday. Raggy Morrison's shop had been closed that afternoon, and in any case some of the colours of materials she had said were available had been sold out earlier in the week. The inference was that Mrs Donald had described a visit she had made to the market the previous week.

This confirmed the police in their suspicions, but was not going to help in the case against Mrs Donald. Under the rules of evidence her statement was likely to be admitted at her trial only if it was not considered incriminating, and no evidence was led to disprove it. This meant that the results of the police investigations at the market could not be used as evidence against her. It meant that if the case against her was to be proved evidence of another kind would have to be proved.

The only possible evidence was medical and scientific.

I was called in on April 30, five days after the Donalds' arrest and ten days after the crime. I went to Aberdeen and met the Fiscal with Professor Shennan and Dr Richards, saw the specimens that had been taken, and visited the scene of the crime. I made a benzidine test for blood on certain articles in the Donalds' house, and some of them responded to the test. I had these sent to my laboratory for closer examination. They were the first of many.

In trying to fix the place of the crime two lines of investigation were open. One was to look among the materials found with the body for anything that could be identified as coming from the Donalds' house. The other was to look for things still in the house that had belonged to the child, and been overlooked when the house was cleaned up.

The materials found with the child were the sack, and inside it a handful of cinders, some household fluff, and a number of hairs: not a great deal to go on, it seemed. The things to look for in the house included Helen's knickers and beret, the bread and the store ticket, the instrument used to inflict the injuries, and traces of vomit and bloodstains. Because of the nature of the injuries the bloodstains might be contaminated with bacteria from the child's intestines.

I hoped that the sack would prove the best connecting link, and no effort was spared to trace its origin. It was an ordinary jute bag with the letters "boss" painted in red. I learned that it had been sent as part of a shipment of cereals from Canada two years before. The movements of the sacks were traced to London, then to agents in Glasgow, and from them to Aberdeen. After the contents had been used, however, the empty sacks had passed into the hands of dealers, and after that they could not be traced. There was some ground for believing that a number of sacks of that kind had been sold to a farmer living near where a brother of Mrs Donald's worked, and it appeared also that this brother had been in the habit of taking potatoes in a sack to Mrs Donald from time to time; but obviously this was not good evidence.

On the outside of the sack there were traces of food matter and black marks caused by pots, suggesting that it had been in use in a kitchen for some time. There was a hole in one corner where it had apparently hung on a hook. We found nine more sacks in the Donalds' house. None of them had the "boss" marks, but five had a hole in the corner similar to that in the murder sack, and three had similar pot-marks. There were no sacks in any other house in the tenement. This, of course, was suspicious, but did not take proof any further.

Inside the sack there was about a double handful of washed cinders. The only person in the tenement who was in the habit of washing her cinders was Mrs Donald, and traces of washed cinders were found in the trap of her sink. The cinders found in the sack were compared, both by the naked eye and microscopically, with cinders taken from each of the eight houses in the tenement. I sent them to the Department of Mines, where they were X-rayed; they were ashed and examined by the spectrograph and by microchemical methods in order to ascertain whether any particular thing peculiar to the Donalds' cinders was in them, but all without result.

Among the cinders there was a small quantity of dust and fluff such as one finds in ordinary household debris, and a few human and animal hairs. The human hairs were not those of the child, but of a different colour, and much coarser. They showed also a remarkable irregularity of contour, and had many defined twists. This peculiarity was caused by rather careless artificial waving. Hair that we obtained from a brush supplied to Mrs Donald while she was in prison showed exactly similar characteristics and a similar waving distortion. As far as I could judge by examination in a comparison microscope, the hairs from the sack and those from Mrs Donald were identical in every detail, but this could not be regarded as proof that it was Mrs Donald's hair. In any one individual it is possible to get hairs of different diameters, different colours, and different lengths; there may be greater variations among the hairs of a single individual than between the hairs of two different persons. So, unless there is something very characteristic about a certain head of hair, not much reliance can be placed upon it for purposes of identification. In this instance there was no doubt that it was not the hair of a child, that it had been artificially waved, and that it bore a striking similarity in all respects to Mrs Donald's hair. Standing by itself, therefore, it was significant, but a good deal of supporting evidence would be needed before it could be of value as proof of identity.

We examined the fluff from the sack microscopically. In all household fluff there are likely to be common fibres, such as wool, cotton, silk, hair, and so on, but also specific fibres more or less characteristic of the household derived from clothing, carpets, and the rest. In the sample in the sack we found numbers of fibres of wool, cotton, linen, silk, and jute dyed different colours — red, brown, pink, green, yellow, and purple; fragments of undyed wool and cotton; fragments of cat and rabbit hair; and bits of human hair. Altogether we separated about two hundred different types of fibre, which we prepared for comparison with the fibres contained in some fluff that we had found among the cinders in the fireplace of the Donalds' house.

For this examination we used a comparison microscope, which enabled us to look at two fibres side by side. In this way we compared fibres in their general form and constituent parts, in width and length, in the characteristics of the cells that went to make up their respective structures, and in the presence and distribution of colour. Where necessary we ascertained the nature of a dye by microchemical and spectroscopic tests and its behaviour under ultra-violet light. Altogether no fewer than twenty-five different fibres were matched. These agreed in all the details I have mentioned, and more than once alternate patches of bright red and pink were found in fibres on both sides of the comparison microscope. In addition there were numerous fine fibres of wool and rabbit and human hair that were identical in both samples.

Household fluff taken from several other houses in the tenement was investigated for comparison, and in no case could we find any similar series of resemblances. The absolute matching of so many different fibres from the two sources was, in my opinion, good evidence that the fluff in the sack was derived from the Donalds' house.

Not surprisingly, the more obvious possible objects were not to be found. Five days had elapsed between the crime and the arrest, leaving ample time for removing the evidence. We never discovered the child's knickers or her beret, or the instrument that had been used to inflict the injuries. Part of a loaf of bread was found, of the type bought by Helen Priestly and not usually eaten by the Donalds, but that was not very good evidence. Among the debris taken from the fireplace we found a fragment of paper that had the same structure and microscopical appearance as the store voucher that the child had held in her hand, and on one side of it there was a green line identical with the green line on the store voucher. However, this bit of material evidence was not used in the case.

We found a number of bloodstains in the Donalds' house. Human blood was found on certain articles of clothing, such as stockings, shoes, handkerchiefs, and gloves; on two newspapers of April 19, the day before the crime; on two washing-cloths, a scrubbing-brush, a packet of soap-flakes, and a piece of linoleum that we took from a cupboard under the kitchen sink. The child's blood was found to be in Group O. The defence refused permission to group the blood of the accused, but her group was obtained from certain stained diapers, and proved to be different from that of the child. Group O blood was found only on the newspapers, one of the washing-cloths, the scrubbing-brush, the soap-flake packet, and the linoleum. The fact that these bloodstains were of the same group as the child's had only a limited value as evidence, since large numbers of people are in that group.

The linoleum under the sink also showed a rectangular mark where a cinder-box had been in the habit of resting, but the cinder-box had disappeared. In view of the fact that a cinder was found between the lips of the child it seemed possible that the body had been placed in this cinder-box, and that the box had become stained with blood, and was destroyed on that account. The kitchen door-knob, the handle of the sink cupboard door, and other parts of the linoleum on the kitchen floor all gave a benzidine reaction only and none to other tests for blood, suggesting that they had been carefully washed.

Because I thought the blood from the child's injuries might have been contaminated with bacteria, as a result of the rupture of the intestinal canal, I sent the bloodstained combinations for investigation and comparison to the Department of Bacteriology together with the bloodstained articles found in the Donalds' house.

The germs found in the child's combinations differed in certain respects from the ordinary intestinal bacteria. Cultures taken from the materials found in the Donalds' house also showed the presence of intestinal bacteria, but those found in bloodstains on articles personal to Mrs Donald were of a more common kind, and quite different from those found in the child's clothing. The bacterial strains from one of the washing-cloths, on the other hand, showed a close similarity to the more unusual strains derived from the child's combinations. By tests of a highly technical nature a definite relationship was established between the strain from the cloth and the strain from the child. This did not in itself prove that the cloth and the combinations had been contaminated from the same source, but it was highly suggestive: "a very small fact if you measure it with a foot-rule, because the thing is microscopic," the judge told the jury at the trial, "but it may be a tremendously significant fact in this case."

During the proceedings counsel for the defence suggested that everything movable in the Donalds' house was removed except the furniture. He did us an injustice, for not all the furniture was exempt, nor did we take only movable articles. The house was searched many times during the six weeks following the Donalds' arrest, and most of the 253 productions in the case came from it. Counsel for the defence described our work as "careful and meticulous preparation unparalleled in the history of this old court." We had to be careful and meticulous, for it was largely on the laboratory examinations of a number of small things that the case for the Crown depended.

The trial of Jeannie Donald began on July 16, 1934. A jury of ten men and five women was empanelled, and 164 witnesses were called.

Mrs Donald showed no sign of emotion as one after another of her former neighbours went into the witness-box. Mrs Priestly sobbed and broke down repeatedly when giving evidence, and still Mrs Donald remained unmoved. Only twice during the whole trial did she betray any emotion at all.

The first time was when her daughter was called to give evidence for the Crown. A good witness was young Jeannie — from the prosecution's point of view. She did not recognize or seem to know the kind of bread that Helen Priestly had bought, and she said a box of cinders had been kept in the cupboard under the sink, but she could not remember when she had seen it last.

The case for the prosecution lasted five days, of which most of the fourth and all the fifth were taken up by medical and other scientific evidence. None of the laboratory findings was conclusive in itself, but the combination of the various points made a fairly strong case. The defence did not put up any expert witnesses against us, but gave us a gruelling cross-examination. Mrs Donald did not give evidence herself. No objection was made when' the prosecution put in her statement to the police before arrest. It was not incriminating as it stood, and the Crown could not lead any evidence to disprove it. Counsel for the defence described the scientific evidence as inconclusive, and stressed the fact that Mrs Donald could have had no possible motive for the crime.

Mrs Donald was charged not only with murdering Helen Priestly but also with "previously evincing malice and ill-will towards her." This is an unusual charge to find in a murder indictment, and the Crown could not lead much evidence to support it. There was a certain amount of bad feeling between the two families, and Helen, although quite a well-behaved girl, had given Mrs Donald the unflattering nickname of "Coconut." It has been suggested also that she had the habit of ringing the bell or knocking on the door whenever she passed the Donalds' house, which was several times a day, although this was not brought out at the trial. Both the Priestlys testified that Helen had told them several times — the last about a month before her death — that "Coconut" followed her with her eyes as she made her way upstairs; but neither the girl nor her parents worried about this. So it was not surprising that when the Crown counsel came to deal with the charge of malice the judge interrupted and said he proposed to direct the jury that there was no evidence of malice or ill-will.

Then what was the motive for this dreadful crime?

Any reconstruction is necessarily speculative, but we may not be far wrong in assuming that it happened in the following way.

Helen, re-entering the tenement, made some objectionable remark to Mrs Donald as she passed her house. Angered, Mrs Donald caught her by the shoulder and shook her. This had a more serious effect than Mrs Donald could have anticipated, for Helen fell unconscious.

Probably the key to the mystery is the fact, discovered at the post-mortem examination, that Helen suffered from an overgrowth of lymphatic tissue. It sometimes happens that a child in that state is liable to lose consciousness more rapidly and more easily than a normal child. A sudden collapse of this sort might easily be mistaken for death....

Terrified by what she thought she had done, Mrs Donald pulled the girl into her house. Thinking that she would be accused of murder, she tried to divert any suspicion from herself by making it appear that the crime could only have been committed by a member of the opposite sex. To fake a rape she forced some instrument into the girl's private parts. Helen was not dead, the pain caused her to recover consciousness, and she screamed. This was the scream heard by the slater at two o'clock. As she screamed she vomited, and she inhaled some of the vomited matter. This may have caused her death, although the bruising of the tissues of the neck rather suggested that when Mrs Donald discovered the child was not yet dead she strangled her with her hands in a fit of panic; the asphyxia from which she died could have been due to either of these causes.

The deed done, Mrs Donald put the body in the cinder-box under the kitchen sink and recovered her self-control so well that within a few minutes she was able to talk quite normally to Mrs Topp, and try to establish an alibi by pretending to have come in from the street. Then she spent the afternoon ironing frocks, and prepared tea for her own young daughter with the dead and mutilated body of Helen still lying in the cinder-box under the sink. Then to the Pavilion, to watch her daughter dance; then back to the tenement, alive with people going in and out, and with the police coming and searching the yard and all the coal-cellars. At last a pause, as the search for Helen came to a temporary halt; a little quiet — and the knowledge that the search would be resumed at five in the morning.

A light was seen in the Donalds' kitchen at about three. By five the body was in the sack in the passage outside their house.

It is difficult to understand why Mrs Donald put cinders into the sack with the child, but possibly it was done with the idea of absorbing any vomit or other matter. With these cinders the incriminating household fluff found its way into the sack. But Mrs Donald cleaned up well after she had disposed of the body, washing blood and probably vomited matter off the floor and various other surfaces, only neglecting to wash the washing cloths properly afterwards. In one of those cloths was found the immensely important bacterial strain.

The jury considered the case for eighteen minutes only, and with the single word of "Guilty" Mrs Donald showed emotion for the second time. She collapsed in the dock, could not rise for the sentencing, and was carried, still moaning, from the court. The death sentence was afterwards commuted to penal servitude for life. I personally never believed Mrs Donald had any idea of murdering the child, and before the trial I suggested that the Crown might be advised to accept the reduced plea of culpable homicide, which is roughly equivalent to the English manslaughter.

This was put to the defence, but they would not hear of it, and went all out for a verdict of "Not Guilty." No doubt they underestimated the medical and scientific evidence.

Considerable public feeling had been aroused by this horrible crime, and to avoid prejudice the trial was held, not in Aberdeen, but in the High Court in Edinburgh. It was estimated to have cost between £2000 and £3000, and I believe that the change of venue was greatly appreciated by the thrifty citizens of Aberdeen, since the expenses in the High Court would be met by the Crown, and not fall on the Aberdeen rates.

15

The Sydney Shark Case

A YEAR OR SO BEFORE I TOOK UP MY POST AT EDINBURGH University in 1928 I was asked by Archer Bey — formerly Assistant Chief Constable in Cairo, but then Assistant Commissioner to the Metropolitan Police in London — to visit the Commissioner at New Scotland Yard to talk to him about the use that could be made of a scientific laboratory in police investigation.

At that time Scotland Yard relied entirely on outside assistance in these matters. This system had its advantages, since it offered a wide choice of specialists from whom to select. A serious disadvantage was that there was no one to advise on the day-to-day work that came before the C.I.D. A special laboratory and staff, always available for consultation, would not only give useful help but would develop skills in dealing with special problems of particular interest to the police. Such a laboratory would also act as a clearing-house, as it were, when outside help was needed.

When I went to Scotland Yard I gave a number of instances from my practical experience of the value of such a laboratory, and expressed the opinion that no modern police force could be considered complete without it. Possibly I did not impress the Commissioner; anyway, he did not take the idea up.

The next Commissioner was Lord Trenchard. Two or three years after his appointment he wrote me this letter:

New Scotland Yard,
S.W.1.
18th May, 1934.

STRICTLY CONFIDENTIAL

Dear Professor Smith,
    I am thinking of starting a Medico-Legal Laboratory for the

Metropolitan Police, and, as you are a great authority on this subject, I would very much like to see you and have a talk to you about it.

Is there any chance of your being able to come and see me shortly?

Please treat this as strictly confidential.

Yours sincerely,
TRENCHARD

I went and saw Lord Trenchard, and as a result of our deliberations he decided to make a start at Hendon, where accommodation was available at the Police College he had founded. We decided to adapt certain buildings there as laboratories, and with the help of Dr C. P. Stewart — who, as a chemist, had assisted me in medico-legal work — I was able to produce complete plans for their development. First-class equipment for all types of scientific work was obtained, and the Metropolitan Police Laboratory got off to a grand start.

Lord Trenchard offered me the post of Director. In his typical way he wrote: "It is hard to put on paper, but I would just like to say that I hope you are attracted by the idea. I am an old man in a hurry!"

Much as I should have liked to accept the proposal, with all its exciting possibilities, I felt that I could not leave Edinburgh at that time. But at the Commissioner's request I kept in touch with the work of the Police College, and lectured there from time to time. Lord Trenchard had a committee appointed to watch progress and advise as to the best steps to be taken to provide for the full development of the scientific side of police work. It is to his enthusiasm, backed by the Home Office, that we owe the present high standard of scientific police work throughout the country.

In 1935 my wife and I decided to make a trip round the world with the excuse of attending a meeting of the British Medical Association in Melbourne. I had been appointed vice-president of the Pharmacology Section, of which Sir William Willcox was president. In order to have extra time in New Zealand we left a month before the official party.

For me it was a month of sheer delight, seeing my own folks and lots of old friends, in both North and South Islands; and, of course, especially in Roxburgh, where forty-two of us sat down to a private family dinner. All too soon we had to leave for Auckland, where we joined the main party and travelled with them to Sydney.

Here I stumbled on one of the most extraordinary cases of my career. There were so many odd coincidences in it that it would be too fantastically improbable for crime-fiction. And anyway, how many thriller-readers would believe that sharks suffer from indigestion?

It began on Anzac Day, April 25, 1935, in the Coogee Aquarium. Just over a week earlier two fishermen had caught a fourteen-foot shark which had become entangled in their lines, and it was put on exhibition in the aquarium. It was a sulky shark, refusing to eat and just swimming incessantly up and down the pool. Then, in the late afternoon of Anzac Day, it suddenly went berserk. It flayed the water into foam, dashed about the pool, threshing wildly with its tail, and finally vomited a mass of matter. Among the objects it disgorged the spectators were horrified to see a human arm.

The arm had apparently been severed at the shoulder, and a piece of rope was bound tightly round the wrist. Fishery experts were astonished at the remarkable preservation of the limb, since in their opinion the strong gastric and intestinal juices of the shark would digest any flesh within thirty-six hours. The explanation they thought most likely was that the shark had been affected by a sudden change in its environment, and that the shock must have halted its digestive processes. Whatever the causes of delayed digestion might be, it was quite clear that it had been in the shark's stomach for at least a week before it was vomited up.

The police began intensive inquiries into the identity of the former owner of the arm. Their task was made easier by the fact that it was tattooed with the pictures of two boxers in fighting poses. Several men with tattoo-marks on their arms had been reported missing, and ultimately the field was narrowed down to two of these. The wife and the brother of one, a billiard-marker named James Smith, positively identified the limb as his. Strangely enough, it turned out to be the only part of his body with any distinguishing mark at all. In the meantime the skin on the fingers of the hands was removed in flakes and pieced together by the finger-print specialists for comparison with Smith's prints, which were in the archives of the police. This arduous operation took some weeks. The prints finally secured were very faint, but sufficiently clear to corroborate the identification made by his relatives.

Smith, a man of forty, had left home on April 8, nine days before the capture of the shark. He had told his wife he was going on a fishing expedition with another man, but he did not say who his companion was to be. His wife did not find anything unusual or remarkable in this and it was not until he had been away two weeks that she began to worry and reported his absence to the police.

Identification of the limb did not necessarily mean that Smith was dead. However, the presence of the piece of rope round the wrist made it unlikely that he had merely had his arm bitten off, and every effort was made to find other parts of his body. The police searched the beaches in the locality where the shark had been caught, and naval divers searched the sea-bed. Even the Air Force joined in, low-flying aircraft making observation patrols. Nothing more was found. The body of the shark — which had died in captivity — was dissected, but it did not contain any other human remains. The rest of Smith had apparently gone for ever.

At this stage the police did not know whether the arm had been ripped off by the shark's teeth or cut off with a knife, and they thought he had committed suicide. Their theory was that he had tied a rope round his arms and body and weighted it with some heavy object before leaping into the sea. This method of suicide by drowning is by no means unusual. Later, however, they began to suspect foul play. They interviewed associates of the dead man, but no one was found who had been fishing with him, or had even seen him set out. The probability was that he had never gone fishing at all. It was suggested that on leaving home he had gone instead to a seaside cottage with another man. It was reported that a tin trunk and a mattress had disappeared from the cottage, and a rope and three mats from the owner's boat.

After three weeks of investigations the police made an arrest and preferred a charge of murder.

The identification of the arm as Smith's was not disputed, but the question was raised whether it might have been bitten off by a shark while he was still alive. This, of course, would have been in favour of accidental death or suicide. Although I had nothing officially to do with the case, I was asked to examine the arm and express an opinion on this point. I found that the limb had been severed at the shoulder joint by a clean-cut incision, and that after the head of the bone had been got out of its socket the rest of the soft tissues had been hacked away. In my opinion it was certain that it had been cut, and not bitten off by a shark. The condition of the blood and tissues further suggested that the amputation had taken place some hours after death.

This opinion fortified that already expressed by Dr Palmer, the medico-legal expert, and Dr Coppleson. I was told that Dr Coppleson was an expert on shark-bites, of which he had seen a great number. It was a new specialty to me, although I looked upon myself as a bit of an expert on the bites of that odd mammal the camel.

My tentative reconstruction of the case was that Smith and his companion had quarrelled over something or other, and it had ended with Smith being killed. His body was probably cut up in the cottage on the mattress and the mats taken from the boat. The parts of the body were placed in the tin trunk, which was completely filled without the arm. Unable to get this in, the murderer cut it off and attached it to the outside of the trunk with the rope from the boat, tying one end of it round the wrist. The trunk and its contents and the blood-soaked mattress and mats were then taken out to sea and dumped. The arm worked loose and was swallowed by the shark.

What a queer series of coincidences it was that brought the crime to light! The trunk was just a little too small to take all the remains, and the only part of the body with a distinguishing mark was the part left out. This part worked loose, and was swallowed whole by a shark — and, out of the thousands of sharks that infest the beaches of Australia, that particular shark had to be caught alive and exhibited in the aquarium. Further, out of all the sharks put in aquaria, that one had to become sick and vomit up the contents of its stomach, including the arm which led to the identification. It is a trite saying, but true, that fact is stranger than fiction.

Meanwhile the arrest and murder charge were followed by formal hearings and adjournments and, after a few weeks, the opening of the inquest on Smith. This was immediately preceded by another piece of drama. A man who was expected to be one of the most important witnesses — a boatbuilder named Reginald Holmes — was murdered the night before the inquest was to start.

Holmes's part in the affair is still one of the many unsolved mysteries in the case. He had known Smith, and according to the dead man's widow had owed him sixty or sixty-five pounds. He was believed to have been with the man accused of Smith's murder shortly after the crime. A few days after the arrest he was seen in a speedboat in Sydney Bay with his head and face covered with blood. He was steering his craft erratically, and so the water police went to intercept him. He recovered, and with superlative skill evaded the police boat for four hours. The police thought he had tried to commit suicide, but when he was finally stopped he said an attempt had been made to murder him. In spite of his important knowledge about the case of Smith, they thought he was just being melodramatic, and did not take him seriously. However, the night before the inquest he was shot in his own car, by some one who was almost certainly a passenger, while it was parked under Sydney Bridge. The spot had been carefully chosen; he had been shot when all noise was drowned by the passing of a train overhead.

The inquest on Smith proceeded without Holmes, but after thirty-nine witnesses had been heard an application was made to the Supreme Court to stop further proceedings. The Supreme Court decided that an inquest could be held only if there was a body, and that one limb alone was not enough; therefore a writ was issued restraining the city coroner from further proceedings.

The man accused of murdering Smith was committed for trial and then released on bail. The case was heard in September, and he was acquitted. Three weeks later an inquest was held on Reginald Holmes, and after the verdict two men were arrested and charged with murdering him.

At their trial the jury disagreed. A retrial was ordered, and this time they were both acquitted. With that the Sydney Shark Case came to an end.

From Sydney we went with our party to Melbourne for the meeting of the British Medical Association. From there we went back to Sydney, and set off on the homeward voyage.

Sir William Willcox, the medico-legal expert to the Home Office, was still with us, and I saw a good deal of him. Willcox, Spilsbury, and Roche Lynch had together built up the subject of forensic medicine in London, and they set a high standard for all future medical experts to aim at. Willcox and Spilsbury had worked together on many cases, beginning with Crippen in 1910. Both were highly skilled witnesses, and enjoyed unassailable reputations with Bench and Bar. Yet as persons they had nothing in common. Spilsbury seemed lacking in all the warmer human attributes with which Willcox was so well endowed, but had a distinguished and imposing appearance which Willcox lacked. One evening, after a particularly good dinner, Willcox surprised me by asking what I considered was the greatest factor in his success. I mentioned several obvious things, but he brushed them aside with the remark, "No, no, nothing like that. I owe most of my success to the fact that I look a fool *and I'm not.*"

At one of the ports on the way home the British newspapers came aboard, and in one of them we read that a collection of human remains had been found in the "Devil's Beef Tub" near Moffat, in Dumfriesshire, and taken to my laboratory in Edinburgh for examination. In my absence they were being examined by my assistant, Dr Millar, and Professor John Glaister of Glasgow University. The remains were reported to be parts of two human beings — a woman of twenty-five, about five feet one in height, and a man of about sixty, about five feet six in height.

In another newspaper was the announcement of the disappearance of two women from Lancaster — the wife of an Indian medical practitioner and her maid. Lancaster is only a hundred miles or so from the place where the human remains were found.

Willcox and I were greatly interested in the reports of these two occurrences, which seemed more than coincidental. Willcox, thinking that he was on a good thing, offered to bet me five pounds that the remains of the man and woman found at Moffat belonged to Mrs Ruxton and her maid from Lancaster. I was not tempted to take the bet.

A few weeks later I was looking at the remains myself.

16

The Ruxton Case

GARDENHOLME LINN, A NARROW STREAM RUNNING INTO THE River Annan, is crossed by a bridge about two miles north of Moffat, on the main Edinburgh-Carlisle road. On Sunday, September 29, 1935, a woman walking over this bridge paused and looked into the gully below, and saw a human arm lying on the bank of the stream. The police searched the ravine and eventually collected seventy pieces of human remains, including two heads and one trunk.

Two local doctors examined the remains the next morning. The following day, October 1, Professor Glaister and Dr Millar arrived on the scene. They were of the opinion that the remains belonged to at least two bodies, but probably not more than two, and that they had been dismembered by some one with anatomical knowledge. The remains had been severely mutilated, presumably to hinder identification. From each of the heads the tissues of the face had been cut away, including the nose, lips, ears, eyes, and skin, and some teeth had been extracted after death. From other parts the organs of sex, external and internal, had been removed. However, the trunk was evidently of a female, and so was the less mutilated of the two heads. The other head was thought to have male characteristics, and that was why the first published statement described one of the victims as a man.

Millar and Glaister had the remains taken to my laboratory for more thorough examination, which they carried out together with Professor Brash of the Anatomy Department of Edinburgh University. Meanwhile the Dumfriesshire Constabulary continued the investigation, with the help of the Glasgow C.I.D. Even without medical evidence the police were able to establish approximately when the remains were deposited in the ravine.

It could not have been before September 15, for that was the date of one of the newspapers in which the remains had been wrapped. On the other hand, it could not have been after September 19, the last day when the stream was in spate. Some portions of the remains were found several hundred yards below the bridge, obviously having been carried down by the stream; there had been heavy rain and flooding on September 17 and 18, followed by several fine days. Some of the parcels just below the bridge had been left stranded when the level of the water subsided because they had been dropped where it had overflowed the banks and not in the stream itself. This suggested that the operation had been performed in darkness, and not by a local man.

The police therefore carried out inquiries over a wide area for persons missing before September 19. As they thought the remains had probably been taken to the bridge by motor-car, they tried to trace any unusual movements by the owners of cars registered in Dumfriesshire, and asked at garages and filling-stations for information about suspicious vehicles. Meanwhile the search of the ravine was continued with the help of bloodhounds. Nothing more came to light as a result of all this activity, and the murderer might have got away with it if he had been more careful — or if the police had been less astute.

After all the trouble he had taken to disfigure the remains of his victims, the murderer had made the elementary blunder of wrapping them up in articles that could be identified. The wrappings included straw, cotton-wool, pieces of a cotton sheet, a pillow-slip, a georgette blouse, a child's woollen rompers, and some newspapers. It was one of the papers — a copy of the *Sunday Graphic* dated September 15 — that gave the police the first and vital clue. One fragment of this paper showed part of a photograph of a girl wearing a crown, and on another fragment was the remains of a headline reading "——AMBE'S CARNIVAL QUEEN — ROWNED." On investigation it was found that these pieces had come from a special 'slip' edition of the paper prepared in connexion with a carnival held in Morecambe, near Lancaster. Only 3700 copies of this edition had been printed, and they had all been distributed in Morecambe, Lancaster, and the immediate vicinity.

This was discovered on October 9, and the Chief Constable of Dumfriesshire at once got into touch with the Lancaster Borough Police. By chance on the same day he had his attention directed to an item in a Glasgow newspaper about the disappearance three weeks previously from Lancaster of Mary Jane Rogerson, a nursemaid employed in the house of Buck Ruxton. Further inquiries brought out that the doctor's wife had left him about the same time. The Chief Constable of Dumfriesshire put two and two together, and asked the Advocate Depute to suggest to the medical experts that what they had been regarding as male human remains might be those of a strongly built female. A description of Mrs Ruxton accompanied the request.

Buck Ruxton was a Parsee. His name was originally Bukhtyar Hakim, and he qualified at the Universities of Bombay and London. After serving in the Indian Medical Service and then working in London, he settled in general practice in Lancaster in 1930. Isabella Ruxton, the woman he called his wife — actually they were never married — had then been living with him for two years. He was thirty-one, she was twenty-nine; and their relationship was both stormy and passionate. "We were the kind of people who could not live with each other and could not live without each other," he said at his trial; and added the French proverb, "Who loves most chastises most." He was excessively jealous and suspicious, and several times he used violence and threatened to kill her. Twice the police had to be called to his house because of his behaviour.

Mrs Ruxton, as she was always called, was alive on Saturday, September 14, 1935. She was at Blackpool with two sisters, for the illuminations. At 11.30 p.m. she drove back to Lancaster by herself. The car was there in the morning, so presumably she arrived; but she was never seen again.

The Ruxtons had three children, aged six, four, and two. They were looked after by the nursemaid, Mary Rogerson, a local girl of twenty. She also was not seen alive after September 14.

During the next few days Ruxton gave various explanations for the absence of the two women, but finally settled on their having gone together to Edinburgh. He gave a message to this effect to Mary Rogerson's stepmother.

Nothing more happened for over a week. Then, on Tuesday, September 24, Ruxton went to the police-station at Lancaster and protested against the questioning of one of his servants about the murder of a woman named Mrs Smalley. He said he knew nothing about Mrs Smalley's death — which was true enough —

and complained of interference in his private affairs. In his excitable, dramatic way he invited the police to search his house. Then he said he was the most miserable man on earth, as his wife had left him a fortnight before. He said he did not know where she had gone, but thought it was to Scotland.

The next day Ruxton saw Mary Rogerson's parents and told them that the girl was pregnant, and that Mrs Ruxton had taken her away to try to get this trouble over. It was now more than ten days since Mary had disappeared, and the girl's father said that if she was not back by the following Saturday — September 28 — he would report her to the police as missing. Ruxton asked him not to go to the police and promised to bring Mary back on the Sunday. In fact the parents waited until the evening of Tuesday, October 1, when they saw Ruxton again and then reported Mary's disappearance to the police.

On Friday, October 4, Ruxton went again to the police-station, complained again about the investigation into the murder of Mrs Smalley, and said his wife had gone to Edinburgh on September 15, taking her maid with her, and that he had not heard from them since. On October 9 he went to Edinburgh and saw Mrs Ruxton's sister, asking her if she was hiding his wife.

The following day he called on a woman named Mrs Hampshire whom he had employed to scrub down his staircase on the day after Mrs Ruxton and Mary Rogerson disappeared. Her husband had helped, and the doctor had given them some carpets, some felt stair-pads, and a suit of clothes, all stained with blood. When he called on Mrs Hampshire on October 19 he was greatly agitated and told her to burn one of the carpets and the suit. Before leaving he asked her if she would stand by him and not make a statement to the police until he had made one himself.

Ruxton went to the police-station the same evening, but not to make a statement. He complained that his name was being connected with the finding of human remains at Moffat. "All this damned nonsense is ruining my practice," he said. "Can nothing be done to stop this talk?" At the request of the police he supplied a full description of his wife and a photograph.

Meanwhile a police-officer took a statement from Mrs Hampshire, who handed over the bloodstained carpets, felt stair-pads, and the suit of clothes.

All this happened on October 10, the day when the Chief Constable of Dumfriesshire asked the Advocate Depute to suggest that the remains might be of two females instead of one female and one male.

The medical experts replied that it was possible.

The next day — October 11 — Ruxton repeated his complaint to Captain Vann, Chief Constable of the Lancaster Borough Police. "Can't you publish it in the papers that there is no connexion between the two" — meaning the bodies found at Moffat, and Mrs Ruxton and the maid — "and stop all this trouble?" Captain Vann made the careful and ominous reply that he would do that when he was satisfied there was no connexion between the two.

The same day the medical experts concluded that both bodies were definitely female. The head they had previously thought to be male was found to belong to the female trunk.

The investigation was now taken over by Captain Vann.

The georgette blouse found with the remains was shown to Mary Rogerson's stepmother, who recognized it at once. She said she had bought it at a jumble sale, mended it, and then given it to her stepdaughter. She identified it positively by the patch she had sewn under one arm.

Mrs Rogerson did not recognize the child's rompers, but said that they might have come from a woman named Mrs Holme, with whom the Ruxtons had stayed in June. Mrs Holme identified the rompers by a peculiar knot she had tied in the elastic. She said she had given them to Mary Rogerson for the Ruxton children when they stayed at her house.

The police found more bloodstained carpets in the possession of Ruxton's charwoman, Mrs Oxley. A local newsagent confirmed that a copy of the 'slip' edition of the *Sunday Graphic* had been delivered at the doctor's house on September 15.

At 9.30 p.m. on October 12 Captain Vann invited Ruxton to the police-station and formally cautioned him. Ruxton said he would be very pleased to make a statement. Their interview lasted until 7 a.m. the next morning, when Vann charged him with the murder of Mary Rogerson.

Later he was charged also with the murder of Mrs Ruxton, and it was on this indictment that he was tried.

The day after Ruxton's arrest Detective-Lieutenant Hammond of the Glasgow C.I.D. went to Lancaster to examine the doctor's house. Hammond stayed there for eleven days. He found a number of fingerprints and palm-prints which proved identical with those taken from the left hand of one of the victims of the murder. These prints were accepted by the court as proof of identity of the body of Mary Rogerson. Hammond also found two impressions of her right thumb, but these were of no value then as her right hand had not been found. However, it was discovered on November 4. Decomposition was so far advanced that the whole of the epidermis and much of the dermis had disappeared, but with great skill Hammond got a dermal print of the thumb. This matched the two impressions he had found in the house. This, I think, was the first occasion in Great Britain where dermal prints were used for identification purposes. For some obscure reason Scotland Yard advised the Director of Public Prosecutions not to lead the second part of the fingerprint evidence at the trial, and Hammond never got the credit he deserved for his work.

The police found straw in Ruxton's house, and samples were examined by agricultural experts and compared with the straw found with the remains; but the results were inconclusive. It was similarly impossible to identify the cotton-wool, although it was learnt that Ruxton had made a special purchase of two pounds on the day after his wife and maid disappeared. The pieces of cotton sheet used to wrap the remains were compared with a sheet on the Ruxtons' bed with much more positive results. The textile expert who examined them found them identical in every respect, even to a peculiar fault in the selvedge that showed they had come not only from the same loom but from the same warp in that loom.

Professor Glaister paid two visits to the house, and found plenty of blood and some human debris in the drains. There was evidence that the bodies had been dismembered in the bath, which the charwoman had found a uniform dirty yellow colour up to about six inches from the top. There were bloodstains on the bathroom door and floor as well as on the stairs and in other parts of the house. There was also evidence that the doctor had tried to burn bloodstained materials, including some of the carpets, in his back yard.

I arrived back in Edinburgh on November 7, and was asked the same evening to meet the Chief Constables of Edinburgh and Lancaster to discuss the case. They wanted me to confer with Professor Brash and report on the identification of the remains, and with Professor Glaister on the pathological findings, including the blood and other stains. By that time a fairly complete examination of the material had been made, and I had comparatively little to do beyond confirming the identification of the two bodies and giving a certain amount of help in general. Since two books have already been written on the case which gave in voluminous detail the medical examinations and the evidence produced at the trial, I do not propose to do more than discuss a few matters that interested me from a medico-legal aspect.

In removing all those parts of the bodies that might have been of use in identification the murderer had undoubtedly tried to destroy evidence of sex. However, with that carelessness which so often leads to the undoing of malefactors, he had left, among the masses of flesh and fat and skin which he had cut away, three female breasts and portions of sex organs which indubitably proved that at least two women were involved. The detailed examination of all the remains indicated with a considerable degree of certainty that there were not more than two.

From the seventy pieces recovered two bodies were reconstructed, complete except for one trunk and various odds and ends. There should have been no room for error about the sex of either. The younger of the two bodies — the one minus the trunk — was quite definitely female: there could be no doubt of that. The older body had certain mixed male and female characters. The head by itself might have caused some difficulty in deciding the sex, but fortunately the cuts in the tissues of the severed head and the cuts in the tissues of the neck attached to the thorax proved that the trunk and the older head were from the same body. For example, one of the cuts had passed through the cartilages of the larynx, leaving part of this in the trunk and the other part in the head. The trunk itself was in two parts, but the cut in the backbone of the chest portion fitted exactly the cut surface in the abdominal portion. The pelvis in the latter was undoubtedly that of a woman. Thus the questionable head, which had caused the first error in identification, was definitely proved to be female.

The ages and stature of the two bodies corresponded with those of Mrs Ruxton and Mary Rogerson, as did the colour of the hair, certain dental details, and other personal points. Ironically, once the identity of the remains was suspected, the mutilations helped to confirm identification by drawing attention to the very characteristics they were designed to conceal. The mutilation of a left foot, for example, was obviously done because Mrs Ruxton had a bunion and toes bent in a recognizable way. (As a matter of fact, it was not done very efficiently, for there was still evidence of a bone deformity that indicated a bunion.) The removal of the skin from Mary Rogerson's right forearm was clearly to prevent identification by a birthmark, and the excision of tissues from part of her right thumb only emphasized the fact that her thumb had borne a scar.

The most interesting aspect of the case to me was the information derived from superimposing a photograph of the skull on a photograph of the head of the missing person. This was done by Professor Brash, with the assistance of Detective-Constable Stobie of the Edinburgh C.I.D., and a very remarkable piece of work it was. The illustrations show how every detail of the skull fits into Mrs Ruxton's photograph. Admittedly it might be argued that there was no certainty about identification by this comparative technique; but Brash never claimed there was. The judge at the trial did not give this piece of evidence much prominence, but to my mind it was the most interesting in the case.

Brash also had flexible casts made from the feet of the two bodies, and these casts fitted accurately into the shoes of the missing women. Although this could not be accepted as proof of identity, it was one more link in the chain of circumstantial evidence.

The trial of Buck Ruxton was held at Manchester and opened on March 2, 1936. The Crown called over a hundred witnesses, of whom I was the last. By the time I went into the box, late on the eighth day of the trial, the case against Ruxton was already very strong. Norman Birkett was counsel for the defence, and Sir Bernard Spilsbury had advised him on the medical evidence. This was the first time I had been cross-examined by Birkett. As usual, he had a remarkable mastery over the technicalities of the case, and he did not miss a point in favour of the accused. Nor did he deviate in any detail from his customary courtesy towards a witness.

A number of medical and medico-legal experts had assisted in the preparation of the defence, and it was expected that Birkett would call them to give evidence. However, in the end he decided to call only the accused, thus reserving the right, as in the case of Annie Hearn, of addressing the jury after the closing speech for the Crown. In the witness box Ruxton, insignificant in appearance and pathetically nervous in manner, cut a sorry figure under cross-examination, and not all Birkett's eloquence could save him from being convicted and hanged.

Exactly how the murders were committed remained uncertain. They did not appear to be premeditated, and I do not think that Ruxton meant to kill. He was jealous and suspicious of Mrs Ruxton's relationship with another man, and I have no doubt that when she returned from Blackpool a quarrel broke out and he killed her in a fit of rage. From the congestion of her lungs it is probable that she died of asphyxia, and a fracture of her hyoid bone suggested this was caused by strangulation.

Mary Rogerson, who probably discovered the crime, was killed as a precautionary measure in order to prevent her from reporting the murder to the police. From the appearance of the wounds in her head it seemed likely that she had lived for a few hours after being rendered unconscious. How she was finally killed could not be ascertained, but she may have had her throat cut.

I estimated that the dismemberment and mutilation of the two bodies must have taken about eight hours. One can well imagine Ruxton's state of mind with that mass of flesh and bones in his bathroom. It looked sufficiently formidable to me when I saw it first in my laboratory. The worry it must have induced was sufficient reason for his overlooking so many details and making so many blunders.

Among the human remains there were, of course, numerous fragments of muscle, fat, and so on which could not be specifically attributed to one or other of the bodies. This was of little importance, since the muscular and fatty tissues had been stripped off the bones in a haphazard manner. Among the debris there was, however, one specimen of more than ordinary interest, which caused a good deal of speculation: a specimen of a cyclopean eye.

This phenomenon is named after the one-eyed monster that Homer described so vividly in the *Odyssey* (Book IX). The Cyclops, as the giant was called, found Odysseus and his men in his cave. After the monster had killed and eaten six of his men, Odysseus encouraged him to drink a large quantity of wine, which caused him to fall into a drunken sleep. Odysseus had already decided to blind the Cyclops by destroying his single eye. To this end he had prepared and sharpened a green olive pole. He had heated its point red-hot, and while four of his men thrust it into the eye of the monster Odysseus twisted it home. By this means the giant was rendered sightless, and Odysseus and his men escaped.

The term 'Cyclops' has since been applied to one-eyed monsters which have resulted from a defect in development of the brain and front of the skull causing the two eyes to become either partially or completely fused into one. This mal-development happens from time to time in sheep and pigs, and more rarely in human beings. As far as I know, these monsters die at birth or shortly afterwards from other malformations.

The specimen found in the Ruxton remains was not specifically identified, but it was certainly not human. It had evidently been preserved soon after its removal from the animal, and it showed no signs of decomposition such as those observed in the other remains. Ruxton at one time had been interested in ophthalmology, and probably he had collected the cyclopean eye as an interesting specimen. It may be that he emptied the preservative in which it had been kept into the human remains and inadvertently threw the specimen in as well.

The defence tried to make a point about this specimen being derived from a human baby, but it was quite definitely not human, and had no importance in the case, except as a red herring.

I expect that I was the only witness in the trial who had taken part in a case in which a human Cyclops was involved, details of which I published in the *Journal of Anatomy*. That has nothing to do with the Ruxton trial. Nor has an oddly prophetic piece by Thomas de Quincey, which Glaister and Brash quoted in their book on the *Medico-legal Aspects of the Ruxton Case*. The piece occurs in De Quincey's essay on "The English Mail-Coach" — Section 11, "The Vision of Sudden Death" — and it is so uncannily appropriate that it seems worth quoting again:

"But what was Cyclops doing here? Had the medical men recommended northern air, or how? I collected, from such explanations as he volunteered, that he had an interest at stake in some suit-at-law now pending in Lancaster."

17

Clues in Clothes

THE RUXTON CASE WAS NOT PARTICULARLY COMPLEX, BUT IT was noteworthy for the evidence, particularly of clothing and newspapers, collected by the police. It was a good example of that teamwork which is so essential in criminal investigation — the close association of medical and other scientific experts with the police.

A medical expert, however, is still a doctor, and though he may place his special knowledge at the disposal of the investigating authority he must be extremely careful when he is examining living people. He should not encourage an accused person to talk about the crime with which he is charged or about the events that led to his arrest. If during a medical examination a person says anything that might incriminate himself it should be neither recorded nor repeated.

There are, however, occasions when a doctor may use an admission to direct the police to certain lines of inquiry and action without actually divulging what has been said.

For example, I was once asked to examine a youth who alleged that he had been the subject of a murderous attack. This young man, according to the police history, had received a number of letters over a long period threatening him with death. He had been placed under police protection, but no open attempt on his life had been made until this occasion. His story was that he had been followed by a man in St Andrew Street, Edinburgh, and when he walked into a stairway he was brutally attacked with a razor. He shouted for help, and his assailant, whom he described in detail, ran away. He was in a weak and frightened state when he reported the matter to the police, and was bleeding from wounds in his back.

When I examined him I found that his 'wounds' consisted of a number of fine cuts just penetrating the skin between his shoulder-blades, more or less parallel to one another and apparently made from below upward by a right-handed man. They were undoubtedly self-inflicted, by means of a sharp instrument such as a razor used very carefully. I asked him how he managed to cut himself in the back with a safety razor without doing more damage. He at first protested that it was an attempted murder, but when I told him not to be silly he admitted he had made the cuts by fixing a razor-blade on the end of a cleft stick and doing the job by adjusting two mirrors. The various threatening letters I found to be in his own handwriting. He confessed to me that the whole thing was a fake.

I called in the sergeant who had accompanied the youth and, without divulging anything of what I had been told, suggested that if he took him into the next room he would hear the whole circumstances of the attacks. This was done in official style, and after being warned he duly confessed.

The police were not in the least amused. The sergeant asked in astonishment why the young man should have kept this play going on for months, wasting valuable police time. To me the explanation was simple enough. Here we had a miserable little runt of a man who had always been bullied and treated with contempt. By means of this fake he became at once a person of interest to the police. He had for months been under the care and protection of hefty constables — what a feeling of importance it gave him, and what interest it brought into his hitherto colourless life! It was only when he translated words into acts and came into the hands of the medical expert that his little world of make-believe blew up.

I felt I had been guilty of a slight breach of confidence, but made amends by recommending to the Procurator-Fiscal that it would be a good idea to let the case drop. He would, I thought, never repeat the offence, and as far as I know he never did.

Another time I received a confidence that later proved a little embarrassing.

I was investigating traces of foreign matter in the clothing of three men who had been arrested on suspicion of safe-breaking. I found quite a lot of incriminating material, such as particles of gelignite and sawdust and fragments of paint from the safe, in the clothing of two of the suspects, but nothing of the kind in the clothing of the third.

At that time I was interested in the manner in which certain physical characters in an individual might be deduced from an examination of his clothing.

I had made casts of the interiors of the boots of the three safe-breaking suspects purely for my own interest, and found that one pair suggested that the wearer had a deformity of the right foot and ankle. I got permission to examine him in prison, and found that my deduction about his condition was quite correct. He was very co-operative, and told me not only how he got his injury but also why he did a "bit of burglary on the side."

He was a cabinet-maker and earned good wages, but every now and then, he said, he got fed up with his work and burgled a house or broke a safe just for the fun of it. He told me how in this case he and two others had taken the safe out of the shop down to the seashore and burst the back open with boulders. I could have told him, but did not, that the particular safe that he had taken so much trouble to break could have been opened by unscrewing the back with an ordinary screwdriver; for it was one of those ridiculous safes that have the back screwed on and then painted over with green enamel to make it look like a welded safe.

The trial of the three men came on, and I duly gave evidence about the laboratory tests I had carried out on the incriminating material found in their clothes. This evidence was largely instrumental in convicting two of the accused. The third was my confidant with the deformed right foot. He elected to cross-examine me, and asked whether anything had been found in his clothes that might incriminate him in any way. I replied, of course, that I had not found anything. Since he knew that I knew exactly what part he had played in the safe-breaking, it was no doubt very amusing to him to obtain this evidence in his favour from the principal Crown witness.

There are few cases of breaking and entering in which the laboratory cannot be of use.

When a house or shop is broken into the intruder is almost certain to leave some marks of his presence, and to take away traces of materials that can prove his association with the scene of the crime. He may leave the tyre-marks of his car on the ground outside, his own footprints and fingerprints, and the marks of the tool he uses to force a window or door. At the same time, that tool is likely to carry away fragments of paint, wood, and glass, all of which can be identified in the laboratory. In general, we may say that no man can go to a place, commit a crime, and come away again without two things happening: he leaves behind him some trace by which he can be identified, and he carries away with him certain traces by which he can be connected with the crime.

The variety of material that may require analysis is almost without limit. At one time or another I have obtained valuable evidence from the examination of glass, sand, earth, paints, varnish, distemper, metal particles, oil, grease, lipstick and other cosmetics, polishes, woods, sawdust, and other vegetable matter such as algæ, fungi, and so on. Frequently several types of material require examination in the same case.

An example of this was a robbery from a bank strong-room, which had been entered by blowing the lock of the door. The putty used for packing the lock was found to be chemically identical, not only in its essential composition but also in its metallic contaminants, with putty found at the home of the suspect. Particles of paint were found in the turn-ups of his trousers and on the floor of his car, and these were found identical in all respects with paint that was scraped off the strong-room door. Gelignite had been used to blow the lock — and traces of gelignite were found in his raincoat pocket and on the fingers of his gloves. These chemical findings were significant enough, and their value was enhanced by the discovery on his trousers of coloured woollen fibres — light blue, dark blue, orange, yellow, green, and red — which could be matched exactly with coloured fibres from a rug on the floor of the bank.

When the case was heard an ingenious defence was advanced to explain the presence of traces of gelignite on the clothing of the accused. He was an owner of racing greyhounds, and, it was said, he used small doses of gelignite, administered in mince balls, to influence the running of his dogs adversely when a poor performance suited his purpose. In cross-examination I was asked by the accused whether gelignite could be used for the dopings. I confess it was something of a surprise question, but since the explosive contains nitrite the possible efficacy of such therapy had to be admitted. However, the plea was of no avail so far as the jury were concerned, and it may have done more harm than good. The presiding sheriff was a dog-lover, and appeared to think doping a dog was even more reprehensible than robbing a bank.

A common method of safe-breaking is to place a wad of gelignite over the keyhole, fix it in position by means of putty, "Plasticine," or something of the sort, attach a detonator with fuse, and cover up the safe with cushions or whatever is available to damp down the noise of the explosion. The force of the explosion disorganizes the lock, and the door can then be opened. Very often an excessive quantity of explosive is used, and then the door is smashed and the ballast or packing is scattered all over the place. This ballast varies in its constitution, but in the cases I have investigated it has usually been sawdust mixed with alum. One advantage of these substances is that if a fire breaks out they form a slag which protects the contents of the safe from being burnt. A disadvantage to the safe-breaker is that they have a habit of finding their way into the turn-ups of his trousers and other parts of his clothing.

One of the most interesting safe-breaking cases that I helped to investigate occurred in Aberdeen in 1938. A laundry was broken into at about half-past six in the morning of July 11, and approximately £300 was stolen from two safes. One of them had been forced open by explosives, the other was opened by means of a key found inside the first safe. Some of the money was contained in envelopes bearing details of their contents and its origin. Many of these had been opened, the money taken out, and the empty envelopes torn up and thrown on the floor. The floor was strewn also with the ballast used in packing the safe, which was the popular mixture of sawdust and alum. Samples of this from the floor of the laundry were sent to my laboratory for examination.

The police suspected that the burglary was the work of one of the toughest safe-breakers in Scotland, Johnny Ramensky. A strong, well-built young man with tremendous vitality, he had already been in the hands of the police on many occasions. He was rather a likeable character really, and even the police, with whom he had waged war since boyhood, regarded him with some respect and even affection. Four years before the laundry case he had gained quite a lot of notoriety by escaping from Peterhead Prison, from which it was said to be impossible to escape. He had got out on a cold winter's night by clinging to a ledge for half an hour by his hands alone and then swinging himself over the outside wall. Clad only in his underpants, he swam the river and lived without food for two days, and slept in a very cold garage until he was re-arrested. A tough fellow, you must admit.

After finishing his sentence Ramensky was released in 1938. During the next month or two safes blown in various places from Clydebank to Manchester were suspected of being his workmanship. He was living in Glasgow at the time of the Aberdeen robbery, but the police got information that a man answering his description had hired a taxi at a stand about two miles from the laundry and been driven in it to Stonehaven. There he had hired another cab, which took him to Perth and put him down at the railway-station. From Perth he had not gone by rail, but hired another taxi which took him to Glasgow.

Photographs of several men, including Johnny Ramensky, were shown to various witnesses, including the taxi-drivers. They all identified him as the man they had seen. Glasgow police were notified, and he was arrested in the early morning of July 12, the day after the robbery. Pretty good police work, but there was more to come.

The Glasgow police found in his possession a Murray's A.B.C. railway time-table, in which there was a small piece of white paper. They did not take much notice of this at the time, being more interested in a crease that had been made to mark the page showing the Perth-Glasgow service. This time-table was later sent to the Glasgow Fingerprint Department, for examination of the crease. The piece of white paper fell out, and Aberdeen police-officers, who were there at the time, examined it and found written on it "8th July, 1938." It occurred to them that this might be part of one of the envelopes taken from the safe and torn up at the laundry, and they took the fragment back to Aberdeen. Sure enough, they found three other pieces of an envelope with which this one made almost a complete envelope.

The police also examined Ramensky's clothes and found some traces of material that they thought might be safe-ballast or packing, although it was evident that the clothing had recently been cleaned and brushed. That was to be expected, for Johnny Ramensky had been through this sort of examination before. In 1934 traces of safe-ballast had been found in the turn-ups of his trousers and in the welts of his shoes, and these had been sent to me for comparison with samples taken from a burgled safe. I had found the specimens identical, and this had helped towards the conviction of Ramensky, who was sentenced to five years' penal servitude. This time it was assumed that he might have taken the precaution of dusting down his clothes, especially the turn-ups of his trousers, to get rid of any incriminating traces. The police therefore examined the interiors of the Aberdeen and Stonehaven taxi-cabs, and from them they collected a quantity of dust and debris. All this material was forwarded to me for examination.

Altogether there were forty-seven items, including all the clothes Ramensky had been wearing at the time of his arrest. Certainly he had brushed out the turn-ups, but I was still able to extract from them a number of small crystals and a few fragments of wood, and I found more crystals on the surface of the right leg. More of these materials appeared in the space between the soles and uppers of his shoes. There were similar minute fragments of wood and crystals in the sealed containers sent by the police, containing traces they had taken from his clothes and from the two taxi-cabs.

The crystals were all composed of alum. The sawdust in the ballast contained four different kinds of wood — Scotch pine, spruce, and two hard woods, probably beech and birch; samples of all four were found in Ramensky's clothes and in the materials from the taxi-cabs.

I passed the wood samples to my colleague, Mr J. L. S. Smith, of the Botanical Department of Edinburgh University. An authority on forest botany, he confirmed the identification of the four woods and made the further and most important discovery that all four varieties were infected by a fungus of the same nature. This fungal infection was found not only in the sawdust from the safe-packing but also in certain of the fragments taken from Ramensky's clothing and in the sweepings from one of the taxi-cabs.

I also received the piece of white paper found in Ramensky's time-table and the three matching pieces from the laundry. As an example of how we examined material of this sort, here is an extract from the report I made to the Procurator-Fiscal at the time:

> When fitted together, the four pieces are found to fit accurately, one portion still being missing which would have completed the envelope. Running across the bottom of the reconstructed envelope there are the words "XA Laundry Drwgs. Friday, 8th July, 1938. £3.11.0." This inscription runs across two of the fragments found

in the laundry and the fragment found on the person of the accused. The junction between one portion of the torn envelope found in the laundry and the portion found in possession of the accused cuts through the figure '8' and across the tail of the 'J' of July. There is also a small pencil spot on one of the fragments which runs into the fragment found on the accused. The paper has been examined by ultra-violet light and by appropriate tests, and all fragments are found to be identical in nature. The marking of the pencil is the same, the writing is in the same hand, and the junction between the fragments is accurately defined. I certify therefore that the three fragments found in the laundry and the fragment found on the person of the accused are all fragments of one envelope.

Ramensky was convicted and sentenced to another five years' imprisonment. In sentencing him Lord Russell said, "I am sure that a man of your ability could earn a livelihood in some honest way."

As it happened Ramensky was able later to prove that this was true. When he came out of prison he joined the Army and became a Commando, and turned his undoubted talents to the service of his country. He was frequently parachuted behind the enemy lines for the purpose of committing sabotage, breaking into head-quarters of the opposing Army Command, and similar missions. It has been stated that when the Allies occupied Rome it was found that the Germans had locked a strong-room in which there were believed to be important documents, and none of the specialists could open the door. Johnny Ramensky volunteered to crack the safe, and, I am told, had it open in less than half an hour.

We were all hoping that he had definitely turned over a new leaf when he returned to civilian life, but eventually the call of the wild was too much for him.

He achieved further notoriety when he escaped from Peterhead in 1952, and again in 1958. Each time he was recaptured within a few days. He is still serving a sentence of ten years' preventive detention that was imposed on him for a safe-breaking exploit in Glasgow at the end of 1955. A pity, for he seemed essentially a good fellow.

No doubt a criminal thinks it hard lines to be convicted on evidence derived from tiny particles of material such as I have spoken of in many of my cases; but it must be even more galling to him to be convicted on evidence from material that he cannot even see. Minute traces of material, too small to be visible to the naked eye, can be identified and compared by means of various types of microscope. Further, their chemical nature can be identified by means of the spectrograph even when in quantities so minute that the ordinary chemical analysis fails. Many common things that look the same can be proved to be of quite different origin by the detection in them of minute traces of foreign matter; for example, most bits of glass or spots of white paint look alike — they may even have the same principal ingredients — but there is usually one or other of the rarer elements in them which can be identified by the spectrograph, and this may prove identity or non-identity of two samples.

An example of this occurred when a young cat-burglar named Coogan was brought to me for examination. A shop had been broken into by cutting through the iron bars protecting a window, and Coogan was suspected of the offence. The police brought him to my laboratory wearing the same clothes as he had on when he was arrested. He was a short young man, and the bars he was said to have filed through were above his head, so that he would have had to stretch up to reach them. It had occurred to the police that some of the filings might have fallen on his cap and coat. I went over both garments with a magnet, and, sure enough, quite a few fragments of iron filings were obtained from each. These were sent to the chemical laboratory for spectroscopic examination and comparison with filings that the police took from the iron bars of the shop.

To the naked eye all iron filings look pretty much alike, although they may have come from widely differing sources, but the chemists found minute quantities of other elements in specimens from each source that proved their common origin. These trace elements may have been accidental impurities, or may have been added deliberately to confer specific properties on the metal for industrial purposes; whichever it was, they served the purpose of establishing identity.

While I was going over Coogan with the magnet I noticed that the right shoulder of his coat and the right side of his cap were wet through, all the rest of his clothing being dry. This was odd, but the young constable in charge of him remembered that the rhone just above the barred window was leaking, and that a drip was falling when they were obtaining samples of filings for comparison. This point might have been of interest, but in fact it was not necessary for the case. When Coogan learnt of the incriminating traces found on him he elected to plead guilty. He admitted it was "a fair cop," though he thought that laboratory methods were not giving shop-breakers a fair deal.

I came into contact with Coogan again some months after his release.

On October 5, 1937, a draper's shop in Edinburgh was broken into after dark, and nineteen ladies' dresses and £2 15s. in cash were stolen. The burglar had got in by climbing up a soil-pipe to a window on the first floor and undoing the snib with a knife. Fingerprints were found on the cash-box from which the money had been stolen and on a bottle that had been removed from a suitcase in the display-room. The fingerprint department identified the impression on the cash-box as the left thumb-print of Coogan. The print on the bottle was not identified from the files.

The following morning Coogan was arrested at his home. In the house with him was a well-known Glasgow housebreaker, and he was arrested as well. His fingerprints were taken and compared with those on the bottle. Nine points of resemblance were found, but as at least sixteen points are required for evidence of identification he was liberated.

The house was searched, but none of the stolen goods were found. The police took possession of a pair of rubber shoes which they thought might have something to do with the case. Coogan said they were his, and his wife backed him up. Eventually the police passed them over to me.

They had flecked grey cotton uppers and rubber soles, the rubber extending for about half an inch on to the uppers: ordinary gym-shoes, in fact, but extraordinarily interesting. On the inner side of the instep of each there was an area about four inches in diameter deeply marked with iron rust. This staining could quite well have been caused by climbing up the soil-pipe of the shop. The iron rust was contaminated with black material. Parts of the rubber soles and the cotton uppers had been worn by friction. I thought that fragments of the shoes might still be sticking to the soil-pipe, especially if there should be a bracket fixing the pipe to the wall.

The police at once made another examination of the pipe, and collected a lot of the sort of material I had expected them to find. In this material, well mixed with iron rust and flecks of black paint, were quite a number of fibres which proved to be precisely similar to the grey cotton fibres of the upper parts of the shoes. There were also bits of rubber that corresponded with the rubber soles.

In the meantime I compared the iron rust on the shoes with the sample of rust taken from the soil-pipe. They appeared identical, and both contained the same kind of lead paint. This was suspicious enough, but hardly amounted to proof of identity. However, on one of the shoes, caught in the broken rubber of the sole, I found several blue and red woollen fibres, and these proved identical with fibres taken from a thick woollen carpet on the floor of the showroom. With the fingerprint evidence this seemed enough to bring Coogan to trial.

The case had its humorous side. When Coogan appeared at the Sheriff Court both he and his wife denied that the shoes were his. This denial was corroborated by the Glasgow housebreaker, who elected to give evidence for his friend. The shoes were his, he said, and he had left them at Coogan's house.

Coogan was convicted on the fingerprint evidence and sentenced to three months' imprisonment. At the conclusion of the trial the Glasgow man was arrested on his own sworn statement that the shoes were his property. He was tried later at the same court and, on the evidence derived from the shoes, supported by the rather blurred fingerprint on the bottle, he also was found guilty, and was sent to prison for six months.

I met Coogan for the third time in the mortuary. I was just asked to look at an unknown body, and there he was. He had fallen from a considerable height when a soil-pipe that he was climbing gave way, and was instantaneously killed. I was interested to find that the cat-burglar had almost prehensile big toes and thick pads of skin on the balls of both feet, indubitably due to constant climbing.

A book could be written on the pathology of clothing. Apart altogether from incriminating traces of materials that may be found on them, clothes themselves can reveal a mass of information about the identity, habits, and actions of their wearer. Some indication of this was given in the Karam case, at Alexandria. An equally interesting case occurred at Falkirk in 1937.

On November 28 of that year a man was arrested after breaking into a shop. He was caught on the premises in his stockinged feet.

He had entered the shop from the back, first climbing a drain-pipe, near which a pair of boots was found. The burglar said these were his.

In the same district two other burglaries had occurred, one on September 14 and the other on November 1. All three had strongly similar features — the method of approach, the mode of entry, the approximate time of breaking in, and the intruder's general conduct on the premises. In each case the burglar had left his footwear behind, near the place where he had broken in. He had apparently taken them off to climb a drainpipe at the back of the premises and after finishing the job had let himself out of the front door. In one of the cases a pair of boots had been left, in the other two a pair of shoes.

The man caught doing the third burglary denied any know-ledge of the other two. The detective who had charge of the case was convinced that the same man had done all three jobs, and he sent the three pairs of footwear to my laboratory for me to find out if they could have been worn by the same man.

This was not a difficult problem, since every individual has his own characteristic way of walking. If boots or shoes are worn long enough changes occur in the soles and heels and also in the uppers by which the wearer can be identified. These were no exception, and it was not hard to prove that they had all been worn by the same feet.

Nor was this the end of the story that the footwear had to tell. In the pair claimed by the accused as his own there were distinct differences between the right and left boots. The right upper was bulged over the base of the great toe; the left showed no such full-ness, but was rather wrinkled at that part. The marks of the laces were more deeply impressed on the right upper part than on the left. These differences suggested the possibility that the right foot was bigger than the left.

The right sole was more worn throughout than the left, and was very thin in the centre; this showed that most of the weight of the body was borne by the right leg. The greatest wearing of the left sole was at the toe and the adjacent inner margin. In the centre of the left sole there was a series of curved concentric lines, indicating that the left foot had rotated while bearing weight. The right heel was much worn, especially at the back and on the outer side; the left heel was comparatively free from wear.

The differences between right and left boots were very well

marked, and gave the impression that the wearer's feet differed in length and breadth. They indicated also the manner in which each foot was used in walking.

When I examined the other two pairs of footwear I found exactly the same characteristic differences between right and left feet. This confirmed the fact that all three pairs had been worn by the same man. I also knew now that he suffered from a deformity of the left foot.

Having deduced this, I thought I would try to glean some more information from the impressions made by the feet inside the boots and shoes. So I had gelatin-glycerine casts prepared of the insides of the three pairs of footwear.

The casts in all three cases were practically identical, and they brought out certain characteristics of the burglar's feet that were of the greatest interest.

The right foot was about an inch longer and half an inch broader than the left. The right cast showed distinct impression of five toes; the ball of the foot made complete contact with the sole of the boot, and pressure areas were seen on the outer side of the instep and the heel. The left cast showed that the great toe made the most marked impression, indicating that most of the weight of the body had been borne on that toe. Only three other toe impressions could be seen; this suggested that either one toe had been lost or that it overrode two of the others. There was practically no impression of the ball of the foot, the instep, or the heel, which showed that the left foot was shrunken and smaller than the right. The fact that the great toe was the main source of support indicated that the left leg was shorter than the right.

So from the examination of his footwear I was now able to build up quite a distinctive picture of the man. It was not at all what one would have expected of a cat-burglar, and it was really quite extraordinary that a man with his disabilities should have taken up such a physically exacting profession.

According to my inferential picture, he had a deformity of the left leg and foot — namely, a short leg and a withered foot, no doubt the result of paralysis of the leg which had occurred in infancy. He had either lost a left toe or had a deformity such as a hammer-toe. He walked with a limp, characterized by a twist of the left foot so as to bring the heel in and the toe out. His left foot drooped, and the tip of the great toe dragged or scraped on the ground when he moved forward. He had a curvature of the spine due to the pelvis being dipped to the affected side. He was probably short in stature.

All this was deduced from the evidence of the boots and shoes. I did not see the man until I gave evidence against him at his trial. I had still not seen him walk when I told the court in some detail how I thought he walked. I remembered wondering then what would have happened if he had stood up and said, "This is all nonsense — I can walk just as well as anyone else." But he did not, and he was convicted of all three burglaries and sentenced to a term of imprisonment. He afterwards frankly confessed, and agreed to let me examine him in prison and take photographs including a slow-motion cinematographic study of his gait. In fact, he appeared to be rather flattered by our attentions.

We found that the story told by the boots was true in every respect. The man was of less than average stature — five feet three and a half inches — and his left leg was two and a half inches shorter than the right. He had been lame since an attack of infantile paralysis in childhood. He had a pronounced lateral curvature of the spine to compensate for the shortness of his left leg. The muscles of the left leg, thigh, and buttock were shrunken, and his left foot was withered and deformed. All the toes were there, but the fourth overrode the third and fifth. His gait corresponded closely to what I had inferred from the markings on the boots and shoes.

I do not know of any previous case in which the impressions of the feet inside footwear were used for identification, but the results seem to have established the usefulness of taking such casts. In this particular case we did not begin our investigations until the man was already under arrest, and the purpose of our work then was to discover proof of his guilt. Had he still been at large, however — or, indeed, had either or both the pairs of footwear left after the first two burglaries been brought to the laboratory when they were found — a good description of the wanted man could have been given to the police.

The same method might also be used in other kinds of investigation. In cases of mutilation or dismemberment, for example, casts from the interior of footwear of a missing person may, on comparison with the feet of the victim, give conclusive evidence for or against identification.

18

Accident, Suicide, or Murder?

THE QUESTION WHETHER A FATAL INJURY WAS HOMICIDAL, suicidal, or accidental is as common in real life as it is in detective fiction.

It arises whenever a person dies from injuries to which there are no reliable eye-witnesses, and sometimes it is extremely difficult to answer. The difficulties may be inherent in the circumstances; they may also be fabricated.

It is natural for a murderer to try to escape detection by making his crime look like suicide or accident, and such attempts have doubtless been going on for a long time. One cannot say how long, for one never hears about them when they succeed. However, records of failures take us quite far back.

There was Sir Edmund Berry Godfrey, for example, who was found impaled on his sword in 1678. At first sight it looked like suicide, as it was meant to. But post-mortem examination showed that he had been strangled, and at the trial which ensued two surgeons testified that the sword-thrust was inflicted after death, and that his death was due to homicidal violence. Three men were found guilty of murder and subsequently hanged.

There was no suggestion of suicide in the case of a farmer whose body I examined in a field, although his hand was on his gun. Here the question was between accident and murder.

The man lived in the farmhouse with his wife. The only other person about the farm was a boy of fifteen, who lived in a bothy close to the house. The farmer was forty-nine years old, addicted to drink, and undoubtedly difficult to live with.

The farmhouse was situated a few miles from a small town. The day before the body was discovered the farmer went into the town, and stayed until the public-houses had closed. Then he took a bus to the road that led to his own house. When he got off the bus, at about 11 p.m., he was definitely under the influence of drink but able to walk. The farm lad told the police the next day that the farmer had entered the bothy, drunk and shouting as usual, and said, "Are you no coming oot wi' me to shoot some cushies?" Apparently he was in the habit of shooting 'cushies' — pigeons — at night. According to his own story, the boy was frightened and hid his head under the bedclothes, and the farmer went away. The boy said he knew nothing more till the next morning, when he found the farmer's body lying in a field. He told the farmer's wife, who did not go to look herself or obtain medical assistance but simply sent for the police. She said she had gone to bed at 10.25 p.m. and heard nothing after that. Her husband ordinarily kept his gun in the kitchen, and he could have taken it out without her being any the wiser. The suggestion was that in his drunken state he had gone out to shoot pigeons, and had accidentally shot himself. However, the doctor who examined the body was suspicious, and he got into touch with me. I was able to be on the spot by two o'clock the same afternoon.

The body lay face downward in long grass, with both arms stretched out in front. The head was lying in the direction of the farm buildings, which were about seventy-five yards away. The cap was on the back of the head, and when we removed it we saw that the scalp was covered with clotted blood. This had come from severe injuries on the crown and left side of the head, which had not been caused by gunshot. In contrast with this heavy bloodstaining, the inside lining of the cap was hardly stained at all. This implied that it had been placed on the head some time after the head injuries had been received.

About the middle of the back of the jacket there was a large patch of blood. This stain was only on the outside of the garment, and there was no wound in that part of the body that could explain it. I lifted the tail of the jacket, and pulled it up over his head. The patch of blood exactly covered the bleeding area of the scalp. It followed that the man's head and the back of the jacket had been in contact shortly after the head wounds were inflicted, and while they were still bleeding.

It was easy to deduce why. The inside of the jacket lining was badly stained with earth, and there were bits of vegetable matter sticking to it. The jacket, waistcoat, and shirt were rucked up towards the shoulders, and in the wrinkles there were earthy stains and fragments of straw and vegetable matter. The braces were smeared with earth, and under the loops and buttons were wedged earth, bits of grass, and a fragment of a plant — a plant, incidentally, that was not growing where the body lay. There was a considerable amount of vegetable matter embedded in and adhering to the blood on the scalp, and many bits of dry and green vegetable matter were embedded in smears of blood on the backs of the hands.

All this could mean only one thing. The body had been dragged along the ground for some distance on its back after the injuries to the head had been inflicted.

The body had probably been grasped by the legs and dragged feet first. As it was drawn along the jacket was pulled up behind the head. Hence the patch of blood in the middle of the back of the jacket — which, no doubt, prevented the blood leaving a trail on the ground.

Lying at right angles to the body was a double-barrelled shotgun. The outstretched left hand touched the stock. The left chamber of the gun held a discharged cartridge; the right was empty, and the hammer on that side was at full cock. As the body was lying, we could see a shotgun wound on the left sleeve. The pellets had passed through the outer side of the arm, and some of them through the left back panel of the coat.

We turned the body over — and there was another characteristic shotgun wound on the left side of the face.

It was a very extensive wound, and had caused profuse bleeding. There was no clear indication of the flow of blood in any particular direction, however, and certainly no evidence of blood running down the neck.

This meant that the wound on the face had not been inflicted when the body was dragged along on its back.

The facial wound had more to tell us than this. It had been drawn upward towards the eye, and it was ingrained with dirt.

The waistcoat, shirt, cardigan, and singlet were rucked up towards the head at the front, just as they were at the back. Again there was considerable contamination of the clothes with earth and loose vegetable matter. Further, the palms of the hands and tips of the fingers were rubbed.

The conclusion was that the body had been dragged along face downward — after the infliction of the wound on the face.

There had been no clothing over this wound to absorb the

blood, and we soon found a distinct trail of bloodstains on the grass. It ran in a fairly straight line from the body towards the bothy and farmhouse. Along this line we found ragged particles of cloth and three cartridge wads. The cloth was later proved to have been blown from the farmer's jacket and shirt-sleeve by the discharge from his gun. The wads of cartridge were identical with wads found in the farmhouse, and were the same brand as the discharged cartridge in the gun.

The bloodstained trail continued for forty-six feet. It ended — or rather, began — close to a post on the edge of a stack-yard which stood between the farm-buildings and the paddock where the body was found.

At the place where the trail ended there was little sign of blood and the surface of earth was smooth — too smooth, I thought, and I dug under it with a penknife. As I had expected, earth had been placed over heavy bloodstains and patted down. There was a good deal of clotted blood an inch or two underneath.

When we had learnt all we could from the body on the spot we had it removed to the mortuary for a post-mortem examination.

It was clear from the loss of blood that all the injuries had been inflicted before death.

The wounds on the head had caused three separate fractures of the skull. They had apparently been caused by a number of blows from a blunt instrument, very possibly the butt-end of an axe. The injuries were severe and likely to cause unconsciousness, but were not in themselves likely to lead to death. From their shape and position, it looked as if they had been struck from above.

The gunshot injury to the face was the immediate cause of death. It had caused not only a considerable degree of shock and hæmorrhage but also asphyxia by inhalation of blood into the lungs. No specific sign of burning or powder-marks was visible to the naked eye, but embedded powder grains could be seen under the microscope. The shot was probably fired from a distance of about two yards.

Even apart from the fact that the gun contained only one spent cartridge, it was clear that the two gunshot injuries could not have been caused by both gun-barrels being discharged simultaneously. The shots had been fired from different positions. The direction of the facial wound was almost horizontal, and went from front to back. The shot that caused the injury to the left upper arm had been fired from about three yards, also from the front, but at a fairly acute angle from above downward and somewhat from left to right. After examining the entrance- and exit-holes in the jacket and shirt, we reconstructed the shooting in the laboratory, and deduced that the farmer was in a reclining position when this shot was fired. The holes in the clothing told us also that it had been fired after the shirt had been rucked up behind by dragging on the back and the tail of the jacket had fallen back into its normal position.

Our next step was to try to deduce the probable time of the injuries and death. For this there were various factors to take into account. The first was the presence and extent of rigor mortis.

When I examined the body at 2 p.m. rigor was complete. It is impossible to fix the time of death with any degree of certainty from this condition, but on the average it usually takes from ten to twelve hours. On this basis death would have occurred some time between 2 a.m. and 4 a.m., or possibly earlier.

The next factor was the retention of heat in the body after death. Its temperature at 4 p.m. was 81 degrees Fahrenheit. Assuming it was about normal at the time of death, it had therefore lost about 17 degrees. The atmospheric temperature at 4 p.m. was 68 degrees. Again, it is not possible to be certain about the rate of cooling of a body, but we could reckon that it would have lost about 8 degrees in the first four hours and about 1 degree an hour afterwards. If this was correct death occurred at about 3 a.m.

Finally, there was the relationship between the alcohol content of the blood and urine. Ordinarily the two figures are approximately the same, or frequently 1:1·3. In this case the amount in the urine was three times as much as in the blood. This was rather extraordinary, but was no doubt due to the fact that whereas the alcohol in the blood gradually diminishes by oxidation, alcohol already excreted into the bladder alters very little. From this and other physiological data we were able to calculate that the farmer had lived for about five and a half hours after he stopped drinking. The public-house closed at 10 p.m., and there was no evidence that he had any more alcohol after that hour; so by this estimate the time of death was about 3.30 a.m.

The farmer left the bus at 11 p.m. If, as we thought, he did not die till about four hours later, what happened in the meantime? When was he injured, and what was the relationship of the injuries to one another?

We knew he must have died quite shortly after the gunshot wound of the face, for the blood was inhaled into the lung, and death must have occurred within a few minutes of that. We knew that the head injuries occurred before both the gunshot wounds. A microscopic examination of the scalp showed that the head injuries were inflicted an hour or so before death. Among the areas of bleeding we found a few leucocytes, or white blood-corpuscles — not a great many, but enough to show that life had continued for some time after the injuries.

With all these facts in our possession it seemed possible to reconstruct the crime. What probably happened was something like the following.

The farmer arrived at the farm a little after 11 p.m. roaring tight. He was attacked and struck several times on the head by a fairly heavy weapon such as the butt-end of an axe. Either he was attacked while sitting or his assailant was at a higher level. The attack probably took place near the bothy or farmhouse, because there were marks of whitewash on his clothes. He fell backward unconscious, bleeding freely from his wounds. He was immediately grasped by the legs and dragged feet first on his back for a considerable distance into the stack-yard. There he was left for dead, and he stayed there for two or three hours. Then the assailant, or assailants, decided to fake a shooting accident. He took the farmer's gun from the kitchen, and went to the stack-yard to place it beside the body. But he found his victim sitting up, or in a kneeling position, trying to scramble to his feet. The assailant decided to finish him off by shooting, and fired from a distance of about three yards. The shot passed obliquely from above downward, through the farmer's left arm. The assailant thought he had missed. So he advanced to a closer range and discharged the second barrel, the shot entering the farmer's face. He fell on his face, bleeding profusely, beside the post on the edge of the stack-yard. His assailant then dragged him on his face, feet first, into the grass paddock. Finally he placed the weapon near his victim's outstretched hands, and the cap, which had fallen off previously, on the back of his head over the already dried blood from the injuries caused by the axe.

The fact that no bloodstained trail was found in the stack-yard had already been explained by the farmer's jacket being pulled up behind his head as he was dragged along. In the stack-yard, about half-way between the bothy and where the body was found — and nowhere else in the vicinity — there was a clump of the same plant that we had found wedged under the loops of the dead man's braces. A considerable number of fine hairs had been found sticking to the patch of blood about the middle of the back of his jacket; identical hairs were found in the stack-yard near the post. Their presence in the bloodstains showed that the farmer's jacket had fallen into normal position after he had been dragged on his back.

If my reconstruction was correct pellets of shot ought to be somewhere in the stack-yard near the bloodstained area by the post. I suggested where they might be found, and the police searched. On digging they obtained twenty-three pellets in almost the exact area where the reconstruction placed them.

It looked as if the murder had been committed by one or more persons in or about the farm. The only two persons in the locality were the farmer's widow and the boy, and they were both arrested.

The boy then made a full confession. He said the farmer's wife had suggested the murder, and they had lain in wait together until the farmer returned. She had attacked her husband with an axe, and together they had dragged the body into the stackyard. The boy said that afterwards they had gone back to the body and that the wife had given him the gun to do the shooting, after which she had cleaned off the fingerprints and removed the fired cartridge in the right barrel. The lad said that after the bloodstained mass at the scene of the crime was cleaned up the woman cleaned the axe and black-leaded round it, and burnt some bloodstained clothing and the spent cartridge.

The police searched the premises and found two axes, one with marks of black-leading round the head and handle as described by the boy. It was stained with human blood, and had a few hairs on the butt-end. The blood was of the same group as the farmer's, and the hair was similar to his. They found also bloodstains on some clothing and a towel belonging to the boy, of the same group as the farmer's but different from the boy's. No traces of blood were found on any of the woman's clothes. The butt-end of a cartridge was found in some debris in the spot indicated by the boy, and it was proved that this cartridge had been fired from the right barrel of the gun. Various other bits of information were obtained, and the boy's story was more or less corroborated. One weak point about it, however, was the fact that if he had carried out the whole thing himself the corroboration would have been just as good. In other words, except for his story, there was nothing that implicated the woman.

However, the Crown charged her with murder, and the boy was cited as the principal witness against her. The defence objected on the grounds that he was mentally deficient, but this objection was overruled. The mental expert for the Crown admitted that such boys were imaginative and inventive, and that in a matter of life and death he was of the opinion that no great reliance could be placed on what he said. When the boy was cross-examined he said that the farmer had been in the habit of getting into bed with him and "playing" with him, which he did not like; and this led to a suggestion that he might have considered revenge. The whole truth of the matter, however, remains a mystery. In the absence of corroboration the woman was, as expected, found not guilty, and the case is still unsolved.

The question whether a death is due to murder or suicide is often complicated by the curious means that people sometimes use to kill themselves. Anyone not familiar with the vagaries of suicides would consider some of these methods impossible. For example, in Egypt it was by no means uncommon for women to commit suicide by saturating their garments with paraffin and setting them alight. Then I have seen a case of attempted suicide by driving a four-inch nail through the forehead into the brain; the nail was removed with the greatest difficulty, and the man made a surprisingly good recovery.

Cutting through the tissues at the back of the neck with a blunt knife might be thought rather an absurd way of attempting to kill oneself, but I saw such a case once. It was not a success. In another odd case a maid in a hospital hacked the front of her head with a hatchet, inflicting twenty cuts; then, finding this ineffective, she filled a bath with warm water and drowned herself. I wonder how often any of us doctors, finding a number of hatchet wounds in the skull, would think of suicide.

Dr Mason of Hull sent me photographs of an equally odd suicide by multiple means. A man was found hanging, and from the surroundings in which the body was found and the general information available it was undoubtedly a genuine case of suicide. The body had, however, a bullet-wound on the right side of the face and another in the palm of the left hand; five cut wounds of the throat; and cuts over the left wrist, dividing the muscle tendons but not the larger blood-vessels. Apparently he had made attempts to shoot himself, to cut his throat, and to open the arteries in his wrist, all of which were ineffective. He then, in desperation, hanged himself — a final and successful effort.

I could recount many other queer cases. When I lectured to my students on multiple methods of suicide I generally finished up by relating the most outstanding case of all, a classic of its kind, which is, unfortunately, not susceptible to confirmation. I might say that it is *not* one of my cases.

The story is that a highly pessimistic individual had determined to take his life, and wanted to make sure that there would be none of the slip-ups he had read about. He decided that hanging would be an efficient means of self-destruction, and selected a tree with a stout branch overhanging a cliff, the sea being fifty feet below. This, he thought, would make a fitting and spectacular finish. In order to prevent any pain in the hanging process he procured for himself a large dose of opium. Although these arrangements seemed fairly complete, he decided that to make certain of a successful result it would be a good idea to shoot himself as well. The noose adjusted, the poison taken, and the revolver cocked, he stepped over the cliff, and as he did so fired. The jerk of the rope altered his aim, and the bullet missed his head but cut partly through the rope. This broke with the jerk of the body, and he fell fifty feet into the sea below. There he swallowed a quantity of salt water, vomited the poison, and swam ashore a better and wiser man.

A very extraordinary suicide case that I saw myself occurred in Aberdeen. I was in the city visiting Dr Richards, the lecturer in forensic medicine, and assisting him in the examination of students at the University. The case occurred while I was there, and Richards took me along. It was suicide by coal-gas, which, as every one knows, is very common, and as a rule hardly worth recording. This case, however, was different. The deceased, who was a plumber, had connected a tube to the gas-pipe before it entered the meter, and so all the way to the room where his body was found. Being an Aberdonian, he must have felt a strong sense of satisfaction in thus committing suicide at the expense of the Corporation. I told this story to our Principal, Sir Thomas Holland, when I got back from Aberdeen, and I'm sure he enjoyed it for the rest of his life, for he retold it to me many, many times.

No doubt there is a motive behind all our actions, and few if any sane persons act without a reason. It would be wrong, however, to assume that the reason can always be appreciated by another person. So well is this understood that the law does not demand that a motive be proved in a case of murder — although, of course, juries are seldom satisfied unless they are presented with sufficient motive or reason for a serious crime.

The motive is often inexplicable in cases of suicide as well as murder, and this aggravates the difficulty of discovering which it was. I recall the case that occurred when I was in Egypt of a young soldier of good character who left barracks with a certain amount of mess money in his possession, and was found dead in a banana plantation some miles away. There was a suspicion of murder combined with robbery, but all the conditions suggested he had shot himself. Beside the body lay a Webley service revolver, from which two shots had been fired. There was an entrance-wound of a bullet in the right temple, and the bullet had traversed the brain from right to left and passed out above and behind the left ear. At the time of firing, the muzzle of the revolver had been been in contact with the skin. It was, in fact, a typical suicidal bullet-wound, and I had no hesitation in deciding it was self-inflicted, although the man had no apparent reason for taking his life.

In another case in Egypt the dead body of a man was found on the beach with a similar bullet-wound, but this time no weapon was found. Again there was no apparent reason for suicide, and the authorities thought it was a case of murder. This view was supported by the medical officer who first examined the body. Owing to the excited state of the public at the time, I was asked to make a re-examination. I found that the wound was situated in the region of the right temple, and was excavated and slightly blackened; the bullet had passed backward and to the left and lodged in the left side of the brain. It was a ·32 calibre lead bullet, with five right-hand grooves such as occur in bullets discharged from a Smith and Wesson revolver. From the injuries I had no doubt that the wound was self-inflicted, and I reported to this effect. My opinion was accepted, not without a good deal of criticism; but shortly afterwards a number of cartridges of the same kind as the bullet in the brain were found in the man's house, and later a letter arrived from his relatives in England saying he had written them that he was "fed up" and "going to finish it." Some one passing the scene had no doubt stolen the weapon after he was dead, an incident by no means uncommon in the East.

A case that baffled us all was the suicide of a personal friend and colleague, a highly successful medical practitioner of senior standing who had but recently been appointed to a high office for which he was well fitted. He was a man of impeccable character, happily married, and with a family all doing well; in fact a normal, successful, and highly respected member of the community. Yet one evening he was heard pacing the floor of his flat until very late, and then a pistol-shot was heard. He was found dying with the weapon still grasped in his hand. All his affairs had been put in order, but as to why he should have killed himself there was not a hint, and no fragment of evidence of motive could be found.

No suicide could be so unaccountable as this. There must have been something of terrible significance occupying his mind as he paced his floor in the stillness of that night, but what it was nobody knew or ever can know.

I have seen and minutely examined the cases and histories of many other suicides and of murders in which no clue to a motive could be found. It seems that pent deep within most of us, unsuspected by others or even by ourselves, lie potentialities that may be released by a certain combination of circumstances and erupt into action, good or bad — but always unpredictable.

In cases of death from injuries of doubtful origin many questions have to be considered besides the primary ones of how, where, and when the injuries occurred. Among the most important are how long the deceased could have survived after the injury, and to what extent he was then able to perform voluntary acts. These arise particularly when the injury affects the head.

It is commonly assumed that when the brain is seriously injured voluntary action is at once suspended, and death will take place within a very short period. This assumption is not necessarily correct, and if uncontested it can lead to mis-direction of an investigation, and even a miscarriage of justice.

Imagine that a body is found with a serious firearm wound of the brain, and this is assumed to be instantly immobilizing and rapidly fatal. Imagine at the same time that the appearance of bloodstains on the body and about the locality indicates that the body has been moved a considerable distance from the place of injury. If the primary assumption of immediate immobilization is accepted, then the fact that the body has been moved involves the further assumption that it is a case of murder. Yet it may have been a case of suicide or accident, the person having walked or crawled from the place of injury to the place where he died. I can illustrate this with one of many such cases in which the facts are beyond dispute.

An elderly professional man walked out of his private hotel in Edinburgh one winter evening and did not return that night. As his habits were somewhat irregular this did not cause any great anxiety. He returned the next morning at half-past seven and rang the bell. When the maid opened the door she saw that he was wearing his overcoat and hat, and carried his umbrella over his arm. She also noticed considerable bloodstains about his face. Alarmed, she called her mistress. The old man, however, said, "Don't worry. I will just go upstairs and have a wash." He placed his umbrella in the hall-stand, hung up his hat and coat, and walked upstairs to the bathroom, where he collapsed and lost consciousness. The police were told, and he was taken to hospital. He did not regain consciousness, and died three hours later without having made any statement.

There was no mystery about the cause of death. The man had been shot in the head. The bullet had entered under his chin; and, while there was no powder-staining round the wound itself, I found powder inside among the slightly disrupted tissues of the floor of the mouth. This meant that the weapon had been placed in contact with the skin under the chin, and suggested self-infliction. The wound tracked upward, passed through the brain, which was severely damaged, and came out on the left side of the frontal bone of the skull. The exit-hole was one and a quarter inches in diameter, and its size and shape suggested a ·45 revolver bullet, which had turned on its side before passing out.

While the body was being examined the police were tracing the man's movements back from the hotel. They followed a trail of blood to a public garden on the opposite side of the street. In these gardens was a shelter, and on the seat in this they found a ·45 revolver, later identified as the property of the dead man —

and in front of the seat a large pool of blood. A bullet-hole, surrounded by fragments of brain and bone, was observed in the roof of the shelter just above the seat. The exact spot at which the event occurred was, therefore, definitely located. The exact time of the occurrence was more difficult to fix.

The man had left the hotel at an unknown time the previous evening, and it seemed probable that he had spent part of the night in the shelter. It had begun to snow at six in the morning, and a track of footprints and blood-spots was clearly outlined in the snow from the shelter to the grass in front, continuing in a circle for about 165 yards, and returning to the shelter. A single track was also visible leading from the shelter to the hotel across the street. An examination of the bloodstains inside and outside the shelter and of the tracks in the snow indicated that the wound must have been inflicted some time before six o'clock. It seemed that after shooting himself he had rested in the shelter with his head hanging forward, and thus had produced the pool of blood in front of the seat. Then he had walked round the gardens and returned to the seat, where he rested again for a while. Finally, at half-past seven, he returned to the hotel.

It was learnt that the man had had considerable financial and domestic difficulties, and he had been under the erroneous impression that he was suffering from cancer. Letters that he had written the day before the tragedy indicated his intention of committing suicide. The fact of suicide was beyond question.

The injury to the brain was quite extensive. Portions of it had been blown right through the top of the skull to the roof of the shelter. I am quite certain that in such a case many of us would be prepared to give an opinion that the injury would lead to instant unconsciousness and rapid death. Yet it is established without the shadow of doubt that this person, after shooting himself, remained alive for several hours, walked about for a considerable distance, made his way home, carried out definite purposeful acts, and spoke reasonably and intelligibly before consciousness was lost. It is a striking example of what can be done after a severe injury to the brain.

I published an account of this case in the *Police Journal* in 1943. Twelve years later it was largely instrumental in obtaining remission of the death sentence in a case heard in Ceylon.

In a certain village a quarrel broke out in which three men were involved. After a good deal of talk of a provocative nature some kind of a fight took place. One of the men ran off to his house, loaded his gun, and returned to the scene of the quarrel. He fired at one of the other men, who turned and ran away. The third man then seized the gun from the first man, recharged it, chased the fleeing man some distance, and fired. The fugitive fell either at once or very soon after, and when examined by the doctor he was found to be dead. The two men who had fired the gun were arrested and charged with murder.

The case would not have caused any problem in this country, for under English or Scottish law both men would have been considered equally guilty without regard to the effectiveness of their respective shots. In Ceylon, however, it was essential to establish who had fired the fatal shot.

There were nine pellets in the kind of cartridge that had been used, and the medical officer performing the post-mortem examination found six entrance-holes, so closely grouped that he thought they had been made by a single discharge. The slugs had struck the victim on the front of the face and shoulder, causing fairly severe damage and hæmorrhage. One of the slugs had penetrated to the frontal lobe of the brain. The medical officer gave the opinion that the injury to the brain must have caused immediate unconsciousness, followed shortly by death. The victim, he said, would not have been able to move after the brain injury. If this was correct it followed that only the second shot could have been fatal.

The two men were tried jointly. There was some question whether there was a common intent to murder, and whether they were acting in concert, but this is of no importance here. Mainly because of the medical evidence, the man who had fired first — and presumably missed — was sentenced to a term of imprisonment for attempted murder, while the man who had fired the second shot was condemned to death. Counsel defending the second marksman appealed against the sentence, but the appeal was dismissed. Nothing could be done except a final appeal for clemency to the Governor-General.

At that time I was in Ceylon on contract with the World Health Organization to inquire into the medico-legal services there and recommend improvements. I was asked to consider the medical and other evidence in this case, and to give my opinion on the cause of death, and in particular on whether he was killed by the first or second shot. This was outside the scope of my job with the W.H.O., but I agreed. The Professor of Forensic Medicine at Colombo University, Dr de Saram — an old student of mine — was asked to confer with me.

We had at our disposal verbatim reports of the medical evidence, the evidence of the various eye-witnesses and of the police who had carried out the inquiry, a sketch of the scene of the crime, and the Commissioner's charge to the jury. We did not receive any description of the bloodstains on the victim's clothing, which might have given some indication of his movements after being wounded; nor was there any evidence of the place where the empty cartridge was found, which might have helped in fixing the movements of the accused.

The medical evidence was much too arbitrary for us to accept. We agreed that wounds of the extent described might have incapacitated the victim immediately, but we disagreed absolutely that such a consequence must have ensued. We had had personal experience of many cases in which far more severe damage to the brain had been inflicted without causing immediate incapacity. Although the brain injury was associated with other injuries, the combination of which might be more likely to produce shock than a brain injury by itself, we were convinced that these were not sufficient to prove that the victim must have collapsed at once. He might have done so, but it would be highly dangerous to assert that he did.

There was, fortunately, certain objective evidence in favour of our opinion in the form of bloodstains found at the scene of the crime. These were described by the investigating police-inspector as "red stains similar to blood leading from the ridge where the deceased was standing when the first shot was fired to the spot where the body was found." It appeared to us very odd that this trail of blood, which was obviously a vital factor in the case, was not the subject of scrutiny either by the Crown or by the defence; for if the inspector's observation was correct it proved that the victim was severely injured by the first shot, and that he ran a considerable distance after being hit.

A subsidiary bit of evidence was the presence of blood in the stomach, which suggested that the victim had lived a short time after the injury. Further, the distribution and position of the various injuries of the head and shoulder were compatible with the effects of a single shot fired from the front and left; if the man had been hit while running away such a distribution could only have been possible if he had turned his head and body almost right round so that he faced his assailant, and he could not have done this while running without losing his balance.

We had to consider the possibility that both discharges struck the victim. Could the injuries on the face and shoulder have been inflicted by the first shot and the brain injury by the second? Such a possibility could not be excluded, but it would have been a singular coincidence if two separate discharges had formed the single pattern that was found.

We therefore came to the conclusion that all the injuries could have been caused by the first shot, and that it was unnecessary to suppose that the second shot had hit the man at all. We appended to our report the account published in the *Police Journal* of the Edinburgh suicide. The fact that severe and gross injuries had been inflicted on the brain in that case, and the proof that the victim had nevertheless been able to carry out considerable purposive movements afterwards, seemed to me sufficient to destroy the value of the medical evidence in the Ceylon case. At any rate our conclusions were apparently accepted, for the sentence of death was commuted to imprisonment.

I am afraid that the appellant was the least interested person in this case. He asked his legal advisers not to attempt to have his sentence remitted — "since at my age, having lost all my money, it is much simpler to hang."

A case with a very different result occurred in Glasgow. A stoker was killed in the furnace-room of a bakery, and his body was found stretched out on a bench and covered with an overcoat. On the night of his death a casual labourer had been assisting him in his work, and this man had since disappeared. He was traced, arrested, and charged with murder.

His story was that while he was working the stoker started to quarrel with him, and attacked him with an ash-raker. In self-defence he hit the stoker on the head with a shovel. The stoker fell on the floor, apparently stunned by the blow; the labourer then dropped his shovel and went away leaving the stoker where he lay.

At the post-mortem examination it was found that the blow from the shovel had severely injured the stoker's brain. The Crown experts maintained that after such an injury no man could have walked to the bench and covered himself up, and that therefore the victim must have been placed in that position by another person.

I was asked to look into the case for the defence, and I came to the conclusion that the accused was probably telling the truth. However, the position of the body on the bench and the way the coat had been wrapped round it presented a problem. It was certainly difficult to suppose that the victim could have so placed and wrapped himself, although it was not impossible that he might have done both. I had known purposive acts performed after more serious injuries to the brain than the stoker received. But I felt sure that the story as the accused told it would have a most unfavourable effect on the jury. I therefore reported to counsel that there was a good defence if the accused would admit he had placed the stoker's body on the bench before he left.

The man's reply was definite. "I hit him," he said, "put on my coat, and left immediately. I did not place him on the bench."

His legal adviser told him it would be simpler and better for him to admit he had.

"Do you want me to tell a lie?" he asked in reply.

Of course, that could not be suggested, and so the accused stuck to his story, and was convicted and hanged.

I feel sure that if he had kept his mouth shut the charge would have been altered to culpable homicide. It would therefore appear that to tell the truth, the whole truth, and nothing but the truth may sometimes be more dangerous for an innocent man than complete silence.

An earlier example of the amount of damage that can be inflicted on the head without causing death or even obvious disability came to my notice when I performed a post-mortem examination on a member of the irregular Egyptian police known as Ghaffirs. These men were country guards, wore uniform, and were armed with Snider rifles firing a characteristic charge of square-shaped slugs. They were not a trained force, but they played their part in public security reasonably well.

One of these men was killed in a quarrel by a stab-wound of the heart, and I did a routine autopsy although the cause of death was perfectly obvious. I was rewarded for my pains by acquiring a skull, which was a wonderful object, unique in its way. I found that he had been the victim of at least three serious head injuries, any of which might reasonably have been expected to kill him. There were old fractures of the forehead region running down to the eye on both sides. On the top of the head there was an old cut wound running from front to back. On the left side there were old fractures causing displacement of two fragments of bone; these had become slightly septic, and had left an area of roughened bone about three inches in diameter. On the top of the head towards the right side there was another fracture with displacement of a large bit of bone and line-like fractures running from it in all directions. Altogether there seemed to have been a complete smashing of the skull.

He was certainly tough, for all these injuries had healed satisfactorily, and there appeared to have been no permanent damage to the brain. Of course, Ghaffirs were not expected to show much evidence of brain-power, and so there may have been some damage that was undetected.

His past history, as far as I could get it, was of some interest. He had been a brigand in his early life, and had been involved in many fights in which he had sustained many injuries. He had recovered from them all in spite of — perhaps because of — lack of medical attention, and eventually was recruited for the Ghaffir force, probably on the principle of setting a thief to catch a thief. His violent death was in keeping with the general violence of his life. But it shows what you can stand and get away with if your head is thick enough.

Another routine autopsy that I performed on an Egyptian had an equally surprising result.

He was an elderly man, and he had been knocked down by a motor-car — actually it was a police car — while crossing the street. He was taken to hospital in a semi-conscious state, and died five days later, without having regained consciousness.

On dissection I found that he had two tumours of the brain. The invasion was extensive, but, so far as I could learn, he had not complained of any symptoms. The case was remarkable from a clinical point of view, and important also from the medico-legal aspect. It showed that a person could be walking about leading an apparently normal life while suffering from an advanced disease of the brain. When such a person was the victim of an accident of the kind that this man had sustained it was at least an open question whether the central lesion played a part, first in contributing to the accident and secondly in leading to a fatal issue. In this particular case I attributed the cause of death to the tumours rather than to the accident.

This case had an amusing sequel. As soon as the man had died the Cairo Chief of Police, Russell Pasha, issued instructions that no post-mortem examination was to be performed on him. When a civilian is run over and killed by a police car it tends to create a bad impression on the public, and Russell naturally wanted as little fuss as possible. I did not hear of Russell's instructions — at least, not officially — until after I had performed the autopsy. It was too late to comply with his wishes then, but I decided the least I could do was to refrain from sending him a copy of my report.

Secrets were not easy to keep in Egypt, and Russell soon heard not only that a post-mortem examination had been performed but that the report was much more favourable to the police-officer involved than he had any reason to expect. When Russell asked me about it I reminded him of the instructions he had issued, and expressed surprise that he should think I would do anything against his wishes. He told me to come off it, and finally I exchanged a copy of the report for a promise that there would be no more high-level police interference with the work of my department. There never was.

The power of voluntary activity after severe injuries other than to the brain can be quite startling. A striking example occurred in the block in which our office in Cairo was situated.

A messenger arrived in a state of great excitement one morning, and asked me to go down to the courts to see an attendant who had injured himself. I hurried to the man, and found him lying on the floor of the lavatory in a pool of blood — but still conscious, able to talk, and, until the moment before, able to walk. He had completely removed his private parts with two cuts of a razor, had sliced his abdomen wide open with two gashes, and had then pulled out a mass of his intestines and cut them off too. This had occurred fully half an hour before I saw him. The greater part of his bowel and a portion of the stomach were outside the abdomen, and the whole place was covered with blood.

I naturally expected the man to die at once, but he was quite conscious and able to tell me why he had done this extraordinary thing. It appeared that he had been sent by one of the judges to change a ten-shilling note and had lost it. He was so worried about this, which to us would seem a trifling incident, that he committed this barbarous assault on himself. He was a Circassian, and had never evinced any signs of mental instability until that moment.

I gave him morphine and, with the help of an assistant, replaced the viscera as far as possible, expecting him to die at every moment. But he didn't, and we bandaged him up and called an ambulance, and it was not until after he had reached hospital that he finally expired.

This, I think, is another good warning not to express opinions too easily on what a human being can do after severe injuries. It is also rather a lesson for us as to what does and does not constitute a motive for human actions.

19

War and Ballistics

DURING THE SECOND WORLD WAR I SPENT SOME TIME INVES-
tigating the ballistic properties of various types of official
ammunition. I experimented with cartridges from our own
ordnance factories, ammunition supplied to our Home Guard,
and ammunition supplied to our regular forces by manufacturers
in the United States of America. I found that the cordite used in
our cartridges gave a good deal less penetrating power than the
United States ammunition. Since it appeared to be much more
expensive to manufacture cordite than the more efficient pro-
pellants, I thought I should communicate my results to the authorities. I was told that cordite had special though unspecified
advantages over other powders, and I have no doubt there is
some reason for its continued use.

It was a personal incident that led me to experiment on the
penetrating power of different types of ammunition. When I was
in one of the English counties the local Home Guard told me
about an armoured car that they had made, and of which they
were very proud. I was asked to examine it. The sides were
armoured with two sheets of iron with a filling between them of
cork and other debris. The sheets were quite thin, and I said that
a ·303 rifle-bullet would go through them. They looked upon this
as a joke, and readily agreed to my suggestion of a practical test.
We found that from about fifty yards an ordinary service rifle
could drive a bullet not only through one pair of plates into the
car but right through both sides. Fortunately, we were making
the tests in a quarry so that the emergent bullets could do no
damage, though we lost them for examination purposes.

An unexpected thing about rifle-bullets which I noted in these
experiments with official ammunition was that when they were

fired through an iron plate they made a hole much larger than the bullet, and the bullet itself was turned inside out. I collected a number of specimens in which the rifling marks from the barrel were to be seen inside the inverted jacket. When a projectile travelling at high velocity suddenly strikes a resistant body the tip of the bullet is checked in flight, whereas the rest of it continues at the original speed. As a result the hinder end passes over the body of the bullet, just as the finger of a glove is turned inside out when it is drawn off the finger by pulling on the wrist portion. At the same time there is a splash back at the point of entrance which gives the appearances of an exit-hole.

These odd effects are readily explicable, but they can cause a lot of trouble to anyone investigating the results of rifle-fire who does not know these facts. The behaviour of high-velocity projectiles at short ranges is rather extraordinary and is also little known.

When a rifle is fired the bullet leaves the barrel at a speed of about 2500 feet per second. It is spinning at between two and three thousand revolutions per second, and at short ranges — that is, between two to three hundred yards — it tends to have a certain degree of wobble. A similar wobble can be seen in the spinning of a top. When a top is spun it first gyrates unsteadily round its centre of gravity, and then settles down and spins without any deviation at all. A bullet does the same; and if it strikes anything while it is still unstable the effects may have all the appearance of an explosion.

If a high-velocity bullet is fired into soft clay it does not, as one might expect, pass through it. After tunnelling in for a few inches it suddenly produces a cavity many times its own diameter, and quite frequently the bullet itself is smashed into fragments. An inexperienced observer might infer that only an explosive or dum-dum bullet could do this. A similar inference could be drawn, with possibly more serious results, when a human body is struck by an ordinary rifle-bullet within two or three hundred yards with the same explosive effects.

An example of these effects was seen in a case that occurred in Edinburgh in 1940.

On July 12, at about midnight, a police-car containing three police-officers and the Assistant Chief Constable was proceeding towards police headquarters at about forty miles an hour. Two of the officers were in the back, and the third was driving. The

Assistant Chief Constable was sitting beside the driver. An air-raid alarm had sounded, and when the car approached the city it was challenged by a sergeant of the Royal Air Force. It did not stop, and the sergeant fired his rifle at the car. The bullet passed through the rear celluloid window of the car and struck the Assistant Chief Constable on the chin. The car was stopped, the sergeant was arrested, and the Assistant Chief Constable was then driven to the Royal Infirmary. He was found to have a severe bullet-wound of the face and a fracture of the lower jaw. Septic infection occurred, and after three days he died.

At the post-mortem examination I found a clean-cut entrance-wound of the bullet on the right side of the lower jaw, and a lacerated exit-wound on the left. This exit-wound was three and a half inches long, and ran up from the level of the chin towards the lobe of the ear. It had the appearance of bursting outward. The lower jaw was smashed into fragments, but the appearance of the entrance-wound showed that the bullet was intact when it struck. It appeared to have merely touched the jaw-bone in the region of the chin, and then its velocity and spin caused complete disintegration of the bone. In among the broken bone there were a few fragments of the bullet, which had itself disintegrated after striking the chin.

When the car was examined not one but a number of bullet-marks were found. There were two holes in the licence-holder and the windscreen under it, each of which looked as if it had been caused by a separate bullet. The upper part of the left traffic-indicator had also been pierced, and there were several other marks apparently produced by the passage of projectiles. On the upper bar of the windscreen frame there was an oval dent about an inch in length, in which some metal had been deposited, and which appeared to have been made by a ·303 bullet. In and round the windscreen, on the woodwork in front of the passenger seat, on the seat and on the hood, the police found more bits of lead and nickel and fragments of human tissue and bone. On the back seat a portion of a ·303 bullet was found, consisting of the aluminium tip and the cupro-nickel jacket.

When the car was first examined it was thought that a number of shots had been fired. From the holes in the windscreen alone it seemed that two or three bullets must have struck the car. However, all the eye-witnesses spoke of only one shot being fired, and one cartridge-case only was found on the scene; out of a clip of five bullets the remaining four were still in the rifle, one in the chamber and three in the magazine. Finally a reconstruction at the scene of the affair, with the actual vehicle and passengers, showed pretty conclusively that not more than one bullet could have entered the car.

A single bullet, then, had produced all these bizarre effects — the bullet that had hit the Assistant Chief Constable on the chin. The jaw is not a very firm structure, but it was enough to cause a high-speed projectile with a low-range wobble to explode and disintegrate. Fragments of the smashed bullet were driven through the victim's cheek, causing a lacerated wound. These fragments, some with human tissues attached, dispersed in various directions, producing numerous fractures in the windscreen and holes in the licence-holder and traffic-indicator. The largest piece found — the bullet-tip, which had come to rest on the back seat — fitted the oval dent on the windscreen frame perfectly; after leaving the victim's jaw it had evidently struck the frame and then ricocheted to the back seat without touching the other three occupants of the car. It must have been travelling fast when it emerged from the victim's face, and the interesting thing was that instead of going forward in the direction of the discharge from the rifle — from right to left and slightly downward — it had, after striking the jaw, flown off at an acute angle, upward and from left to right. The deflection of this piece of bullet almost at right angles to the line of flight shows the danger of assuming that any fragment of a bullet that disintegrates will necessarily continue in the line of flight of the parent missile.

The R.A.F. sergeant was charged with assault and culpable homicide and tried by the High Court of Justiciary. Lord Aitchison, who presided, ruled that although subject to Service discipline he was still within the reach of the ordinary law of the land, and that if he committed a crime punishable by the criminal courts he could not escape the consequences by pleading that he was in the Services, and therefore exempt.

The sergeant had been on forty-hours leave at the time of the affair. The reason why he was armed was that at that period of the war — shortly after Dunkirk, when the danger of invasion was at its height — all Servicemen had to take their weapons and ammunition with them when they went on leave. This man had spent part of the evening with some friends in a roadhouse, and had drunk four half-pints of beer and two or three small whiskies.

He had left the roadhouse about 10 p.m., taking with him two bottles of beer. What became of these was not found out.

About midnight the air-raid sirens sounded and, on his own authority, the sergeant took up his stand on a main road leading to the centre of the city. He stopped a car driven by an A.F.S. patrol officer, who was on duty, and forced the driver to put out his lights and go into a side-road by pointing his rifle and threatening to shoot. Then came the police-car, which the sergeant claimed he challenged repeatedly, although he was not heard by any of the occupants. When he was arrested he protested vehemently, and according to some witnesses he boasted of his powers as a marksman and said he had brought down two Heinkels. He said that no car was entitled to be on the road while an air-raid warning was on, and that he was obeying his wing-commander's instructions. Witnesses varied greatly in their estimate whether he was drunk or sober at the time of arrest.

The sergeant's defence was that he had been acting on general verbal instructions given by a wing-commander, but he did not bring any evidence to prove this; and in his charge to the jury Lord Aitchison said he could not conceive any responsible officer telling his men that if cars did not answer their challenge to stop during an air-raid they were entitled to fire on them. The sergeant was found guilty of assault and culpable homicide, but the verdict was coupled with a strong recommendation for leniency. He was sentenced to six months' imprisonment, which could hardly be called unduly severe.

In the case I have just described the bullet exploded after merely touching the bone at the chin. Shortly afterwards I saw a similar case of a bullet exploding when no solid substance was struck at all.

A young deserter was fired at from a distance of about ten to fifteen yards by a Service rifle. The bullet passed through both legs, and the man collapsed and died from hæmorrhage in about an hour. Unfortunately, his clothes were destroyed before I had a chance to see them, but I had the opportunity to observe the wounds.

The bullet went in from the outer side of the left thigh, and the entrance-wound was clean-cut and characteristic. The bullet traversed the fleshy part of the thigh, passing below the femur. The tissues were severely lacerated, and although the great vessels were not damaged the muscle was pulped. This damage to the muscle increased as the track approached the exit, which was made on the inner side of the thigh. The exit-hole itself was two and a half by two and a half inches; the skin was torn, and tags of muscle and tissue were projecting from it.

The bullet then entered the inner side of the right thigh. The entrance-hole was a lacerated wound six by three inches in size. After destroying skin and fibrous tissue and pulping more muscle the bullet struck the lower end of the femur, smashed it into fragments, reduced a portion of it to powder, and destroyed the femoral artery and nerve. A few fragments of the bullet made their exit on the outer side of the right thigh. Other fragments, innumerable and minute, were found in the tissues among the damaged muscle and bits of bone. It was evident not only that the bullet had completely disintegrated but that it had broken up in the muscles before it struck the bone.

Anyone without experience or knowledge of the circumstances of the shooting might, on looking at the wounds, have assumed that two shots had been fired, one from the left and the other from the right. In another case, similar in some respects, it could have been still more difficult to discover what had happened by examining the injuries.

This time the soldier was wounded in all four limbs. There were an entrance- and an exit-wound in each, so one might have thought four bullets had been fired. In fact there was only one shot. The soldier had been bending down tying his boot-lace or adjusting his puttees when a comrade's Lewis gun accidentally went off at a range of about a yard. The bullet entered the outer side of his left leg below the knee, came out on the inner side and entered his left arm below the elbow, went through that and then through his right leg, finally entered his right arm and reappeared on its outer side. One of the interesting features of the case was that the bullet did comparatively little damage in the first three limbs, and only exploded and disintegrated after striking the bone in the right arm.

One shooting case that I had to deal with during the Second World War recalled the case of the Egyptian postman whose murderer was traced by Bedouin trackers, which I related in an earlier chapter. Again it was for me a matter of identifying a rifle by the cartridge-case found at the place where the shooting took place.

One Sunday afternoon in the summer of 1942 certain man-
œuvres were held near Edinburgh. A mock battle was in progress
between a detachment of the Home Guard, defending a wooded
slope on the south side of a road, and an attacking force composed of Regular soldiers who were hidden in a wood on the
north side. The opposing forces were fully armed, but, of course,
had been issued with blank ammunition only. Suddenly one of
the Home Guard men jumped up, collapsed, and rolled over a
retaining wall on to the grass verge of the roadway. He was
found to be seriously wounded, apparently by a rifle-bullet.
The exercise was stopped at once, and the military authority on
the spot made every endeavour to trace the person who had fired
the shot, but without success. The civil police were then called in.

The man died shortly afterwards, and his body was submitted
to me for post-mortem examination. I found that a bullet had
grazed his chin, entered his body above the right breast, and
driven a portion of bone outward through the right shoulder-
blade. Fired at high velocity and close range, the bullet had disintegrated in the body, and the portions remaining were too
small to enable me to identify the firearm from which it was fired.
The direction of fire, however, could be fairly accurately fixed.

Before he jumped up — which he presumably did when hit —
the man had been lying on his stomach with his head and shoulders
raised slightly, pointing his rifle in the direction of the attacking
force on the opposite side of the road. Officers of the Edinburgh
C.I.D. went to the site of the shooting and, from the information
derived from the post-mortem examination, made a reconstruction of the incident. As a result, it was definitely established that
the shot must have been fired from behind a wall on the north
side of the road, within a limited area. The area was searched, and,
among many empty blank cartridges, they found one ·303 cartridge case from which a live round had been fired.

Further inquiries revealed that a platoon of twenty-six men
had made up the attacking party in that area of the wood. The
police collected all the rifles of the men in the platoon, fired
sample shots, and compared each cartridge-case with the one
found at the scene of the affair..The preliminary examination was
carried out in the Photographic and Fingerprint Department of
the Edinburgh City Police. A series of photographs of the
cartridges was taken, and these were submitted to me. From
specific marks made on the percussion cap by the firing-pin, and

impressions made by the bolt of the rifle on the base of the cartridge, I was able to identify the rifle from which the fatal shot had been fired.

The soldier who had fired the shot apparently had no personal grudge against the man he had killed, but just thought it would be a good idea to add a little realism to the exercise by discharging a live cartridge from time to time. He was examined by a psychiatrist, who found that by reason of his mental condition he had to be considered to have a diminished sense of responsibility. He was therefore tried summarily by the military authorities on a charge of firing ball ammunition without authority. He was found guilty, sentenced to twenty-eight days' detention, and transferred to a branch of the Service in which he would not be required to bear arms.

During the War I acted as consultant in medico-legal cases to the Army authorities, and saw some interesting cases in Edinburgh. One of the less usual of these was a young woman in the A.T.S. who had been examined by her medical officer on account of a swelling that had appeared in her groin. It had at first been attributed to hernia. However, during the examination the medical officer noticed that the development of the girl's external organs did not appear normal, and the case was submitted to me for consultation.

When I examined her I found that although she had all the appearance of a rather nice-looking girl of about eighteen or nineteen, her organs indicated that she was really a male.

The characters that decide the sex of the child are observable quite soon after the egg starts to develop in the womb, and gradually a typical male or female is formed. In some cases, which are relatively rare, this process is interrupted or altered, and a child may be born whose sex cannot be determined. Such children are registered as males, and if later the true sex can be determined an application is made to the Registrar-General and an official change of sex is allowed.

In every normal child the rudiments of both sexes are present, but male or female characters are predominant and the characters of the other sex rudimentary. As the child grows up the predominant characters develop while the rudimentary characters of the other sex remain vestigial. In this particular case the predominant characters were male but had not developed properly, and the appearance of the external sex organs was not unlike the normal appearance of the female organs. This resemblance, however, did not extend beyond appearance, and there was no room for doubt about the person's true sex. The question was what should be done.

First of all, I decided it would be best to tell the young 'woman' frankly that she was really a man. I asked whether she had noticed that she was different from other girls, and she said that she had, but that she did not take a great deal of notice of it. Then I told her the facts. She was a very common-sense young person, and accepted it all without much sentiment or emotion. Her main trouble was that she was being courted by a young man, and it was their intention to get married. Of course, it was obvious that this could not occur, and she accepted this without demur.

I reported the matter to the Army authorities, and I had an interview with a senior officer to discuss what should be done. He suggested that the best thing would be to have her discharged from the women's corps and, since she was eligible for service, to re-enlist her immediately in the Army. I was appalled at this crude way of dealing with a highly complicated problem. I tried to explain the inevitable psychological damage to a girl in love with a young man on suddenly discovering that she was really a man herself. I pointed out that this by itself was sufficient of a shock for anyone, without having it aggravated by immediate recruitment into a male corps. I managed to have my point of view accepted, and at my suggestion a job was obtained for her on the land. I thought this might be suitable, as so many land girls were in trousers, and she might not feel the change in her relationship so heavily if she was gradually introduced to her new sex in this way.

About a year or so later I was visited in my office by a rather spruce, well-set-up young man who asked me if I remembered him. His face was familiar but I could not place him. "I seem to have seen you before, but I am not sure where," I said. He then explained that he was the A.T.S. 'girl' whom I had seen a year before.

He was now obviously masculine, just as before he had had all the appearance of femininity. His main object in seeing me was to ask my advice about marriage — to a girl. He said he had told her something of the facts of the case, and she was willing to marry him.

In his condition marriage was obviously impossible, and I recommended him to dismiss the matter from his mind. However, I offered to have him seen by one of our surgical specialists to ascertain whether a reconstruction operation could be performed. The surgeon reported that an operation could be done which would probably be successful, but as far as I know it was never carried out and I saw nothing more of the young man.

A remarkable feature of the case was the way the psychological effect of the discovery of change of sex produced active physical change. The case was of interest also for the official attitude to the problem.

Early in 1946 I was asked to attend a meeting in Frankfurt to consider the participation of German medical authorities in certain war crimes. Several meetings were held, and we received a great deal of information, mostly about medical experiments on Jews in concentration camps.

Some of these experiments were concerned with combating particular medical problems associated with the war. There were the freezing experiments, for example, carried out for research into the effects of cold and possible treatment; human beings were exposed to extremes of temperature under varying conditions, and then resuscitated. Other experiments involved the inoculation of immunized and non-immunized subjects with disease-germs, such as virulent typhus bacteria, tubercle bacilli, and virulent bacteria producing gangrene. Another type of experiment in this category was on the effects and treatment of phosphorus burns.

Other experiments were connected with Nazi racial theories. These included experiments on women with reference to insemination and abortion, and experiments on men and women with reference to the effects of sterilization. A third category seemed to have no aim except sadistic curiosity.

What struck me particularly about most of the experiments in all three groups was the lack of planned objectives and of discrimination in the choice of experiment, the absence of controls, and the crudity of technique.

The experiments were not merely carried out with gross indifference to the value of human life and callous disregard of human suffering, but were incompetent in both conception and execution from a purely scientific point of view.

One would have thought that with the wealth of human experimental material at their disposal, and with their complete freedom from restraint imposed by ordinary ethics — not to mention the strongest prohibition imposed by medical ethics — a great deal of valuable scientific work could have been done and much unique information obtained. Unfortunately, this was not the case, and all this unethical experimentation on human beings produced little of any value. Possibly the elimination of so many of their scientists of Jewish extraction left the field open to men whose scientific attainments were small though their party sympathies were sound. No doubt also some men with the necessary ability had more scruples than their masters and somehow secured exemption from this inhuman work.

20

A Murder in Ceylon

IN DECEMBER 1952 I RECEIVED A LETTER FROM A FIRM OF solicitors in Ceylon which began as follows:

DEAR SIR,

Regina v. Sathasivam

We are the Proctors for the accused Sathasivam in the above case. Sathasivam stands indicted in the Supreme Court with the murder of his wife. Their former servant, WILLIAM, who stood charged as second accused together with him at the preliminary inquiry in the Magistrate's Court, has since been pardoned and is now a witness for the Crown.

In the course of the lengthy preliminary inquiry, there arose an important, and even vital conflict of medical opinion in respect of which we are anxious to obtain your opinion if possible. This "conflict" was really in the nature of an attack developed by the Crown itself on its own Judicial Medical Officer – Dr G. S. W. de Saram – *after* he had given his considered medical opinion in evidence. We may say that we would regard as helpful every point which would help to sustain Dr de Saram's main evidence....

This letter interested me to a great extent because, as I have mentioned, Professor de Saram was a former pupil of mine, and I had formed a high opinion of his ability and his undoubted probity. I agreed to read the evidence, which was brought to me personally by Mr Nadarajah, the junior counsel.

From it I concluded that the case against the accused was by no means good, and that there was every prospect of putting up a successful defence. I reported to this effect, and some time later the senior counsel, Dr Colvin de Silva, came to Edinburgh for consultation.

The facts of the case were simple. The accused was a man of

good family and an excellent sportsman, and he had captained Ceylon at cricket. He had married in 1940, and there were four children. However, his relationship with his wife deteriorated until finally she decided to divorce him on the grounds of desertion. He was in England when proceedings were started, but returned home on September 22, 1951. In spite of the impending proceedings he was admitted by his wife, and stayed for about a fortnight. Early in October she insisted he leave, and on October 8 he was served with divorce papers at a friend's house. He returned home that night, which he spent with his wife.

Their home was a villa in a pleasant part of Colombo, and the domestic staff consisted of an ayah, or children's nurse, and a cook. The ayah was an old and trusted servant of the family.

The next morning the ayah and the two older children had breakfast and left for school at about 8.15, their usual time. Mrs Sathasivam was then in the younger children's room reading her letters and the morning paper. Her husband was apparently still asleep. The only other person in the house was the cook, so called — the boy William, eighteen years old, whom Mrs Sathasivam had engaged without references about a week before. He was in the kitchen.

At 3 p.m. the ayah and the older children returned home. Neither Sathasivam nor William was in the house. The two younger children were playing in the kitchen. In the garage, which was adjacent to it, their mother lay dead on the floor.

Sathasivam was found at the house of the friend with whom he had previously stayed. At 5 p.m. he was arrested and charged with the murder of his wife.

An hour later Professor de Saram made a preliminary inspection of the body in the garage. Early the next morning he performed the post-mortem examination and stated, among other things, his estimate of the time of death.

This was crucial. Sathasivam had left the house by taxi at 10.35 a.m., and he could prove it; and he had a complete alibi for the rest of the day. Therefore he could have had no part in the murder if it occurred after that time. If, on the other hand, death occurred before he left the house he must have been concerned in it. The question was as simple as that — before or after 10.35; an interval of time as fine as a hair but as deep as a grave, as Lord Hunter said on another occasion.

For the time being the question remained open; for Professor de Saram said he thought death had occurred some time between 10 and 11.30 a.m.

Ten days after the crime William was tracked down. Eventually he 'confessed' that he had helped his master to kill the lady of the house — before 9 a.m.

He said also that after the murder the master had removed his wife's bangles and rings and the gold casket and chain round her neck — the Thali Kodi, a Hindu wife's most sacred possession, placed there by her husband at the marriage ceremony and never to be removed during his lifetime — and given them to William, with three rupees, as a reward for his services. Then, William continued in his 'confession,' he went to a jeweller's and sold the objects — at 9.30 a.m.

Two men at the jeweller's admitted the purchase and confirmed the time. Three other witnesses, however, asserted independently that they had seen or heard Mrs Sathasivam alive an hour or more later.

The first of these was the traffic manager of the taxi company that had supplied Sathasivam with a cab. He said that a woman had phoned for the cab at 10.30, and he thought he had recognized her voice as that of Mrs Sathasivam. Then the driver of the taxi said that when he called at the house five minutes later he saw Mrs Sathasivam, whom he knew by sight, at the door when her husband left. Finally the son of Mrs Sathasivam's legal adviser, who was familiar with her voice, said he had a telephone conversation with her at some time between 10.25 a.m. and 12 noon.

It seemed unlikely that all three were mistaken, and none of them had any reason for inventing an untruth. The two jewellers, on the other hand, were known to be receivers of stolen goods, and had bought Mrs Sathasivam's bangles and rings from William in the course of their illicit business. I suggested to the defence that these men had been either mistaken or deliberately lying in their estimate of the time of the deal.

The Crown based its case against Sathasivam on William's evidence. As Professor de Saram's estimate of the time of death did not support this, the Crown called in a considerable array of other experts to try to show that Mrs Sathasivam could have been killed an hour before the earliest time allowed in the report of the post-mortem examination. My own opinion was that this erred, if anything, in the other direction.

There were three main facts to be considered in fixing the time of death by the medical evidence. These were the temperature of the body, the extent of rigor mortis, and the state of food in the stomach and bowel.

At some time after 8.15 on the morning of the death Mrs Sathasivam had breakfast, consisting of string hoppers — a kind of macaroni — grated coconut, and milk. Exactly when she had this meal could not be discovered. She was in the habit of taking breakfast quite late, and her husband said that on that day she ate her meal when he was dressing, probably not long before 10 a.m.; but, of course, his evidence alone was not worth anything. It was known that she had not had breakfast when the ayah and older children left for school, and, indeed, that at that time the string hoppers were still tied up in their bag. It was known also that she had breakfast some time before she died, because semi-digested string hoppers and coconut were found in her stomach and intestines at the post-mortem examination. From the evidence in the digestive tract de Saram gave an opinion that the meal had been taken about three hours before death. It is difficult to be precise about a matter such as this, but it was agreed the time would be something in that order. If this was right death could not have occurred before 11.15 a.m.

This estimate was roughly confirmed by the extent of rigor mortis at the time when Professor de Saram examined the body. Stiffening then — at 6 p.m. — was complete, except for the fingers and toes. Under the conditions in which the body was found such a degree of rigor would take place in six or eight hours. This put the time of death between 10 a.m. and 12 noon, but with a strong probability that it was nearer twelve than ten.

Finally there was the temperature of the body. When Professor de Saram took this, at about 7 p.m., it was 93·2 degrees F. — that is, a loss of only 5·2 degrees if the temperature had been normal at the time of death. The atmospheric temperature in the garage at 7 p.m. was 81·5 degrees. The body was small and poorly nourished, the clothing was thin and rucked up, and it lay on a cement floor — all factors that favoured rapid cooling. I did not think it could have taken ten hours to lose a little over 5 degrees. As the time of death would certainly be the deciding factor in proving or disproving the guilt of the accused I told the defence to ask Professor de Saram to make certain observations on the cooling of recently dead bodies in Colombo.

The other important question was the place where the murder

was committed. According to William, it was done in the bedroom upstairs. Mrs Sathasivam, he said, was sitting on the bed when her husband held her hair with his left hand and grasped her by the throat with his right, and pulled her to the floor. She fell face upward. The master squatted down with his hand still holding her throat and as she struggled he called to William, "Hold her legs, you devil." William obeyed, and the master held her throat until she died. Then he rose and stamped on her throat with his shod foot. William claimed that he heard the voice-box crack. The master removed the bangles and rings and the chain round her neck. Then they raised the body, the master holding it under the armpits and the boy by the feet, and carried it down the stair — which was in view of the street — through the kitchen to the garage.

William's account of the murder was detailed and precise, and much of it substantiated the medical evidence. This was not surprising, and it did not necessarily mean that it was true. He, of course, was there, and obviously could give a wealth of corroborative detail. If his accusation was false — if instead of being Sathasivam's unwilling accomplice he had committed the crime himself alone — he needed only to switch his part in it to the person he was accusing in order to give his evidence a specious air of corroboration.

There was no doubt that Mrs Sathasivam had died as a result of manual strangulation. The post-mortem examination showed that clearly enough. There was no doubt, either, that the voice-box was broken. Both horns of the thyroid cartilage were found to be fractured. Whether, however, a bystander could have heard the breaking seemed to me doubtful; on the other hand, it could certainly have been felt by anyone who caused the damage with his bare foot.

There was an abrasion on the left side of the dead woman's jaw and neck where the trampling had apparently been done. Adhering to it were fragments of a fine dark powder and a few coconut fibres, both of which the Government analyst had found identical with similar material taken from the floor of the kitchen. Unfortunately neither Sathasivam's shoes nor William's feet were examined at the time, but to me the dirt-stained abrasions curving down over the jaw-bone suggested a bare foot that could take the contours of the face.

Two other bruises found at the post-mortem examination

seemed to me at variance with William's story. One was a very severe bruise on the right side of the head, which the Crown experts said could have been caused by bumping the victim on the floor. I could not agree with them; in my opinion it was caused by a blow from a blunt object such as a poker or stick. The other bruise was on the back between the shoulder-blades, and the Crown explained this in the same way. Again I could not agree. I thought the bruise could only have been produced by forcing the body against a narrow projection which could fit into the hollow between the shoulder-blades. If there had been a brick or something like that on the floor it would have been sufficient, but there was nothing of the kind. I thought it might have been caused by thrusting the victim while upright against something projecting from a door or wall.

There was only William's word for it that the unfortunate woman had been strangled while lying on her back. Against this there was the evidence of the Government analyst of urine stains on her petticoat running almost to the hem. The victim of manual strangulation frequently urinates just before death, and the stains were not likely to have run so far if she had been lying flat on her back.

William, again, was the only authority for the theory that the murder had been committed in the bedroom upstairs — other evidence suggested that it was more likely to have been done in the kitchen adjacent to the garage. One of the most important points was the fact that the soles of the woman's feet were coated with the same dark material that had been found with the coconut fibres adhering to the abrasion on the left side of her jaw and neck. On analysis again it was found to be identical with similar material taken from the kitchen floor. The Government analyst also noticed drag-marks on the kitchen floor. William had said quite positively that when he and Sathasivam carried the woman's body through the kitchen it did not touch the floor. The material was easily scaled off her feet — indeed, it was removed as a crust by touching it with a sheet of paper before the body was taken from the garage — and it would surely have readily fallen off if the woman had walked about. It seemed to me clear proof that she had walked into the kitchen that morning, and never walked out.

Among the victim's lesser injuries was a superficial bruise behind the left ear. It was caused before death, and was due, no doubt, to the pressure of her ear-stud, which was bent, presumably by a blow. A pearl that had been mounted in it had dropped out. Twelve days after the murder this pearl was found in the garage about a foot from where the body had been lying. If the injury had occurred upstairs the pearl, loosened by the blow, would almost certainly have fallen either in the bedroom or during the jolting of the body on the way down. Since the injury was inflicted while the woman was still alive, this was additional evidence in favour of the kitchen or the adjacent garage as the scene of the crime.

Another point that told against William's story was that he was scratched on the face and arm, while Sathasivam, who was examined immediately after the crime, was not. William's scratches were still visible when he was arrested, and they looked about ten days old. He admitted he had got them during the murder, and said it was when he was obeying the master and trying to hold the lady's legs. I thought he was more likely to have got them while strangling the woman himself.

William had been charged with murder on his arrest, and it was only after he learnt that the sale of the jewellery had been discovered that he made his 'confession.' He was given a conditional pardon on turning Queen's Evidence, which seemed to me rather odd. It was no business of mine, but I thought that it would have been much simpler if both men had been tried for the murder. As it was, every point made in favour of Sathasivam was inevitably evidence against William, who was not on trial.

If William had committed the crime himself it seemed unlikely that it was for the jewellery and three rupees. The dead woman's saree was torn in several places, and a large stain of seminal matter was found on her petticoat. I thought it likely that the murder was an unintentional sequel to an indecent assault.

When I had read all the evidence, examined the photographs, and discussed the matter with counsel for the defence, I carried out a reconstruction of the crime in the way I thought it had occurred. I did this in my laboratory in Edinburgh, the scene of many other such reconstructions. I had the benefit of the assistance of the two defence counsel — although they were of surprisingly little help when I asked them to show me how a saree was arranged.

I wanted to know whether the tears in the victim's saree coincided with the position of the wounds on her back. The saree is wrapped round the body in a particular way and fastened at the side. Neither of the lawyers knew how it was done, although both were married men. In the end we had to seek the help of a young lady from Ceylon who was working in the department above my laboratory.

According to my reconstruction, some time after Sathasivam had left the house his wife had gone down to the kitchen, where William was preparing coconut. As she stood scantily clad before the window the boy became sexually excited and attempted to assault her indecently. As she turned to resist he grasped her by the neck and forced her up against the wall or the doorway between kitchen and garage, bruising her back against some projection and tearing her saree. She partially lost consciousness and passed urine as she sagged down. He then dragged her into the garage and either killed her there at once or after an indecent assault.

I assumed that she had not been on her back in the kitchen, otherwise black stains from the floor would have been found on the back of her saree as well as the soles of her feet. I thought my reconstruction accounted for the drag-marks found in the kitchen, which had been reported on by the Government analyst, but which had apparently been given no importance. Everything seemed to fit perfectly, and with the help of the two defence counsel the crime was reconstructed with considerable realism. My typist, who played the part of the murdered woman, looked quite terrified when Dr de Silva pushed her up against the door and pretended to throttle her.

The defence counsel agreed with my reconstruction, so I asked them to have the scene of the crime examined again with the express purpose of seeing whether there was a projection such as a hook or staple somewhere about three and a half feet from the floor in the kitchen or on the door between the kitchen and garage.

The accused had already been in custody well over a year when I was consulted about the case, and there was a further delay before the trial began.

Dr de Silva considered it essential that I should go to Ceylon to give oral evidence. This was difficult, since I had a very heavy programme of work in front of me.

I was completing my final year in the University before retiring in September, and I had to give the Promoter's address at the Graduation in June. I had accepted an invitation to go to Canada to give the Shepherd Memorial Lecture at McGill University on May 1, to represent Edinburgh University at the laying of the foundation stone of the new Montreal General Hospital, and to attend a meeting of the Canadian Medical Association. I was also due to represent the University at the Coronation of Her Majesty. Finally I was under contract to the World Health Organization to go to the Lebanon and Ceylon after my retiral and report on the medico-legal services there. I was also engaged in advising the defence in an interesting case of alleged murder in Kenya.

A fairly tight programme — but I found that I could fulfil all these engagements provided that my evidence in Colombo was taken between certain dates. This was agreed to. I could not go to Nairobi as well, but was able to give the defence full advice about their case, which I am glad to say they won. I flew to Montreal on April 29 and returned on May 11; flew to Colombo on May 20, gave evidence in court on various days from May 21, and returned to London on May 30 in time for the Coronation on June 2.

At Colombo the defence, led by Dr de Silva, met me at the airport and wanted to take me to my hotel. I asked them if the kitchen in the house had been examined for a projecting hook or staple, and they said this had not been done. I asked if we could go there then, and they said it was easy enough to reach from the airport, so off we went. The house had long since changed hands, and the new owners were living there, but they allowed us to look round the kitchen. I was rather pleased to find, just 3 feet 6 inches from the ground, on the wall between the kitchen and garage, a staple which had been used for hooking the door back. It was exactly the sort of thing I had expected to have caused the bruise on Mrs Sathasivam's back.

This little detour from the airport aroused some comment at the trial. I was asked, among other things, if I had gone to the scene of the crime before having breakfast or a bath. The judge was impressed because none of the medical experts appearing for the Crown — except Professor de Saram, of course — had ever bothered to go to the house. His Honour said he had had to have the bed brought to the court to get them to examine it.

While I had been at the house I had been able to see the upstairs bedroom where William said the crime had been committed,
the staircase, the kitchen, and the garage, so that I had a fairly
clear picture of the case. But the thing that created the greatest
impression was the fact that I had deduced the existence of the
wall staple while reconstructing the case in Edinburgh, and then
come to Ceylon and gone straight to the house and found it just
where I expected it to be.

As we had anticipated, the issues on which the case depended
were where and when the murder had been committed. The place
of the crime was important as showing whether William's confession was true or not. The question of time was vital.

Sathasivam was charged specifically with having murdered
his wife "before 9.30 on the morning of the 9th October, 1951."
The Crown thus relied entirely on William's evidence and rejected that of Professor de Saram wherever the two disagreed.
The disagreement was sometimes so profound that the Solicitor-
General sought and obtained permission from the court to cross-
examine Professor de Saram as a hostile witness.

The long delay in bringing the accused to trial was in itself
somewhat unfair to him, as it meant that his life had to depend
on the memory of witnesses concerning events that had happened
over eighteen months before. However, the jewellers' evidence
was, as I had expected, proved false. William's evidence about
the time of the murder was therefore unsupported, except by the
medical experts mustered by the Crown.

There was quite a large array of these, including specialists in
physiology, anatomy, pathology, medicine, and surgery — and
including even a Professor of Mathematics. Among all these
experts was a radiologist, who had taken a number of X-ray
photographs of the abdomens of a number of women at different
times after taking a barium meal. These experts expressed their
opinion that the food in the woman's stomach and bowel had
been taken immediately before her death. This, if true, would
have constituted serious evidence against the accused. However,
the time food takes to pass from the stomach along the twenty-
two feet of the small intestine varies very considerably, being
affected by many circumstances — physiological, psychological,
and physical.

When I was cross-examined I was asked how long it took for
food to pass from the mouth to the lower end of the small intestine.

I replied that though it was simple enough to give an average time, that average could not apply to a particular case. It was much the same as asking how long it took a horse to run a mile. It depended, I said, on the breed of the horse, its condition at the time, upon the trainer and upon the jockey; whereupon his Lordship, who had some interest in horse-racing, leant over to me and said, "And the owner, Sir Sydney, and the owner!" This was received with much amusement by the local audience, knowing as they did the vagaries of horse-racing in Ceylon.

The experiments on the cooling of recently dead bodies that I had suggested had been carried out. Professor de Saram had been fortunate in obtaining three bodies of young murderers immediately after they had been executed. Dressed in petticoats and sarees, the bodies were kept under conditions as close as possible to those in which the body of the murdered woman had been placed, and their temperatures were taken every half-hour. Approximately seven hours were required for these bodies to lose 5·2 degrees. This information was of crucial importance, for it was obvious that the much lighter body of the dead woman would have taken less time to cool to the same extent; and, therefore, she would have died much later than 10.30 a.m. The Crown's answer to this was the suggestion that her temperature at death was higher than normal on account of the struggle with her murderer. The Crown produced an enormous amount of literature concerning the onset of convulsions during strangulation and their effect on the temperature. Many books on forensic medicine were quoted, including my own — which fortunately could not be used in evidence against me as I had stated that in cases of asphyxia convulsions were common but not inevitable.

I was cross-examined heavily about the injury to the dead woman's ear. I, of course, had not seen it, but de Saram had, and he said in evidence that it was inflicted before death. His opinion was not subjected to cross-examination, and in reply to a question I said I was prepared to accept it. I was then asked why I could accept the opinion of the Crown expert in this case when, in the Fox case in England, I had refused to accept the evidence of a much more distinguished person, Sir Bernard Spilsbury. The conditions were, of course, entirely different. In the Fox case I saw the specimen myself and could therefore speak with assurance. In this case neither I nor anyone else, except Professor de Saram, had seen the injury, and therefore his evidence had to be accepted if he was a reliable witness, as he was. It is queer how these things recur — I had quite forgotten the Fox case until it was mentioned to me at this trial.

The Crown, realizing the importance of the soiling of the feet, suggested to me that the accused could have taken the material from the kitchen and daubed it on the feet in order to confuse the issue. Asked if that was possible, I said shortly, "Yes." The absurdity of the suggestion was elaborated by Mr Justice Grataien in his extremely fair summing up. Although the trial had then been going on for over three months, the jury came to a unanimous verdict of "Not Guilty" within a very short time after the closing of the case.

At the beginning of the trial local opinion in Colombo was strongly against Sathasivam, and I personally received a number of letters cursing me for interfering with the course of justice, which apparently meant the hanging of the accused. One writer said that he was praying to the Almighty to strike down the aeroplane in which I was travelling back to Britain. This seemed a bit unfair to the other forty or so passengers on the 'plane, but by Divine Providence they and I were spared.

The Coronation was an unforgettable experience and a forceful reminder of the authority of the Church. As the Queen, loaded with emblems of State, moved almost automatically at the behest of the clerical dignitaries, I felt that the majesty and authority of the Church dominated the majesty and authority of the Monarchy. The civil significance of the occasion was completely overshadowed by ecclesiastical splendour and sacramental ritual.

On my way back from the Abbey I failed to find my taxi, and walked from Westminster to Piccadilly in my University robes — scarlet gown with hood and black velvet berette. As I neared my hotel the crowds became more and more dense, and I expected to have a very long delay in crossing the street — not a pleasant thought, since I had been in the Abbey since seven o'clock in the morning. However, a Cockney in the crowd saw my scarlet robes and shouted, "Make way there, make way, here comes a bloody bishop." I did my best to look like one of that eminent body, sanguinary or otherwise, and walked through comfortably to my hotel. Another example of the power of the Church!

After the Coronation came my seventieth birthday, and then my retiral from the Chair of Forensic Medicine. Immediately afterwards I set off on my advisory mission for the World Health Organization. I went to the Lebanon first and then to Ceylon, where my wife and I stayed for nine months.

We returned to Edinburgh in 1954, and I had the honour of being presented with my portrait painted by Sir William Hutchison. I was deeply touched by this gesture from my old students in many parts of the world, my medical and legal colleagues, and the University.

Very shortly afterwards I was asked to stand for election as Rector of the University. I agreed, and, after the usual spirited contest among the student body, was duly elected to that high office. This, I felt, was the highest honour that could be paid to me, and I greatly appreciated it. In July 1955 the University conferred on me an honorary Doctorate of Laws, thereby further enhancing my feeling of kinship with my *alma mater*. As undergraduate, graduate, assistant, lecturer, professor, Dean of Faculty, and Acting Principal, I had been associated with her over a period of nearly half a century.

Immediately thereafter my wife and I set out on another trip round the world. On that trip I became involved, by mere chance, in what proved to be a most interesting case of arsenical poisoning.

21

The Auckland Arsenic Mystery

THE CASE OCCURRED IN AUCKLAND, IN MY NATIVE NEW
Zealand, where a man named James Wilson ran a petrol
service station with the help of his wife. He was fifty-four,
she was fifty-six, and they had been married for seventeen years.
There were no children. They were both diligent and hard-
working, and had built up a good business and bought a nice
home. They were apparently a reasonably happy couple.

Mrs Wilson was an attractive woman, fastidious about her
appearance, and had an extensive wardrobe and a wide range
of cosmetics. She also had quite a collection of medicines and
ointments, mostly of patent origin. She had once been a physician's receptionist, and among her belongings was a large
American book entitled *Domestic Medical Practice*, which gave
information on so many aspects of "medical practice" that it
should have rendered the ordinary doctor quite superfluous.
This book — which was the only book in the house — was well
thumbed and appeared to have been in considerable use.

During 1954 Mrs Wilson had bouts of vomiting and diarrhœa
which she put down to "gastric flu." She had four such attacks,
each lasting a day or two, within a period of six months. She suffered from insomnia also, and a chemist whom she consulted gave
her a sedative mixture. This contained twenty grains of sodium
bromide and a quarter of a grain of phenobarbitone per half-
ounce, which was a pretty heavy dose. She took this regularly
each night for three or four months.

In the early hours of August 31, 1954, Mrs Wilson had an
attack of vomiting and diarrhœa. When her husband left for
work soon after 7 a.m. she asked him to have some medicine sent
to her from the local chemist. He phoned the chemist, who made

up a simple bismuth mixture but could not deliver it. Wilson was alone at the station — formerly he had had a lad to help — and so asked a customer, Mrs Thomas, to collect the medicine and take it to his wife. She agreed and delivered the "stomach medicine," as it came to be called, at about 11 a.m.

Mrs Wilson opened the door, and then went back to bed. She seemed bright and cheerful, although a little "washed out."

She and Mrs Thomas conversed normally for about ten minutes; Mrs Wilson said she was feeling better, and spoke of returning to the garage the next day. Mrs Thomas poured out a glass of water for her to take with the stomach medicine, which Mrs Wilson only tasted while Mrs Thomas was there.

Mrs Wilson had no more known visitors until three o'clock in the afternoon. Then a man named Ball, an acquaintance of the Wilsons, paid a call. He had been to the garage, and Wilson had said his wife was ill and asked Ball to see how she was and if she wanted anything. Mrs Wilson unlocked the door to let him in, but she seemed to him "pretty sick." She vomited while he was there, and expressed doubt as to whether she would be at work the next day. She took a tablespoonful of the stomach mixture in a glass patterned with red tulips — to be known as the 'tulip glass' — which was different from the glass she had used in the presence of Mrs Thomas. She diluted it with what Ball assumed was water from a cup under the bed, and drank it in his presence. He went back to the garage and told Wilson that his wife was pretty sick but a bit better when he left.

Wilson got back home at 7 p.m. to find the house dark and cold and the fire in the range out. The statements he made afterwards varied as to his wife's condition then. On one occasion he said she spoke or mumbled to him. At other times he said he looked in and as she was asleep he did not disturb her. However, he got the fire lit and cooked his meal.

About 8.15 Wilson realized that his wife was seriously ill, and went next door and phoned the doctor. A few minutes later the doctor arrived and found Mrs Wilson in coma and nigh unto death. He summoned an ambulance which took her to hospital; but she was dead when it arrived. That was at 8.45 p.m.

The doctor, meanwhile, had asked Wilson if his wife had been taking any medicine. Wilson told him about the sleeping-medicine. The doctor then suggested that Wilson should take the bottle to the hospital. Actually there were three twelve-ounce bottles of the sleeping-medicine in the kitchen. One was full to the cork, another half full, and the third empty except for an inch of the mixture. Wilson took the half-full bottle to the hospital.

Nothing significant was found at the autopsy apart from deep congestion of the stomach. As a routine the stomach, a portion of the liver, the kidneys, and a portion of the brain were sent to the Government analyst. He found arsenic in all of these. The body had meanwhile been buried, but it was exhumed on September 11, and further samples — including portions of the shroud, soil, hair, and nails — were taken and sent for analysis. Again arsenic was found. It was computed from the weights of the liver, kidneys, and brain that 1·52 grains of arsenic were present in these tissues, and the death was reported to be due to arsenical poisoning.

Meanwhile a few days after Mrs Wilson died the police had searched the house. They found the bottle of stomach medicine in Mrs Wilson's bedroom, which had not been touched. Under the bed they found the so-called tulip glass containing some dregs. These and the three bottles of sleeping-medicine were all analysed, with interesting results.

The bottle of stomach medicine, from which two doses had been taken, contained no arsenic at all. The full bottle of sleeping-medicine contained 1 per cent.; the half-full bottle, which Wilson had taken to the hospital, 8·4 per cent.; the almost empty bottle, none at all. The dregs in the tulip glass contained some of the stomach medicine and 7 per cent. of arsenic — but no bromide at all. Therefore arsenic in the tulip glass had not come via any of the bottles of medicine.

The cup that Ball had seen Mrs Wilson take from under the bed had disappeared.

In March 1955 — six months after all these facts were known — Wilson was arrested and charged with the murder of his wife. The trial was held at Auckland in May.

The Crown's case was that Wilson had been trying to poison his wife with arsenic for some months, that he gave her the fatal dose during the evening or night before her last attack of vomiting and diarrhœa, and that possibly he gave her another dose about an hour before she died. It was suggested that the arsenic found in the dregs of the tulip glass had been planted by Wilson after his wife's death in an attempt to make it look as if she had taken the poison herself while he was out.

The case for the prosecution rested almost entirely on the medical and scientific evidence. No more arsenic of any kind was found in the house, and there was no evidence of a purchase of arsenic in weed-killer or any other form by either of the Wilsons. There appeared to be no motive. There was no money involved, no other woman in the case, no evidence of any serious quarrels, no suggestion that Wilson wanted to get rid of his wife.

Two pathologists were called by the prosecution. The first was Dr Francis Cairns, who had performed the autopsy; the second was the senior Crown expert, Dr P. P. Lynch — no relation to Dr Roche Lynch, but like him a man whose opinion was greatly respected. Both Cairns and Lynch thought that a toxic dose was taken during the evening or night of August 30-31, and that a second dose might have been taken shortly before death; although both said that if that had been the case they would have expected to find more arsenic in the stomach and lower bowel.

Both experts also thought that Mrs Wilson had received repeated small doses of arsenic for some months before she died. This was important, because if the Crown could prove that previous attempts had been made to poison her the case against her husband would be greatly strengthened. In fact, however, it was not easy to prove.

The clinical evidence was meagre. The four attacks of vomiting and diarrhœa could have been caused by arsenical poisoning — or by food-poisoning or bacterial infection. Without laboratory evidence — and there was none — arsenic could not be presumed. Further, on one of these occasions Wilson was as badly affected as his wife, while another, after investigation by the Public Health authorities, was found to be due to food-poisoning.

If, moreover, arsenic had been given in toxic doses over this period there should have been symptoms and signs of chronic poisoning — inflammation of the eyes, nose, and throat, skin rashes or discolorations, thickening of the skin of the feet, and the tingling and cramps in the legs characteristic of peripheral neuritis. Loss of weight and emaciation, with marked loss of appetite, would also have been expected. But of all these signs of chronic arsenical poisoning Mrs Wilson had shown none whatever.

The chemical evidence was more positive. The results of the analysis of the dead woman's hair and nails showed that arsenic had been taken in small doses for several months. But the doses were small, and could well have been medicinal. It was true that arsenic had not been prescribed for Mrs Wilson by any doctor — but that book *Domestic Medical Practice* was apparently her main source of medical information. Significantly it contained the information that the taking of bromide is liable to cause skin rashes, and that such rashes could be prevented by taking small doses of arsenic. With her great concern about her appearance, and her tendency to self-medication, Mrs Wilson could very well have added arsenic to her bromide sleeping-mixture.

The defence suggested that the arsenic may have been taken in this way, but called no evidence. They, however, put the matter to Lynch, and referred to a paper which Dr E. B. Hendry and I had published over twenty years before dealing with arsenic absorption.

In my account of the Annie Hearn case I mentioned that there was a gap in my knowledge of the absorption of arsenic by the hair and nails. I knew quite well that these tissues would readily absorb arsenic and retain it for long periods; but I was not at all certain that they were able to take up so much arsenic that the concentration could become greater than that in the arsenical fluid in which they were immersed. Hendry and I made controlled experiments to try to find out. These experiments showed conclusively that arsenic found in the hair and nails after soaking in a solution of arsenic could be many times greater than in the mother fluid. We published our report in the *British Medical Journal* in October 1934, and it was on this that Lynch was questioned by counsel for the defence.

As in the case of Annie Hearn's sister, the Crown's main evidence to support the theory of systematic poisoning over a period of months was the distribution of arsenic in Mrs Wilson's hair and nails. The average length of her hair was four and a half inches, and the analysts divided it into three portions and tested each. In the first inch, nearest the skull, they found a concentration of eighteen parts per million; in the next inch, five parts per million; and in the rest, three parts per million. The Crown held that this was proof of systematic poisoning, and that the concentration was too large to have been the result of taking medicinal doses even over a long period of time.

If arsenic was given in therapeutic doses in the form of Fowler's solution, one dose every day for two months, how much, Lynch was asked, would he expect in the hair?

"None or just a trace," he replied.

Would he agree that five milligrams (5 mg.) of arsenic was a therapeutic dose?

Yes; he agreed.

Then defence counsel referred him to our paper in the *B.M.J.* of 1934, quoting this sentence from it:

"For example, a number of individuals were given 5 mg. of arsenic per day for two months; on examination the hair of these men was found to contain from 2 to 5 mg. of arsenic per 100 grams of hair."

Lynch agreed that this was equivalent to twenty to fifty parts per million. He went on, "That, I think, must be an error. Because that is a very high concentration...I think the mistake there must be one of a decimal point."

"You criticize as a misprint this article on the hair?" counsel asked.

"I don't criticize it," Lynch replied. "I merely say that because the concentration is so high, there must be an error of a decimal point. I don't accept the figure at all."

"This article written in 1934 would have been corrected by now?"

"I don't know if it has or not...I can't believe that a mistake hasn't been made."

There, for the time being, the matter rested.

The defence did not call any witnesses, and after the final speeches and the summing-up the jury retired. They came back six hours later and said they could not agree, so the judge ordered a retrial. I had still not even heard of the Wilsons then.

I often receive letters from former assistants and students asking for my opinion on cases in which they are interested. Dr Lindsay Brown, who had worked in my department in Edinburgh for some years, was now working as a pathologist in Auckland, and it was he who suggested to Wilson's solicitors that I should be asked to say whether or not the figures published in the *B.M.J.* were correct. The request came shortly before we left on our world tour. I was told that my reply might be put to Lynch in cross-examination on the retrial.

I was able to answer that the figures were correctly printed, and I pointed out that they were not only twenty but over fifty years old! In addition to the figures relating to our experimental work in the laboratory, I had recorded in my paper a number of cases that had been officially reported by the Royal Commission on Arsenical Poisoning set up in 1904 after an epidemic of beer-poisoning in the Midlands. A large number of patients in skin hospitals, who had been under treatment by arsenic for varying periods, allowed their hair to be examined. Many of these officially reported cases showed that a course of ordinary medical doses of arsenic over a period could lead to a concentration in the hair of over seventy parts per million — compared with the maximum of eighteen in Mrs Wilson's hair — and I suggested to the defence that they should make sure that a copy of the Report of the Commission was available at the trial.

I also said that the analysis showed that Mrs Wilson had taken arsenic in small doses over a period of several months, and that the amount had been increased a month or so before her death. It was impossible to say definitely that the arsenic was given in medicinal doses, but it could very well have been the result of conservative self-medication.

Then, on the basis of the information sent by the solicitors and by Lindsay Brown, I gave my opinion of the time the fatal dose had been taken.

I was convinced that it could not have been taken through the medium of the sleeping-medicine the night before Mrs Wilson died. The half-full bottle had been found to contain over 8 per cent. of arsenic, so that if she had taken the stated dose of one tablespoonful she would have swallowed approximately twenty grains of arsenic, or ten times the fatal dose. Such a dose in solution would inevitably have lead to very severe vomiting, diarrhœa, and collapse, followed by death. Even if a smaller but still toxic dose had been taken that evening, I should still have expected severe symptoms of vomiting and diarrhœa to occur within half an hour or so, and, subject to slight remissions, to continue with evidence of prostration and collapse until her death.

No evidence of any such severe symptoms had been offered. The only evidence of vomiting and diarrhœa was that given by the accused himself, who said that his wife had had "a stomach upset." Neither in the room nor in any of the bedroom utensils was there any trace of soiling by either vomit or diarrhœa. There was, however, a splash of vomited matter on the cardigan that Mrs Wilson had been wearing the night before her death — and the analyst had found this quite free from arsenic. This point had not been the subject of comment at the trial, but it seemed important to me. We were led to believe that Mrs Wilson was rather a fastidious person, so it was unlikely that she would have worn the cardigan in its soiled state. It seemed safe to infer that since the splash on it was free from arsenic, there had been no arsenic in her stomach when she vomited the night before her death. This single bit of evidence, in my judgment, seriously discredited the suggestion of the Crown that the stomach upset of the night before her death was due to a poisonous dose of arsenic.

Apart from this there was Mrs Thomas's evidence that at 11 a.m. Mrs. Wilson had seemed bright and cheerful, and was obviously not seriously ill. If she had been given a toxic dose of arsenic the night before she certainly would not have appeared normal at eleven o'clock the following morning. Remissions in arsenic poisoning are known, but not such a recovery as this. Altogether, therefore, I thought it extremely improbable that she had received a poisonous dose of arsenic the night before her death, or, indeed, that she had taken any arsenic at all at that time.

On the other hand, I did not believe the fatal dose could have been given as late as 7 p.m. the next day, when Wilson returned home. His wife was in a state of coma when the doctor arrived at 8.15, and dead half an hour later. No doubt cases are on record in which death occurs with great rapidity after very large doses of arsenic, but not as quickly as this. Nor did this theory receive any support from the analyst's report. Quite a small amount of arsenic was found in the stomach, and the distribution over the whole length of the gut was fairly uniform, being about fifteen parts per million, or approximately one-tenth of a grain per pound weight. This was quite inconsistent with the ingestion of a fatal dose within about an hour of death. The quantity in the liver — sixty parts per million, or about two-fifths of a grain to the pound — confirmed that the fatal dose must have been given several hours before.

So both the clinical and chemical evidence made it fairly certain that the fatal dose was taken after 11 a.m. and some hours before 7 p.m.; probably, it seemed, in the early afternoon. It could very well have been at 3 p.m., when the witness Ball saw Mrs Wilson take a dose of the stomach medicine diluted with what he assumed was water from the cup under the bed. In any case it was at a time when her husband was at work. Of course, he might possibly have set a trap, leaving a solution of arsenic for her to mistake for water, and use in diluting the medicine, but there was nothing to support that. On the evidence I had been sent, and from what I knew about arsenical poisoning, it seemed physically impossible for Wilson to have poisoned his wife.

The retrial of James Wilson had been fixed for August. By then I was in Canada, on my way round the world. I had sent my report to Auckland before leaving home, and thought no more about it. Actually I had other things on my mind. On my arrival in Montreal I had a slight heart-attack which put me on my back for a few weeks, and gave me my first opportunity of seeing hospital practice from the inside. While I was being deluged with Canadian kindness — I have never been so cared for and cosseted in my life — I received a cable from Lindsay Brown:

COUNSEL ADVISE YOUR OPINION CRUCIAL AND PROPOSE REQUESTING POSTPONEMENT OF TRIAL ENABLING YOUR ORAL TESTIMONY STOP PLEASE CABLE URGENTLY WHETHER YOU WILL TESTIFY AND TO WHAT DATE TRIAL SHOULD BE POSTPONED.

I cabled back that I was due to arrive at Auckland anyway in September, and that I was willing to prolong my visit if necessary to give oral evidence. The trial was therefore put off until October 3.

Again Cairns and Lynch gave evidence for the Crown, but the report of the 1904 Royal Commission on Arsenic Poisoning had been made available, and it was conceded that the arsenic found in Mrs Wilson's hair could have been the result of medication. The Crown case was therefore limited to the administration of the fatal dose; and Lynch, when cross-examined, admitted that he considered it unlikely that it was taken as late as 7 p.m.

I was the only witness called by the defence. When asked about my credentials I confessed that I had been over ten years in Egypt, where I said arsenical poisoning was "quite common." Asked how many cases I had seen there, I replied, "One does not, of course, see all the cases one deals with. I don't suppose I saw more than one a week."

One of the most important features of the case was what the judge called "the mystery of the tulip glass," with its contents of arsenic which the Crown said Wilson had planted after his wife's death. Since this glass might bear fingerprints, it was obviously one of the most important productions in the case. If Wilson's prints had been on it this would have been a serious piece of evidence against him; on the other hand his wife's prints alone would have been strongly in his favour.

No evidence was given by the Fingerprint Department, although they had examined the tulip glass, and it was a member of the jury who asked if any prints had been found. The answer given was that no prints at all were found. Since a smooth surface like glass cannot be handled without leaving prints, their complete absence implied that the surface had been wiped clean. This, of course, was a strong point in favour of the Crown.

However, in his closing address counsel for the defence said he had discovered, in consultation with the Crown prosecutor, that the evidence of the fingerprint investigator was "not entirely correct." A negative report had been returned on the tulip glass, he said. "That doesn't mean there was nothing on the glass——"

Here the judge stopped him on the ground that he was introducing a construction not on record, and adjourned the hearing to consult with both counsel in his Chambers. After this consultation His Honour told the jury he proposed to exercise his discretion and call the police-constable who had examined the glass when the Wilsons' house was searched on September 3. This constable, who had not previously been called, said that he had examined the glass and found no finger-prints "that would be suitable for identification purposes or for comparison purposes," and had made a verbal report to that effect. He admitted that the outside of the glass was not clear, but could not recall whether there were smudge-marks on it. Under cross-examination he said the marks on the outside appeared to have been made by lips and by medicine. He agreed the glass looked as if it had been drunk from. He said also, "Marks on the outside could have been fingerprints, but they were of no interest to me because they were not suitable for comparison." This evidence constituted quite a score for the defence, and in summing up the judge described the first evidence on fingerprints as misleading.

The source of the arsenic remained a mystery. It was not the duty of the defence to elucidate it, but counsel advanced a theory that is at least interesting. Advised by her medical compendium to take arsenic to prevent bromide rashes, he suggested Mrs Wilson was faced with the problem of getting a supply. She could not buy a liquid arsenical solution without a doctor's prescription — but she could make it herself. For this she needed only arsenical weed-killer, which could be bought in New Zealand without any formality at all; the regulations were so lax that most people did not even sign the poisons register — which, of course, would explain why the purchase, whether by her or her husband, had proved impossible to trace.

If she had prepared a mother liquor of arsenic from weed-killer for use with her bromide that liquid might have been used to add to the sedative mixtures on the last day. I say the last day, because one tablespoonful dose of the doctored mixture would have killed her, and therefore it could not have been used before the fatal day. It is not too fanciful to assume that the constant over-dosage with bromide and phenobarbitone could have produced a condition of mental confusion and loss of memory. Such confusion might have caused her, on the day of her death, to add too much of her stock solution to the medicine, and to pour the rest of it into the cup which the witness Ball spoke of as "a cup of water under the bed." This might well have been the last of her stock solution of arsenic, and thus no source of the arsenic was found. It does not sound very convincing, but at least it advances one theory about this mysterious happening.

What happened to the cup remains unexplained.

It took the jury one and three-quarter hours to make up their minds. This time the verdict was not guilty, and after over six months under the shadow of death the accused stepped out of the dock a free man.

We spent three months in New Zealand, and received a warm welcome from my relatives. In Dunedin we met two of my colleagues from Edinburgh University — Professor Brash of the Anatomy Department and Professor Drennan of Pathology. Both were in Dunedin ostensibly to take part in the University examinations but actually to fish. The Dean of the Faculty of Medicine, Sir Charles Hercus, gave a dinner at the Fernhill Club to celebrate the occasion. When toasting our health he slyly remarked that they in Dunedin rarely had a visit from an Edinburgh professor. Now and again they had an odd professor, but to have three odd professors all at once was unprecedented, and well worthy of a celebration.

My meeting with Brash and Drennan was not a matter for

surprise, since their impending arrival in Dunedin was amply heralded in the daily Press on account of a dramatic incident which took place at sea. An unfortunate Greek, in a small vessel, injured himself pretty badly, and since no medical assistance was available on board, an SOS was sent out. In response the liner in which my two friends were travelling offered to help. The lucky chance of having two medical professors from Edinburgh University on board seemed almost providential. Of course, the specialities of the two professors — anatomy and pathology — hardly lead to any intimate association with living patients, but they agreed to do their best. Fortunately, there was a doctor on the liner, and between the three of them they carried out the requisite operation. The Greek patient survived — a tribute to the toughness of that hardy race.

We left New Zealand in December 1955, and returned home, spending a few weeks in Australia, a hectic day in Colombo, and three months in Egypt, where we found the people as hospitable as ever.

As an example of the proverbial Egyptian friendliness, I was surprised to receive, on my departure from Cairo, a cheque for my services as a visiting professor. I protested that I had done nothing beyond giving a lecture or two and having many conferences with the staff, which I thought did me more good than them, but there it was, and I had to accept it or embarrass them considerably. I had the cheque paid into my account in Cairo, and, as that foolish and abortive matter of the Suez Canal occurred shortly after we left for this country, I have heard nothing further about it. I have no doubt, however, that when in due course I visit Egypt again I will find that my cheque is still available.

When we returned to Edinburgh we were greatly affected by the welcome afforded to us by the students of the University, including a reception and dinner by the Students' Representative Council.

So much for fifty years in the study of medicine and thirty years' association with crime and criminals. This period has produced greater advances in human knowledge, especially in science, than the whole of the rest of recorded history. The use of scientific aids in the investigation of crime has kept more or less in pace with scientific advances but they seem to have had little effect, if any, in discouraging crooks. On the contrary, according to the annual statistics all forms of indictable offences known to the police in England and Wales have increased throughout these years. The total has risen from something over 80,000 in 1900 to about 500,000 in 1957, and the increase has been particularly marked since 1938.

Whatever the value to society of the advances in forensic science and, in particular, forensic medicine, it has provided me with a life of infinite variety of human interest. It has not been highly lucrative, to be sure, for the medico-legal practitioner is in the majority of cases very poorly recompensed. Even when he is acting for the Crown the statutory fees are rather ridiculous — in Scotland, anyway — and when acting for the defence an adequate recompense is exceptional.

I well remember one such exception, a case of alleged murder in which the evidence against the accused seemed very black. He was a man of substance. I found that the case against him was very shaky, and the defence was able to discredit much of it at the trial. The result was that the jury, after a very short retiral, brought in a verdict of not guilty. The accused man's solicitors wrote and asked me my fee, and I suggested a hundred guineas — little enough, one might think, for the amount of trouble taken, and less than one might pay for losing an appendix. They replied that they did not suggest I was asking too much, but the usual fee for highly skilled medical and other scientific men whom they had previously employed ranged round about ten guineas. I wrote on their letter, "What is your client's life worth?" and returned it. The cheque was forwarded the next day.

That was a rare event, for it is an unfortunate coincidence that persons most in need of assistance of this kind are usually the least able to pay for it. Looking back, I find that with few exceptions those cases for the defence in which I agreed to help were undertaken without a fee. I knew that a scientific witness could not expect an adequate reward for his services, and in my private cases I never insisted on payment when acting for the defence. I sometimes had instead the satisfaction of elucidating a problem and the feeling that I had done what was right; and the gratefulness of 'the patient' although ephemeral, was an additional source of pleasure. At the same time, it was a good thing I was a salaried official, and not dependent on fees.

It was certainly a good thing for our children, or they would not have had much education. We sent our son from Egypt to a preparatory school in Swanage, and from there he went to Malvern. He did not appear to have any special ideas about his future, so I decided to put him into the study of medicine at Edinburgh.

I soon discovered, however, that he had no bent in that direction, and transferred him to Oxford, where he read history and literature. He left with a good knowledge of books, a taste for painting and poetry, and an excellent palate. He writes, strangely enough for a New Zealander, in broad Scots, inclined somewhat to obscurity and occasional bawdiness, but is now recognized as one of the leading modern Scots poets.

My daughter, at her own desire and against my advice, studied medicine and, not long after qualifying, married a fellow-doctor. They emigrated to the wilder parts of western Canada, where they enjoy a happy, healthy life with unlimited if little used opportunities for the outdoor activities of shooting, fishing, and hunting, and social relaxations confined mainly to the 'roaring game' of curling in the winter and baseball in the summer.

This book has been mainly about murder, which is of the greatest interest to the public but of only minor significance in the general problem of crime. We have in Great Britain something between 130 and 150 murders a year, an average of about three per million of the population, which is infinitesimal compared with the annual half-million or so indictable offences known to the police. Murder is not a great problem in this country, and whether murderers are hanged or imprisoned seems to be a matter of little general importance. The attention directed to this crime is out of proportion to its social significance.

There does not appear to be any common factor in the make-up of murderers. Like other criminals, they have been found generally to be mentally backward; but it should be remembered that such findings are, inevitably, based on the study of convicted criminals, and it is perhaps reasonable to think that the brighter ones are bright enough to escape conviction. I have known more murderers than most people, and in my recollection they have been devoid of the characteristics they are commonly credited with, and quite ordinary individuals such as you and me. So ordinary, indeed, that sometimes when I have watched them going to execution I have been inspired to echo the famous words uttered on a similar occasion by the sixteenth-century divine,

John Bradford, and say, "But for the grace of God there goes Sydney Smith." I have always refrained, however, lest I tempt Providence, knowing the fate of John Bradford. The grace of God apparently deserted him in the end, for he was convicted of heresy and burnt alive.

INDEX

INDEX